SACREDSPACE

the prayer book 2010

acknowledgement

The Publisher would like to thank Piaras Jackson, S.J., and Alan McGuckian, S.J., for their kind assistance in making this book possible. Correspondence with the Sacred Space team can be directed to feedback@sacredspace.ie where comments or suggestions relating to the book or to www.sacredspace.ie will always be welcome.

The Scripture quotations contained herein are from the *New Revised Standard Version* Bible, Copyright © 1989 by the Division of Christian Education of the National Council of Churches of Christ in the U.S.A. and are used with permission. All rights reserved.

First published in Australia, 2009, by Michelle Anderson Publishing Pty Ltd.

Founded in 1865, Ave Maria Press is a ministry of the Indiana Province of Holy Cross.

www.avemariapress.com

ISBN-10: 1-59471-194-1   ISBN-13: 978-1-59471-194-7

Cover design by Andy Wagoner.

Text design by K. Hornyak.

Printed and bound in the United States of America.

how to use this book

We invite you to make a sacred space in your day and spend ten minutes praying here and now, wherever you are, with the help of a prayer guide and scripture chosen specially for each day. Every place is a sacred space so you may wish to have this book in your desk at work or available to be picked up and read at any time of the day, whilst traveling or on your bedside table, a park bench. . . . Remember that God is everywhere, all around us, constantly reaching out to us, even in the most unlikely situations. When we know this, and with a bit of practice, we can pray anywhere.

The following pages will guide you through a session of prayer stages.

Something to think and pray about each day this week
The Presence of God
Freedom
Consciousness
The Word (leads you to the daily scripture and provides help
  with the text)
Conversation
Conclusion

It is most important to come back to these pages each day of the week as they are an integral part of each day's prayer and lead to the scripture and inspiration points.

Although written in the first person the prayers are for "doing" rather than for reading out. Each stage is a kind of exercise or meditation aimed at helping you to get in touch with God and God's presence in your life.

We hope that you will join the many people around the world praying with us in our sacred space.

Sarum Primer, 16th century

God be in my head,
and in my understanding;

God be in my eyes,
and in my looking;

God be in my mouth,
and in my speaking;

God be in my heart,
and in my thinking;

God be at my end
and at my departing.

contents

november 29–december 5

Something to think and pray about each day this week:

Counting the days

It is a delight to find Advent calendars in the shops at this time of the year. They encourage us to count off the days of waiting and pray for Jesus' coming—which is what Advent means. In most of the West, every evening's television reminds us how many shopping days are left before Christmas. Suppose we take these advertisements as a call to pray rather than to purchase. I'll put myself in the mind of Mary and Joseph, focused on the expected baby, wondering what he will be like and how he will affect my life. Try imagining the preparation that Mary made. She spent three months helping her cousin Elizabeth with an unexpected pregnancy. Then she had to face the awful crisis with Joseph, who could not understand how his fiancée could be pregnant (Mt 1:19). Then when things seemed to be on an even course for the birth, she found they had to pull up roots, harness the donkey, and trek up to Bethlehem, where they could find no room in the inn. Mary's main preparation was adjusting to the unexpected and unwished-for. The best patron for Christmas is the quiet and imperturbable Joseph.

The Presence of God

Lord, help me to be fully alive to your holy presence.
Enfold me in your love.
Let my heart become one with yours.

Freedom

Many countries are at this moment suffering
the agonies of war.
I bow my head in thanksgiving for my freedom.
I pray for all prisoners and captives.

Consciousness

At this moment, Lord, I turn my thoughts to You.
I will leave aside my chores and preoccupations.
I will take rest and refreshment in your presence, Lord.

The Word

The word of God comes down to us through the scriptures.
May the Holy Spirit enlighten my mind an my heart to respond
to the gospel teachings. (Please turn to your scripture on the
following pages. Inspiration points are there should you need
them. When you are ready, return here to continue.)

Conversation

Sometimes I wonder what I might say
if I were to meet You in person, Lord.
I might say "Thank You, Lord" for always being there for me.
I know with certainty there were times when you carried me.
When through your strength I got through the dark times in
my life.

Conclusion

Glory be to the Father, and to the Son, and to the Holy Spirit,
As it was in the beginning, is now, and ever shall be,
World without end. Amen

Sunday 29th November,
First Sunday of Advent   Luke 21:25–28, 34–36

"There will be signs in the sun, the moon, and the stars, and on the earth distress among nations confused by the roaring of the sea and the waves. People will faint from fear and foreboding of what is coming upon the world, for the powers of the heavens will be shaken. Then they will see 'the Son of Man coming in a cloud' with power and great glory. Now when these things begin to take place, stand up and raise your heads, because your redemption is drawing near." "Be on guard so that your hearts are not weighed down with dissipation and drunkenness and the worries of this life, and that day catch you unexpectedly, like a trap. For it will come upon all who live on the face of the whole earth. Be alert at all times, praying that you may have the strength to escape all these things that will take place, and to stand before the Son of Man."

- Apocalyptic visions no longer move me, Lord. But I hear your warning, that I do not let my heart be weighed down with dissipation and drunkenness and the worries of this life. The mother of dissipation is not joy, but joylessness.
- In you, Lord, I find the basis of my peace, enabling me to stand up and raise my head.

Monday 30th November,
St. Andrew, Apostle   Matthew 4:18–22

As he walked by the Sea of Galilee, he saw two brothers, Simon, who is called Peter, and Andrew his brother, casting a net into the lake—for they were fishermen. And he said to them, "Follow me, and I will make you fish for people." Immediately they left their nets and followed him. As he went from there, he saw two other brothers, James son of Zebedee and his brother

4

John, in the boat with their father Zebedee, mending their nets, and he called them. Immediately they left the boat and their father, and followed him.

- "And Andrew his brother . . ." It was the fate of Andrew always to be introduced as the brother of Simon Peter. Andrew is the patron saint of younger, usually less significant siblings.
- Do we ever outgrow that self-perception, seeing ourselves as somebody's brother or sister? Maybe with jealousy, maybe with a feeling we are not quite as good, maybe with a clinging dependence that makes it hard for us to make our own way, maybe with an unfeigned and joyful love?
- Lord, you are the brother I need never feel bad about, less than, or inferior to. I know I have a good place in your mind and heart.

Tuesday 1st December   Luke 10:21–24

At that same hour Jesus rejoiced in the Holy Spirit and said, "All things have been handed over to me by my Father; and no one knows who the Son is except the Father, or who the Father is except the Son and anyone to whom the Son chooses to reveal him." Then turning to the disciples, Jesus said to them privately, "Blessed are the eyes that see what you see! For I tell you that many prophets and kings desired to see what you see, but did not see it, and to hear what you hear, but did not hear it."

- What have I learned in prayer? What is it that is hidden from the wise and the prudent that I have learned in the heart of prayer? Can I think over the mystery of prayer and in my life and wonder what it has done for me?
- How has prayer made me who I am? What have I "seen" and "heard" in prayer that I desired? Can I give thanks for all this?

Wednesday 2nd December — Matthew 15:29–37

Jesus went on from there and reached the shores of the Sea of Galilee, and he went up into the hills. He sat there, and large crowds came to him bringing the lame, the crippled, the blind, the dumb and many others. The crowds were astonished to see the dumb speaking, the cripples whole again, the lame walking and the blind with their sight, and they praised the God of Israel. But Jesus called his disciples to him and said, "I feel sorry for all these people; they have been with me for three days now and have nothing to eat. I do not want to send them off hungry, they might collapse on the way." The disciples said to him: "Where could we get enough bread in this deserted place to feed such a crowd?" Jesus said to them: "How many loaves have you? Seven, they said, and a few small fish." Then he instructed the crowd to sit down on the ground, and he took the seven loaves and the fish, and he gave thanks and broke them and handed them to the disciples who gave them to the crowds. They all ate as much as they wanted, and they collected what was left of the scraps, seven baskets full.

- Things happened around Jesus. People got better, physically and spiritually. In this scene they are healed, fed, and taught.
- Things happen when we pray, when we journey to a new destination in ourselves, to the part of ourselves where we sing and dance, weep and laugh, cry and reach out to others.
- Prayer is an adventure. My time of prayer each day is a venture into the uncharted land of love of self, others, and God.

Thursday 3rd December, St. Francis Xavier — Matthew 28:16–20

Now the eleven disciples went to Galilee, to the mountain to which Jesus had directed them. When they saw him, they worshipped him; but some doubted. And Jesus came and said to them, "All authority in heaven and on earth has been given to me. Go therefore and make disciples of all nations, baptizing them in the name of the Father and of the Son and of the Holy Spirit, and teaching them to obey everything that I have commanded you. And remember, I am with you always, to the end of the age."

- "They worshipped him; but some doubted." When I intend to praise God, to pray, I may also find doubt presses in on me. Can I include those doubts in my prayer?
- Can I hear the Lord saying to me, "remember, I am with you always?"

Friday 4th December   Matthew 9:27–31

As Jesus went on his way, two blind men followed him, crying loudly, "Have mercy on us, Son of David!" When he entered the house, the blind men came to him; and Jesus said to them, "Do you believe that I am able to do this?" They said to him, "Yes, Lord." Then he touched their eyes and said, "According to your faith let it be done to you." And their eyes were opened. Then Jesus sternly ordered them, "See that no one knows of this." But they went away and spread the news about him throughout that district.

- How could these men, who were blind, follow Jesus if they could not see?
- How did they know what to ask for?
- Their faith in him opened their hearts to appeal to him. Their faith opened them to the power in Jesus, and they were healed. They knew their need—of God and of others—and did not hide their need and were healed.

Saturday 5th December **Matthew 9:35–10:1, 5–8**

Then Jesus went about all the cities and villages, teaching in their synagogues, and proclaiming the good news of the kingdom, and curing every disease and every sickness. When he saw the crowds, he had compassion for them, because they were harassed and helpless, like sheep without a shepherd. Then he said to his disciples, "The harvest is plentiful, but the laborers are few; therefore ask the Lord of the harvest to send out laborers into his harvest." Then Jesus summoned his twelve disciples and gave them authority over unclean spirits, to cast them out, and to cure every disease and every sickness. These twelve Jesus sent out with the following instructions: "Go rather to the lost sheep of the house of Israel. As you go, proclaim the good news, 'The kingdom of heaven has come near.' Cure the sick, raise the dead, cleanse the lepers, cast out demons. You received without payment; give without payment."

- This seems to be a really outgoing gospel: we are to look at the big harvest, the sick, the dead, the outcasts; all the needs of people are part of prayer. It is in care and compassion that the kingdom of heaven comes near.
- Prayer is one door into the kingdom of heaven, with a door outwards to the world of great need. Advent is a time to notice and to respond to the needs of people in our immediate circle as well in the wider world.

Something to think and pray about each day this week:

John's way

When John the Baptist heard in prison what the Messiah was doing, he sent word by his disciples and said to him, "Are you the one who is to come, or are we to wait for another?" (Mt 11:2–11). There is real comfort in this story. John the Baptist, the powerful, austere man who held such sway among the Jews, still had his moments of darkness. Imprisoned in Herod's dungeon, he wondered, "Am I a fool? Is this all there is? Was I wrong about Jesus?" He does not just brood on the question. He sends messengers to Jesus. Jesus does not send back reassurances; he just asks the messengers to open their eyes and see the evidence of Jesus' life.

Lord, in my moments of doubt and darkness, may I fill my eyes with you. Are you the one, Lord? I am staking my life on it. I am not waiting for anyone else. Politicians, gurus, and celebrities come and go, with promises and new solutions, but I am sticking with you. You show me how to make this world better, by tackling suffering and sickness, and reaching out to the unfortunate. In my doubts and difficulties, I fill my eyes with the sight of you, your person, and your works.

The Presence of God

God is with me, but more,
God is within me, giving me existence.
Let me dwell for a moment on God's life-giving presence
in my body, my mind, my heart,
and in the whole of my life.

Freedom

God is not foreign to my freedom.
Instead the Spirit breathes life into my most intimate desires,
gently nudging me towards all that is good.
I ask for the grace to let myself be enfolded by the Spirit.

Consciousness

Help me, Lord, to be more conscious of your presence.
Teach me to recognize your presence in others.
Fill my heart with gratitude for the times your love
has been shown to me through the care of others.

The Word

I read the word of God slowly, a few times over, and I listen to
what God is saying to me. (Please turn to your scripture on the
following pages. Inspiration points are there should you need
them. When you are ready, return here to continue.)

Conversation

How has God's word moved me? Has it left me cold?
Has it consoled me or moved me to act in a new way?
I imagine Jesus standing or sitting beside me,
I turn and share my feelings with him.

Conclusion

Glory be to the Father, and to the Son, and to the Holy Spirit,
As it was in the beginning, is now, and ever shall be,
World without end. Amen

Sunday 6th December,
Second Sunday of Advent

Luke 3:1–6

In the fifteenth year of the reign of Emperor Tiberius, when Pontius Pilate was governor of Judea, and Herod was ruler of Galilee, and his brother Philip ruler of the region of Ituraea and Trachonitis, and Lysanias ruler of Abilene, during the high priesthood of Annas and Caiaphas, the word of God came to John son of Zechariah in the wilderness. He went into all the region around the Jordan, proclaiming a baptism of repentance for the forgiveness of sins, as it is written in the book of the words of the prophet Isaiah, "The voice of one crying out in the wilderness: 'Prepare the way of the Lord, make his paths straight. Every valley shall be filled, and every mountain and hill shall be made low, and the crooked shall be made straight, and the rough ways made smooth; and all flesh shall see the salvation of God.'"

- The Gospel positions John the Baptist in the history of his time, sign-posting the date of God's intervention in human history. It was not a one-off intervention; it continues through every one who works to prepare the way of the Lord.
- My time is now, and John's path is laid out for me. How am I responding? Have I accepted this "way"?

Monday 7th December

Isaiah 35:1–4

The wilderness and the dry land shall be glad, the desert shall rejoice and blossom; like the crocus it shall blossom abundantly, and rejoice with joy and singing. The glory of Lebanon shall be given to it, the majesty of Carmel and Sharon. They shall see the glory of the Lord, the majesty of our God. Strengthen the weak hands, and make firm the feeble knees. Say to those who are of a fearful heart, "Be strong, do not fear! Here is your God.

He will come with vengeance, with terrible recompense. He will come and save you."

- The passages in Isaiah which we read in Advent often bring us to the experiences of parched and lifeless wilderness.
- Can I bring to prayer a part of me that feels arid and withered? Can I see the flowering of new life in my situation? Can I accept the promise of glory and majesty?

Tuesday 8th December, The Immaculate Conception of the Blessed Virgin Mary   Luke 1:26–38

In the sixth month the angel Gabriel was sent by God to a town in Galilee called Nazareth, to a virgin engaged to a man whose name was Joseph, of the house of David. The virgin's name was Mary. And he came to her and said, "Greetings, favored one! The Lord is with you." But she was much perplexed by his words and pondered what sort of greeting this might be. The angel said to her, "Do not be afraid, Mary, for you have found favor with God. And now, you will conceive in your womb and bear a son, and you will name him Jesus. He will be great, and will be called the Son of the Most High, and the Lord God will give to him the throne of his ancestor David. He will reign over the house of Jacob forever, and of his kingdom there will be no end." Mary said to the angel, "How can this be, since I am a virgin?" The angel said to her, "The Holy Spirit will come upon you, and the power of the Most High will overshadow you; therefore the child to be born will be holy; he will be called Son of God. And now, your relative Elizabeth in her old age has also conceived a son; and this is the sixth month for her who was said to be barren. For nothing will be impossible with God." Then Mary said, "Here am I, the servant of the Lord; let it be with me according to your word." Then the angel departed from her.

- The world would never be the same because of Mary's "yes" to the invitation to be the mother of God. Because of Mary, God is with us in a totally new way in the world, in the person of the human and divine Jesus.
- Later in their lives, Jesus would praise Mary not just for being his physical mother, but because she "heard the word of God and kept it." In prayer we may ask her to bring the word of God to life in us, as the word became flesh in her.

Wednesday 9th December   Matthew 11:28–30

Jesus said, "Come to me, all you that are weary and are carrying heavy burdens, and I will give you rest. Take my yoke upon you, and learn from me; for I am gentle and humble in heart, and you will find rest for your souls. For my yoke is easy, and my burden is light."

- Christmas can be busy. Preparations—social and otherwise—can bring stress. But Advent is the time to come and rest, to find comfort and peace in our God
- The invitation from God is to find security, depth, and peace in belonging to him. Our mutual belonging rests in the God-child of Advent, Jesus the Christ.

Thursday 10th December   Matthew 11:11–15

"Truly I tell you, among those born of women no one has arisen greater than John the Baptist; yet the least in the kingdom of heaven is greater than he. From the days of John the Baptist until now the kingdom of heaven has suffered violence, and the violent take it by force. For all the prophets and the law prophesied until John came; and if you are willing to accept it, he is Elijah who is to come. Let anyone with ears listen!"

13

- Jesus is not a complete surprise! He has been expected and his life is intertwined with the prophets and with John the Baptist. Later it will be with his apostles, and with the other men and women who accompanied him on his mission.
- Our Christian life is intertwined with the community of the Jesus' followers. Friends, co-workers, family, the wider church—all share the journey with Jesus to God. Our Advent prayer is a prayer that welcomes into our lives the people God sends across our path.

Friday 11th December   Matthew 11:16–19

Jesus spoke to the crowds, "But to what will I compare this generation? It is like children sitting in the marketplaces and calling to one another, 'We played the flute for you, and you did not dance; we wailed, and you did not mourn.' For John came neither eating nor drinking, and they say, 'He has a demon'; the Son of Man came eating and drinking, and they say, 'Look, a glutton and a drunkard, a friend of tax collectors and sinners!' Yet wisdom is vindicated by her deeds."

- When we don't like what's going on, we can so easily misjudge people. Or we put on them what we don't like about ourselves.
- Jesus looks more at what people do for each other than what others may say about them. This is not easy to pray. But if we focus on John and Jesus, we can go beyond what people say of them to what their deeds were: the blind could see, the lame could walk, and freedom was the gift to the human heart.

Saturday 12th December   Matthew 17:10–13

And the disciples asked him, "Why, then, do the scribes say that Elijah must come first?" He replied, "Elijah is indeed coming and will restore all things; but I tell you that Elijah has already come, and they did not recognize him, but they did to him whatever they pleased. So also the Son of Man is about to suffer at their hands." Then the disciples understood that he was speaking to them about John the Baptist.

- This child, soon to come, will suffer. Some Eastern Christmas icons have the manger in the form of a coffin. The crib is at its most realistic when the cross is somewhere in the background.
- The following of Jesus will challenge us on all the areas of our life—how we love, how we treat the poor and needy, and how we give some time in our lives to God and the things of God.

Something to think and pray about each day this week:

Embracing the future

John the Baptist was the older cousin of Jesus, and he was, in that region, famous. He had many disciples. But when his cousin came to him (Jn 1:29), instead of saying, "That's a young cousin of mine from down the country," John used a phrase which we hear at Mass, "Behold the Lamb of God." He said it with such reverence that two of his disciples left John and went to follow Jesus. Later John's disciples remarked to John, with a hint of jealousy, that Jesus was now drawing the crowds. John replied, "This is how my own happiness is made complete. He must increase, and I must decrease."

This was a more remarkable feat than living on locusts and wild honey. John was turning away from the cult of personality and from the fame and celebrity he enjoyed, and watching his followers move away from him towards Jesus. He was preparing for redundancy, for accepting that even he, with Jerusalem at his feet, was dispensable. Handing over a job is not dying. It is the start of a new phase of living. If that phase means what we call retirement, then making a go of retirement takes as much energy as initiation into any job. You need to find a new rhythm in your everyday, and you need to ask for help—it is there if we look for it—in finding new occupations.

The Presence of God
What is present to me is what has a hold on my becoming.
I reflect on the presence of God always there in love,
amidst the many things that have a hold on me.
I pause and pray that I may let God
affect my becoming in this precise moment.

Freedom
There are very few people
who realize what God would make of them
if they abandoned themselves into his hands,
and let themselves be formed by his grace. (St. Ignatius)
I ask for the grace to trust myself totally to God's love.

Consciousness
In the presence of my loving Creator,
I look honestly at my feelings over the last day,
the highs, the lows, and the level ground.
Can I see where the Lord has been present?

The Word
God speaks to each one of us individually. I need to listen to
hear what he is saying to me. Read the text a few times, then
listen. (Please turn to your scripture on the following pages.
Inspiration points are there should you need them. When you
are ready, return here to continue.)

Conversation
What is stirring in me as I pray?
Am I consoled, troubled, left cold?
I imagine Jesus himself standing or sitting at my side,
and share my feelings with him.

Conclusion
Glory be to the Father, and to the Son, and to the Holy Spirit,
As it was in the beginning, is now, and ever shall be,
World without end. Amen

Sunday 13th December,
Third Sunday of Advent   Luke 3:10–18

And the crowds asked John the Baptist, "What then should we do?" In reply he said to them, "Whoever has two coats must share with anyone who has none; and whoever has food must do likewise." Even tax collectors came to be baptized, and they asked him, "Teacher, what should we do?" He said to them, "Collect no more than the amount prescribed for you." Soldiers also asked him, "And we, what should we do?" He said to them, "Do not extort money from anyone by threats or false accusation, and be satisfied with your wages." As the people were filled with expectation, and all were questioning in their hearts concerning John, whether he might be the Messiah, John answered all of them by saying, "I baptize you with water; but one who is more powerful than I is coming; I am not worthy to untie the thong of his sandals. He will baptize you with the Holy Spirit and fire. His winnowing fork is in his hand, to clear his threshing floor and to gather the wheat into his granary; but the chaff he will burn with unquenchable fire." So, with many other exhortations, he proclaimed the good news to the people.

- For all the austerity of his life, John spoke to people in words they could grasp. It was his austerity that drew people's respect and trust. Here was a man who cared nothing for comfort, money, or fame, who could not be bought, and who could speak the truth without fear.

- What is my reaction? Where does this lead me?

Monday 14th December   Matthew 21:23–27

When Jesus entered the temple, the chief priests and the elders of the people came to him as he was teaching, and said, "By what authority are you doing these things, and who gave you this authority?" Jesus said to them, "I will also ask you one question; if you tell me the answer, then I will also tell you by what authority I do these things. Did the baptism of John come from heaven, or was it of human origin?" And they argued with one another, "If we say, 'From heaven,' he will say to us, 'Why then did you not believe him?' But if we say, 'Of human origin,' we are afraid of the crowd; for all regard John as a prophet." So they answered Jesus, "We do not know." And he said to them, "Neither will I tell you by what authority I am doing these things."

- There is a big mystery about Jesus: where he came from, why he does what he does. Everything about him makes people think, doubt, get confused, or find faith. He wants us to mull over his life, savor it, even take our doubts seriously.
- Prayer is our daily insertion—personal or communal—into the mystery of the life and the purpose of Jesus in his life on earth. In him heaven and earth are mingled. In prayer, heaven mingles with earth. Praise God!

Tuesday 15th December   Matthew 21:28–32

Jesus said, "What do you think? A man had two sons; he went to the first and said, 'Son, go and work in the vineyard today.' He answered, 'I will not'; but later he changed his mind and went. The father went to the second and said the same; and he answered, 'I will go, sir'; but he did not go. Which of the two did the will of his father?" They said, "The first." Jesus said to them, "Truly I tell you, the tax collectors and the prostitutes are going into the kingdom of God ahead of you. For John came to you in the way of righteousness and you did not believe him, but the tax collectors and the prostitutes believed him; and even after you saw it, you did not change your minds and believe him."

- The gospel calls to faith. Faith calls on trust. We are challenged to believe, just as people were challenged to believe in John and Jesus. Faith grows and waxes and wanes. Trust is difficult; and we are called to total trust. Not just a bit here and there.
- Prayer can grow trust in us; human love does the same. In prayer we can thank God for those we trust and who trust each of us. Prayer—a daily dose of trust in God!

Wednesday 16th December   Isaiah 45:5–8

I am the Lord, and there is no other; besides me there is no god. I arm you, though you do not know me, so that they may know, from the rising of the sun and from the west, that there is no one besides me; I am the Lord, and there is no other. I form light and create darkness, I make weal and create woe; I the Lord do all these things.

- The Lord is the all powerful one, the Lord of all creation who holds each of us in the palm of his hand. This is the one true God who is about to enter the human story, as a babe in arms cradled child.
- Our Advent journey allows us to prepare to receive this child. Am I prepared? Is there more I should do?

Thursday 17th December   Matthew 1:1–11

An account of the genealogy of Jesus the Messiah, the son of David, the son of Abraham. Abraham was the father of Isaac, and Isaac the father of Jacob, and Jacob the father of Judah and his brothers, and Judah the father of Perez and Zerah by Tamar, and Perez the father of Hezron, and Hezron the father of Aram, and Aram the father of Aminadab, and Aminadab the father of Nahshon, and Nahshon the father of Salmon, and Salmon the father of Boaz by Rahab, and Boaz the father of Obed by Ruth, and Obed the father of Jesse, and Jesse the father of King David.

And David was the father of Solomon by the wife of Uriah, and Solomon the father of Rehoboam, and Rehoboam the father of Abijah, and Abijah the father of Asaph, and Asaph the father of Jehoshaphat, and Jehoshaphat the father of Joram, and Joram the father of Uzziah, and Uzziah the father of Jotham, and Jotham the father of Ahaz, and Ahaz the father of Hezekiah, and Hezekiah the father of Manasseh, and Manasseh the father of Amos, and Amos the father of Josiah, and Josiah the father of Jechoniah and his brothers, at the time of the deportation to Babylon.

- The list places Jesus in the mainstream of human life and his people. It includes all sorts of people, the devout as well as public sinners, outcasts, and people you wouldn't associate with.
- This list is God's list of favorites and of co-workers. All can be partners with God in the coming of the kingdom—and that includes me and you, as well as all sorts of people you might normally not invite home to dinner or have coffee with.
- God enters fully into our human history, without reservation.

Friday 18th December   **Matthew 1:18–25**

Now the birth of Jesus the Messiah took place in this way. When his mother Mary had been engaged to Joseph, but before they lived together, she was found to be with child from the Holy Spirit. Her husband Joseph, being a righteous man and unwilling to expose her to public disgrace, planned to dismiss her quietly. But just when he had resolved to do this, an angel of the Lord appeared to him in a dream and said, "Joseph, son of David, do not be afraid to take Mary as your wife, for the child conceived in her is from the Holy Spirit. She will bear a son, and you are to name him Jesus, for he will save his people from their sins." All this took place to fulfill what had been spoken by the Lord through the prophet: "Look, the virgin shall conceive and bear a son, and they shall name him Emmanuel," which means, "God is with us." When Joseph awoke from sleep, he did as the angel of the Lord commanded him; he took her as his wife, but had no marital relations with her until she had borne a son; and he named him Jesus.

- Advent is seldom seen as a time of the Holy Spirit, but in the annunciation to Joseph, and to Mary earlier, the Spirit is alive and at work. The Spirit's action brings the gift to the world of the God-person, in a totally physical and spiritual way. In the humanity of Mary, Jesus is growing from embryo to child.

- In the faith of Joseph, the call first came to all of us to believe the mystery. In prayer we might picture Mary and Joseph talking together about all that has happened, brought alive by the Spirit. Can I bring the presence of the Spirit into my life, today?

Saturday 19th December   **Luke 1:5–25**

In the days of King Herod of Judea, there was a priest named Zechariah, who belonged to the priestly order of Abijah. His wife was a descendant of Aaron, and her name was Elizabeth. Both of them were righteous before God, living blamelessly according to all the commandments and regulations of the Lord. But they had no children, because Elizabeth was barren, and both were getting on in years. Once when he was serving as priest before God and his section was on duty, he was chosen by lot, according to the custom of the priesthood, to enter the sanctuary of the Lord and offer incense. Now at the time of the incense-offering, the whole assembly of the people was praying outside. Then there appeared to him an angel of the Lord, standing at the right side of the altar of incense. When Zechariah saw him, he was terrified; and fear overwhelmed him. But the angel said to him, "Do not be afraid, Zechariah, for your prayer has been heard. Your wife Elizabeth will bear you a son, and you will name him John. You will have joy and gladness, and many will rejoice at his birth, for he will be great in the sight of the Lord. He must never drink wine or strong drink; even before his birth he will be filled with the Holy Spirit. He will turn many of the people of Israel to the Lord their God. With the spirit and power of Elijah he will go before him, to turn the hearts of parents to their children, and the disobedient to the wisdom of the righteous, to make ready a people prepared for the Lord." Zechariah said to the angel, "How will I know that this is so? For I am an old man, and my wife is getting on in years." The angel replied, "I am Gabriel. I stand in the presence of God, and I have been sent to speak to you and to bring you this good news. But now, because you did not believe my words, which will be fulfilled in their time, you will become mute, unable to speak, until the day these things occur." Meanwhile, the people were waiting for Zechariah, and wondered at his delay in the sanctuary. When he did come out, he could not speak to them, and they realized that he had seen a vision in the sanctuary. He kept motioning to them and remained unable to speak. When his time of service was ended, he went to his home. After those days his wife Elizabeth conceived, and for five months she remained in seclusion. She said, "This is what the Lord has done for me when he looked favorably on me and took away the disgrace I have endured among my people."

- Zechariah was speechless through lack of faith. His obstinacy to belief made him like a remote island.
- But Zechariah was never deserted by God; with the birth of John his faith returned and God looked favorably on him. A child may often bring us to faith where faith is missing.
- Watch a child today, think of a child today, remember childhood today, and be close to life, to mystery and to God!

Something to think and pray about each day this week:

The song of salvation

Mary's Magnificat (Lk 1:46) is a prayerful hymn to savor. It echoes the song of Hannah in 1 Samuel 2:1. It places us at the cusp of the Old and New Testaments, charged with the longing of the Old, and savoring the fulfillment of the New. In the whole history of salvation, this is the moment of unalloyed joy. Mary is pregnant not merely with her child, but with dreams about a glorious future. A young mother overflows with gratitude for being the channel of God's grace to humankind.

Yet the prayer is charged with dynamite. It points to a society in which nobody wants to have too much while others have too little. The hungry are fed and the lowly are raised up. Lord, may I never be seduced by sweet devotion while I have more than I need and others have less.

The Presence of God
God is with me, but more, God is within me.
Let me dwell for a moment on God's life-giving presence
in my body, in my mind, in my heart,
as I sit here, right now.

Freedom
A thick and shapeless tree-trunk would never believe
that it could become a statue, admired as a miracle of sculpture,
and would never submit itself to the chisel of the sculptor,
who sees by her genius what she can make of it. (St. Ignatius)
I ask for the grace to let myself be shaped by my loving Creator.

Consciousness
Knowing that God loves me unconditionally,
I can afford to be honest about how I am.
How has the last day been, and how do I feel now?
I share my feelings openly with the Lord.

The Word
I read the word of God slowly, a few times over, and I listen to
what God is saying to me. (Please turn to your scripture on the
following pages. Inspiration points are there should you need
them. When you are ready, return here to continue.)

Conversation
Do I notice myself reacting as I pray with the word of God?
Do I feel challenged, comforted, angry?
Imagining Jesus sitting or standing by me,
I speak out my feelings, as one trusted friend to another.

Conclusion
Glory be to the Father, and to the Son, and to the Holy Spirit,
As it was in the beginning, is now, and ever shall be,
World without end. Amen

Sunday 20th December,
Fourth Sunday of Advent   Micah 5:2–5a

Thus says the Lord: But you, O Bethlehem of Ephrathah, who are one of the little clans of Judah, from you shall come forth for me one who is to rule in Israel, whose origin is from of old, from ancient days. Therefore he shall give them up until the time when she who is in labor has brought forth; then the rest of his kindred shall return to the people of Israel. And he shall stand and feed his flock in the strength of the Lord, in the majesty of the name of the Lord his God. And they shall live secure, for now he shall be great to the ends of the earth; and he shall be the one of peace.

- Micah spoke out passionately on behalf of the poor against their exploitation by the rich and corrupt. Alone among the prophets, he names Bethlehem as the place the Messiah will be born; he will come from among the poorest, to represent their cause.
- Let me sit and think about the poverty, the vulnerability of the Christ-child, and what it means for my life, today.

Monday 21st December   Luke 1:39–45

In those days Mary set out and went with haste to a Judean town in the hill country, where she entered the house of Zechariah and greeted Elizabeth. When Elizabeth heard Mary's greeting, the child leapt in her womb. And Elizabeth was filled with the Holy Spirit and exclaimed with a loud cry, "Blessed are you among women, and blessed is the fruit of your womb. And why has this happened to me, that the mother of my Lord comes to me? For as soon as I heard the sound of your greeting, the child in my womb leapt for joy. And blessed is she who believed that there would be a fulfillment of what was spoken to her by the Lord."

- Mary has just learned that she is to be the mother of God. She does not bask in being a celebrity, but puts on sandals and cloak and walks to Judea to help her pregnant cousin.
- I can recall times when I served and took joy in it—not as a paid job but as a labor of love—and the delight that comes from thinking more about others than about myself.

Tuesday 22nd December   1 Samuel 1:24–28

When Hannah had weaned Samuel, she took him up with her, along with a three-year-old bull, an ephah of flour, and a skin of wine. She brought him to the house of the Lord at Shiloh; and the child was young. Then they slaughtered the bull, and they brought the child to Eli. And she said, "Oh, my lord! As you live, my lord, I am the woman who was standing here in your presence, praying to the Lord. For this child I prayed; and the Lord has granted me the petition that I made to him. Therefore I have lent him to the Lord; as long as he lives, he is given to the Lord."

- The Lord answered Hannah's request for a son, Samuel, whom she promised to God. She then gives praise to God in words that foreshadow Mary's Magnificat.
- Praise is a natural response to God; it wells up from the hidden depths of our hearts. Praise and thanks go hand in hand; praise for what is great, thanks for what is ordinary.

Wednesday 23rd December   Luke 1:57–66

Now the time came for Elizabeth to give birth, and she bore a son. Her neighbors and relatives heard that the Lord had shown his great mercy to her, and they rejoiced with her. On the eighth day they came to circumcise the child, and they were going to name him Zechariah after his father. But his mother said, "No; he is to be called John." They said to her, "None of your relatives has this name." Then they began motioning to his father to find out what name he wanted to give him. He asked for a writing tablet and wrote, "His name is John." And all of them were amazed. Immediately his mouth was opened and his tongue freed, and he began to speak, praising God. Fear came over all their neighbors, and all these things were talked about throughout the entire hill country of Judea. All who heard them pondered them and said, "What then will this child become?" For, indeed, the hand of the Lord was with him.

- We already know the end of this story. We know what this child will become—the Lord's herald, who is then beheaded by Herod. We know that the one he heralds will be killed also, but will rise again. We may know too much; we may be burdened with the knowledge of so much pain and evil in the lives of these people.
- We ask in prayer that our knowledge go from head to heart, that our lives may follow the love by which each of these children would live.

Thursday 24th December — Luke 1:67–79

Then his father Zechariah was filled with the Holy Spirit and spoke this prophecy: "Blessed be the Lord God of Israel, for he has looked favorably on his people and redeemed them. He has raised up a mighty savior for us in the house of his servant David, as he spoke through the mouth of his holy prophets from of old, that we would be saved from our enemies and from the hand of all who hate us. Thus he has shown the mercy promised to our ancestors, and has remembered his holy covenant, the oath that he swore to our ancestor Abraham, to grant us that we, being rescued from the hands of our enemies, might serve him without fear, in holiness and righteousness before him all our days. And you, child, will be called the prophet of the Most

High; for you will go before the Lord to prepare his ways, to give knowledge of salvation to his people by the forgiveness of their sins. By the tender mercy of our God, the dawn from on high will break upon us, to give light to those who sit in darkness and in the shadow of death, to guide our feet into the way of peace."

- Most of us have to we live with parental expectations. Zechariah was full of hope as he saw in his son a prophet of the Most High.
- Lord, I know I'm still discovering what I am to become. The road is still open before me.

Friday 25th December,
Feast of the Nativity of the Lord   Luke 2:1–14

In those days a decree went out from Emperor Augustus that all the world should be registered. This was the first registration and was taken while Quirinius was governor of Syria. All went to their own towns to be registered. Joseph also went from the town of Nazareth in Galilee to Judea, to the city of David called Bethlehem, because he was descended from the house and family of David. He went to be registered with Mary, to whom he was engaged and who was expecting a child. While they were there, the time came for her to deliver her child. And she gave birth to her firstborn son and wrapped him in bands of cloth, and laid him in a manger, because there was no place for them in the inn. In that region there were shepherds living in the fields, keeping watch over their flock by night. Then an angel of the Lord stood before them, and the glory of the Lord shone around them, and they were terrified. But the angel said to them, "Do not be afraid; for see—I am bringing you good news of great joy for all the people: to you is born this day in the city of David a Savior, who is the Messiah, the Lord. This will be a sign for you: you will find a child wrapped in bands of cloth and lying in a manger."

And suddenly there was with the angel a multitude of the heavenly host, praising God and saying, "Glory to God in the highest heaven, and on earth peace among those whom he favors!"

- From this beginning, Jesus accepted the constraints of poverty. His parents had no influence and no money to find a proper lodging for him in Bethlehem.
- Mary's joy as a mother must have been underpinned by sadness at the conditions of the birth, and her powerlessness to make things better. From the very beginning, from his first moments, Jesus was among the poor.

Saturday 26th December,
St. Stephen, the first martyr   Acts 7:54–8:1a

When those in the synagogue heard these things, they became enraged and ground their teeth at Stephen. But filled with the Holy Spirit, he gazed into heaven and saw the glory of God and Jesus standing at the right hand of God. "Look," he said, "I see the heavens opened and the Son of Man standing at the right hand of God!" But they covered their ears, and with a loud shout all rushed together against him. Then they dragged him out of the city and began to stone him; and the witnesses laid their coats at the feet of a young man named Saul. While they were stoning Stephen, he prayed, "Lord Jesus, receive my spirit." Then he knelt down and cried out in a loud voice, "Lord, do not hold this sin against them." When he had said this, he died. And Saul approved of their killing him.

- Violence already, and on the morning after the birthday of the Prince of Peace! Such an horrific occasion, when men who call themselves god-fearing take up stones to kill Stephen.

- All through history, people have yielded to the temptation to use violence in this way, but it is in the name of a god of their own creation.
- Lord, teach me to turn towards you; even as you did with Saul who looked on at this murder, and approved.

december 27–january 2

Something to think and pray about each day this week:

Moving forward

The week after Christmas can be a time of anticlimax, of crackers cracked, of presents opened, of empty bottles binned, the fun and excitement just a cold memory. We cannot live our whole life in a buzz of exhilaration, even religious exhilaration. Even a charismatic service, with ecstatic crowds and catchy music, can leave a morning-after feeling. As Joseph brought Mary and Jesus down to Egypt, dodging soldiers and footpads, the adoring shepherds and the jubilant angels were just a memory. In Jesus' parables, the kingdom of God advances not by fireworks and peak experiences, but by trickling increment, by quiet, organic growth like the mustard seed or the leaven in the lump. Thank you, Lord, for the high moments; but when they are past, let me be good leaven.

The Presence of God

As I sit here, the beating of my heart,
the ebb and flow of my breathing, the movements of my mind
are all signs of God's ongoing creation of me.
I pause for a moment and become aware
of this presence of God within me.

Freedom

I ask for the grace
to let go of my own concerns
and be open to what God is asking of me,
to let myself be guided and formed by my loving Creator.

Consciousness

In the presence of my loving Creator,
I look honestly at my feelings over the last day,
the highs, the lows, and the level ground.
Can I see where the Lord has been present?

The Word

I take my time to read the word of God, slowly, a few times, allowing myself to dwell on anything that strikes me. (Please turn
to your scripture on the following pages. Inspiration points are
there should you need them. When you are ready, return here
to continue.)

Conversation

Remembering that I am still in God's presence,
I imagine Jesus himself standing or sitting beside me,
and say whatever is on my mind, whatever is in my heart,
speaking as one friend to another.

Conclusion

Glory be to the Father, and to the Son, and to the Holy Spirit,
As it was in the beginning, is now, and ever shall be,
World without end. Amen

Sunday 27th December, Holy Family   Luke 2:41–50

Now every year his parents went to Jerusalem for the festival of the Passover. And when he was twelve years old, they went up as usual for the festival. When the festival was ended and they started to return, the boy Jesus stayed behind in Jerusalem, but his parents did not know it. Assuming that he was in the group of travelers, they went a day's journey. Then they started to look for him among their relatives and friends. When they did not find him, they returned to Jerusalem to search for him. After three days they found him in the temple, sitting among the teachers, listening to them and asking them questions. And all who heard him were amazed at his understanding and his answers. When his parents saw him they were astonished; and his mother said to him, "Child, why have you treated us like this? Look, your father and I have been searching for you in great anxiety." He said to them, "Why were you searching for me? Did you not know that I must be in my Father's house?" But they did not understand what he said to them.

- Let me take this scene slowly, Lord. Jesus is coming of age, entering his teens, and as an eager student, questioning his teachers. To his mother's query: "Your father and I," he points gently to another paternity: "I must be in my Father's house."
- No Gospel scene shows more clearly the gradual process by which he grew into a sense of his mission. Let me savor it.

Monday 28th December,
The Holy Innocents   Matthew 2:13–18

Now after they had left, an angel of the Lord appeared to Joseph in a dream and said, "Get up, take the child and his mother, and flee to Egypt, and remain there until I tell you; for Herod is about to search for the child, to destroy him." Then

Joseph got up, took the child and his mother by night, and went to Egypt, and remained there until the death of Herod. This was to fulfill what had been spoken by the Lord through the prophet, "Out of Egypt I have called my son." When Herod saw that he had been tricked by the wise men, he was infuriated, and he sent and killed all the children in and around Bethlehem who were two years old or under, according to the time that he had learned from the wise men. Then was fulfilled what had been spoken through the prophet Jeremiah: "A voice was heard in Ramah, wailing and loud lamentation, Rachel weeping for her children; she refused to be consoled, because they are no more."

• Today we pray for the mourning mothers of the Holy Land, weeping to this day for their dead children because they are no more. Arabs and Jews, all of them Semites, continue to kill one another, in the delusion that bombs and blood will help.

• We pray for a spirit of peace in that holy land.

Tuesday 29th December   Luke 2:22–35

When the time came for their purification according to the law of Moses, they brought him up to Jerusalem to present him to the Lord (as it is written in the law of the Lord, "Every firstborn male shall be designated as holy to the Lord"), and they offered a sacrifice according to what is stated in the law of the Lord, "a pair of turtle-doves or two young pigeons." Now there was a man in Jerusalem whose name was Simeon; this man was righteous and devout, looking forward to the consolation of Israel, and the Holy Spirit rested on him. It had been revealed to him by the Holy Spirit that he would not see death before he had seen the Lord's Messiah. Guided by the Spirit, Simeon came into the temple; and when the parents brought in the child Jesus, to do for him what was customary under the law, Simeon took him in his arms and praised God, saying, "Master, now you are dismissing your servant in peace, according to your word; for my eyes have seen your salvation, which you have prepared in the presence of all peoples, light for revelation to the Gentiles and for glory to your people Israel." And the child's father and mother were amazed at what was being said about him. Then Simeon blessed them and said to his mother Mary, "This child is destined for the falling and the rising of many in Israel, and to be a sign that will be opposed so that the inner thoughts of many will be revealed—and a sword will pierce your own soul too."

- Jesus comes as a baby in his mother's arms, not just the glory of his people Israel, but a light for revelation to the Gentiles.
- Lord, I am one of those Gentiles. I see you here in the vulnerable flesh of a child, knowing you share my humanity fully. May the favor of God be with me as with you.

Wednesday 30th December   **Luke 2:36–40**

There was also a prophet, Anna the daughter of Phanuel, of the tribe of Asher. She was of a great age, having lived with her husband for seven years after her marriage, then as a widow to the age of eighty-four. She never left the temple but worshipped there with fasting and prayer night and day. At that moment she came, and began to praise God and to speak about the child to all who were looking for the redemption of Jerusalem. When they had finished everything required by the law of the Lord, they returned to Galilee, to their own town of Nazareth. The child grew and became strong, filled with wisdom; and the favor of God was upon him.

- Here, in a few words, scripture captures thirty years—Jesus grew strong, was filled with wisdom, and favored by God. The life of the God on earth was hidden away in a small village.

- The life of prayer is the hidden life—time of prayer could seem to be time wasted, as the life of Jesus before his gospel ministry could seem wasted.
- Prayer gives us time to "waste" with God, for it is time with love. It helps us too to grow strong and wise, and to know that God looks on us with love.

Thursday 31st December   John 1:1–5

In the beginning was the Word, and the Word was with God, and the Word was God. He was in the beginning with God. All things came into being through him, and without him not one thing came into being. What has come into being in him was life, and the life was the light of all people. The light shines in the darkness, and the darkness did not overcome it.

- At the end of the calendar year we go back to the beginning of St. John's gospel, and to the beginning of time. As we cross the bridge to 2010, we recall that the greatest thing of all happened at the beginning, and that God is eternal.
- A time of prayer may enable us to reach back in the time-span of our own life and to give thanks that, all along the years of our life, God has been present, guiding us and guarding us.

Friday 1st January, Solemnity of Mary, Mother of God   Luke 2:16–21

So they went with haste and found Mary and Joseph, and the child lying in the manger. When they saw this, they made known what had been told them about this child; and all who heard it were amazed at what the shepherds told them. But Mary treasured all these words and pondered them in her heart. The shepherds returned, glorifying and praising God for all they had heard and seen, as it had been told them. After eight days had passed, it was time to circumcise the child; and he was called

Jesus, the name given by the angel before he was conceived in the womb.

- We celebrate the most passionate and enduring of all human relationships, that of mother and child. As Mary looked at her baby, and gave him her breast, she knew that there was a dimension here beyond her guessing.
- Christians thought about it for four centuries before they dared to consecrate the title, Mother of God. Like Mary, I treasure the words spoken about Jesus, and ponder them in my heart.

Saturday 2nd January   **John 1:19–28**

This is the testimony given by John when the Jews sent priests and Levites from Jerusalem to ask him, "Who are you?" He confessed and did not deny it, but confessed, "I am not the Messiah." And they asked him, "What then? Are you Elijah?" He said, "I am not." "Are you the prophet?" He answered, "No." Then they said to him, "Who are you? Let us have an answer for those who sent us. What do you say about yourself?" He said, "I am the voice of one crying out in the wilderness, 'Make straight the way of the Lord,'" as the prophet Isaiah said. Now they had been sent from the Pharisees. They asked him, "Why then are you baptizing if you are neither the Messiah, nor Elijah, nor the prophet?" John answered them, "I baptize with water. Among you stands one whom you do not know, the one who is coming after me; I am not worthy to untie the thong of his sandal." This took place in Bethany across the Jordan where John was baptizing.

- John the Baptist knew there was little he could do himself, on his own. The one to come was the one all were waiting on. John's life was dependent on Jesus for meaning.
- We are not self-made, but are all God-made, at the beginning of life and all during our lives. Let me pray about this.

january 3–9

Something to think and pray about each day this week:

The weakness of Jesus

The Letter to the Hebrews (2:1 and 5:2) has a striking reference to the weakness of Jesus, "Because Jesus himself has suffered and been emptied, he is able to help those who are tempted. He can deal gently with the ignorant and wayward since he himself is beset with weakness."

What does weakness mean here? Not the experience of sin, but almost its opposite. Weakness is the experience of a peculiar liability to suffering, a profound sense of inability both to do and to protect. Weakness is inability, even after a great effort, to perform as we should want, or to achieve what we had determined, or to succeed with the completeness that we might have hoped. It means openness to suffering. It means that we are unable to secure our own future, or to protect ourselves from any adversity. When we are weak we are not as able to live with easy clarity and assurance, or to ward off shame, pain, or even interior anguish. In his final agony in Gethsemani, Jesus looked repeatedly to his friends for comfort, and prayed for an escape from death. He found neither. Finally he won control over himself and moved into his death in isolation and silence, even into the terrible interior suffering of the absence of God.

The Presence of God
I pause for a moment
and reflect on God's life-giving presence
in every part of my body, in everything around me,
in the whole of my life.

Freedom
Many countries are at this moment suffering
the agonies of war.
I bow my head in thanksgiving for my freedom.
I pray for all prisoners and captives.

Consciousness
Knowing that God loves me unconditionally,
I look honestly over the last day, its events and my feelings.
Do I have something to be grateful for? Then I give thanks.
Is there something I am sorry for? Then I ask forgiveness.

The Word
God speaks to each one of us individually. I need to listen to
hear what he is saying to me. Read the text a few times, then
listen. (Please turn to your scripture on the following pages.
Inspiration points are there should you need them. When you
are ready, return here to continue.)

Conversation
How has God's word moved me? Has it left me cold?
Has it consoled me or moved me to act in a new way?
I imagine Jesus standing or sitting beside me,
I turn and share my feelings with him.

Conclusion
Glory be to the Father, and to the Son, and to the Holy Spirit,
As it was in the beginning, is now, and ever shall be,
World without end. Amen

Sunday 3rd January,
The Epiphany of the Lord Matthew 2:1–12

In the time of King Herod, after Jesus was born in Bethlehem of Judea, wise men from the East came to Jerusalem, asking, "Where is the child who has been born king of the Jews? For we observed his star at its rising, and have come to pay him homage.". . . Herod secretly called for the wise men and learned from them the exact time when the star had appeared. Then he sent them to Bethlehem, saying, "Go and search diligently for the child; and when you have found him, bring me word so that I may also go and pay him homage." When they had heard the king, they set out; and there, ahead of them, went the star that they had seen at its rising, until it stopped over the place where the child was. When they saw that the star had stopped, they were overwhelmed with joy. On entering the house, they saw the child with Mary his mother; and they knelt down and paid him homage. Then, opening their treasure chests, they offered him gifts of gold, frankincense, and myrrh. And having been warned in a dream not to return to Herod, they left for their own country by another road.

• We remember the wise men and their gifts. They highlight that each of us has gifts we can bring to God, no matter who we are. The gift most worth giving at any age is our love.

• The Magi are remembered also for their journey and their search for God. A star guided them. As we sit with you, Lord, teach us to be grateful for those whose stars brought us to God—through the love, their teaching, the example of their lives.

Monday 4th January 1 John 3:22–4:3a

And we receive from him whatever we ask, because we obey his commandments and do what pleases him. And this is his commandment, that we should believe in the name of his Son Jesus Christ and love one another, just as he has commanded us. All who obey his commandments abide in him, and he abides in them. And by this we know that he abides in us, by the Spirit that he has given us. Beloved, do not believe every spirit, but test the spirits to see whether they are from God; for many false prophets have gone out into the world. By this you know the Spirit of God: every spirit that confesses that Jesus Christ has come in the flesh is from God, and every spirit that does not confess Jesus is not from God.

- We are each called to belief in Jesus, the Son of God, and to demonstrate our belief by how we live, and love one another. This is how we come into an intimate relationship with the Lord.
- How do others see this in my life, Lord? Teach me how to love my brothers and sisters so that I come closer to you.

Tuesday 5th January   1 John 4:7–10

Beloved, let us love one another, because love is from God; everyone who loves is born of God and knows God. Whoever does not love does not know God, for God is love. God's love was revealed among us in this way: God sent his only Son into the world so that we might live through him. In this is love, not that we loved God but that he loved us and sent his Son to be the atoning sacrifice for our sins.

- "In this is love, not that we loved God but that he loved us and sent his Son to be the atoning sacrifice for our sins." Can I sit and think about what this means for me?
- We do not and cannot earn God's love, but we are invited constantly to receive it, through our love for one another.
- Lord, teach me to turn towards you and accept your gracious gift.

Wednesday 6th January   1 John 4:11–16

Beloved, since God loved us so much, we also ought to love one another. No one has ever seen God; if we love one another, God lives in us, and his love is perfected in us. By this we know that we abide in him and he in us, because he has given us of his Spirit. And we have seen and do testify that the Father has sent his Son as the Savior of the world. God abides in those who confess that Jesus is the Son of God, and they abide in God. So we have known and believe the love that God has for us. God is love, and those who abide in love abide in God, and God abides in them.

- "No one has ever seen God." But through the gift of the Son, we have far greater intimacy than sight can bring—in our love for one another, "God lives in us."
- Each of us is invited to respond daily, to show in our own lives that "Jesus is the Son of God." Teach me to grow in love, Lord.

Thursday 7th January   Luke 4:16–21

When Jesus came to Nazareth, where he had been brought up, he went to the synagogue on the sabbath day, as was his custom. He stood up to read, and the scroll of the prophet Isaiah was given to him. He unrolled the scroll and found the place where it was written: "The Spirit of the Lord is upon me, because he has anointed me to bring good news to the poor. He has sent me to proclaim release to the captives and recovery of sight to the blind, to let the oppressed go free, to proclaim the year of the Lord's favor." And he rolled up the scroll, gave it back to the attendant, and sat down. The eyes of all in the synagogue were fixed on him. Then he began to say to them, "Today this scripture has been fulfilled in your hearing."

- Luke notes for us that with the "good news" the Spirit anoints, freedom is announced to people who are stuck, blind people see, and the year of God's goodness is announced. The good news of God is not just words, but a person—Jesus himself.
- Can you recall moments and times when the gospel words lifted your heart, calmed fears, renewed hope, and refreshed your whole life? Then it is good news and the good news is Jesus in your life. Let us give thanks for good news.

Friday 8th January　　　　　　　　　Luke 5:15–16

But now more than ever the word about Jesus spread abroad; many crowds would gather to hear him and to be cured of their diseases. But he would withdraw to deserted places and pray.

- At the key times of his life, Jesus prayed: before calling the twelve, at the time of temptation, and the struggle at his Passion and death. Very often he went to quiet places to pray, to be with the Father.
- Like Jesus, we need the energy of prayer to enhance family life, friendship, and work or ministry for others. In prayer, something happens to being us deeper into the source of our convictions and commitments to God and others.

Saturday 9th January　　　　　　　　1 John 5:14–15

And this is the boldness we have in him, that if we ask any-thing according to his will, he hears us. And if we know that he hears us in whatever we ask, we know that we have obtained the requests made of him.

- We often see people on television—actors, athletes, and political leaders come to mind perhaps—who thank God for their victory. Sometimes they seem to be saying, "I know that God is on our team; this is why we are winners."

- "If we ask anything according to his will, he hears us." In prayer there is a catch, though. It is not our will, our personal desire, that God responds to. Instead we are invited to be at one with the will of God. In this unity lies our confidence, our hope, our victory, our boldness.

january 10–16

Something to think and pray about each day this week:

Yes

This week the church celebrates Jesus' baptism. The water of baptism recalls the other waters in which we begin our lives, in our mother's womb. Birth is signaled by the breaking of the waters, the amniotic fluid, and emergence into a less protected life outside mother's body. The waters of the womb reflect the church's sense of what baptism means. At Easter the great Paschal Candle dips into the baptismal font as a vivid image of the act of love which precedes the birth of a child. When Jesus accepted John's baptism, and came out of the water, a voice from heaven was heard: "This is my beloved son." The Spirit came down on him. This symbolism of rebirth, as a child of God and member of the Church, is central in our own christenings.

The Presence of God

The world is charged with the grandeur of God (Gerard Manley Hopkins).
I dwell for a moment on the presence of God
around me, in every part of my body,
and deep within my being.

Freedom

"In these days, God taught me
as a schoolteacher teaches a pupil" (St. Ignatius).
I remind myself that there are things God has to teach me yet,
and ask for the grace to hear them and let them change me.

Consciousness

How do I find myself today?
Where am I with God? With others?
Do I have something to be grateful for? Then I give thanks.
Is there something I am sorry for? Then I ask forgiveness.

The Word

I read the word of God slowly, a few times over, and I listen to
what God is saying to me. (Please turn to your scripture on the
following pages. Inspiration points are there should you need
them. When you are ready, return here to continue.)

Conversation

Sometimes I wonder what I might say
if I were to meet You in person, Lord.
I might say "Thank You, Lord" for always being there for me.
I know with certainty there were times when you carried me.
When through your strength I got through the dark times in
my life.

Conclusion

Glory be to the Father, and to the Son, and to the Holy Spirit,
As it was in the beginning, is now, and ever shall be,
World without end. Amen

Sunday 10th January,
The Baptism of the Lord   Luke 3:15–16, 21–22

As the people were filled with expectation, and all were questioning in their hearts concerning John, whether he might be the Messiah, John answered all of them by saying, "I baptize you with water; but one who is more powerful than I is coming; I am not worthy to untie the thong of his sandals. He will baptize you with the Holy Spirit and fire. Now when all the people were baptized, and when Jesus also had been baptized and was praying, the heaven was opened, and the Holy Spirit descended upon him in bodily form like a dove. And a voice came from heaven, "You are my Son, the Beloved; with you I am well pleased."

- This is like a second beginning for Jesus. At thirty he has left home, and starts his adult life with this symbolic birth, coming up out of the water, and hearing God claim him as his son.
- Lord, I know you are well pleased with me, not for anything I have done, but because I, too, am your child. Help me to live like Jesus, with a sense of your calling.

Monday 11th January   Mark 1:14–20

Now after John was arrested, Jesus came to Galilee, proclaiming the good news of God, and saying, "The time is fulfilled, and the kingdom of God has come near; repent, and believe in the good news." As Jesus passed along the Sea of Galilee, he saw Simon and his brother Andrew casting a net into the sea—for they were fishermen. And Jesus said to them, "Follow me and I will make you fish for people." And immediately they left their nets and followed him. As he went a little farther, he saw James son of Zebedee and his brother John, who were in their boat mending the nets. Immediately he called them; and they left their father Zebedee in the boat with the hired men, and followed him.

- It was an ordinary working day for James and John, Simon and Andrew. Jesus interrupted that when he came past and called them to follow him.
- So it is for us—in the midst of work, family life, or illness will come the call deep inside to follow him, care for others, to give him a priority place in our lives.
- Can I bring to mind a recent time when that might have happened for me?

Tuesday 12th January   Mark 1:21–28

Jesus entered the synagogue and taught. They were astounded at his teaching, for he taught them as one having authority, and not as the scribes. Just then there was in their synagogue a man with an unclean spirit, and he cried out, "What have you to do with us, Jesus of Nazareth? Have you come to destroy us? I know who you are, the Holy One of God." But Jesus rebuked him, saying, "Be silent, and come out of him!" And the unclean spirit, convulsing him and crying with a loud voice, came out of him. They were all amazed, and they kept on asking one another, "What is this? A new teaching—with authority! He commands even the unclean spirits, and they obey him." At once his fame began to spread throughout the surrounding region of Galilee.

- From the beginning of his ministry Jesus is on a collision course with evil. Evil knows Jesus came to destroy it.
- Where in my life or in my immediate circle can I pray that good will overcome evil?

Wednesday 13th January   Mark 1:29–31

As soon as they left the synagogue, they entered the house of Simon and Andrew, with James and John. Now Simon's mother-in-law was in bed with a fever, and they told him about her at once. He came and took her by the hand and lifted her up. Then the fever left her, and she began to serve them.

* Jesus touched the hand of Simon's mother-in-law and she was healed of fever. Behind the gesture there is more than healing—there is calling. She then ministered to them.

* Have you ever been surprised by the person who ministered the grace of God to you? Are you surprised that Jesus takes you, weakness and all, by the hand and calls you to service?

Thursday 14th January   Mark 1:40–45

A leper came to Jesus begging him, and kneeling he said to him, "If you choose, you can make me clean." Moved with pity, Jesus stretched out his hand and touched him, and said to him, "I do choose. Be made clean!" Immediately the leprosy left him, and he was made clean. After sternly warning him he sent him away at once, saying to him, "See that you say nothing to anyone; but go, show yourself to the priest, and offer for your cleansing what Moses commanded, as a testimony to them." But he went out and began to proclaim it freely, and to spread the word, so that Jesus could no longer go into a town openly, but stayed out in the country; and people came to him from every quarter.

* Jesus takes on the limitations of a leprosy sufferer. Having cured the man, he then would be suspected of being contaminated, so he himself could no longer go into the town, but must stay outside like the person suffering from leprosy.

- Jesus' incarnation means he really is one of us, is "made flesh." He knows and feels for us from the inside.
- Who are outsiders in my small world? Can I let them come to mind and feel with them what it must be like to be treated as scum, poor, different?

Friday 15th January   Mark 2:1–7

When Jesus returned to Capernaum after some days, it was reported that he was at home. So many gathered around that there was no longer room for them, not even in front of the door; and he was speaking the word to them. Then some people came, bringing to him a paralyzed man, carried by four of them. And when they could not bring him to Jesus because of the crowd, they removed the roof above him; and after having dug through it, they let down the mat on which the paralytic lay. When Jesus saw their faith, he said to the paralytic, "Son, your sins are forgiven." Now some of the scribes were sitting there, questioning in their hearts, "Why does this fellow speak in this way? It is blasphemy! Who can forgive sins but God alone?"

- In our prayer with Jesus, we are meeting God. In him, God is near, not as a vague presence, but the one who forgives, heals guilt, and strengthens weakness.
- Can I now bring into the presence of Jesus what is mean, sinful, or the dark side of my life which tries to use or control others? Can I believe that the words of forgiveness, of healing and light are spoken to me?

Saturday 16th January   Mark 2:13–17

Jesus went out again beside the sea; the whole crowd gathered around him, and he taught them. As he was walking along, he saw Levi son of Alphaeus sitting at the tax booth, and he said to him, "Follow me." And he got up and followed him. And as he sat at dinner in Levi's house, many tax collectors and sinners were also sitting with Jesus and his disciples—for there were many who followed him. When the scribes of the Pharisees saw that he was eating with sinners and tax collectors, they said to his disciples, "Why does he eat with tax collectors and sinners?" When Jesus heard this, he said to them, "Those who are well have no need of a physician, but those who are sick; I have come to call not the righteous but sinners."

- Jesus is beginning to teach his followers, and he highlights that disciples are learners. Their time with Jesus is a time of learning his wisdom, as much from what he says as from what he does.
- Without words he teaches something unusual in this passage—that he has come for the sinner, the weak. The custom of the time was not to eat with sinners or keep their company.
- Let me watch Jesus' actions of in silence. This is how he teaches all of us today.

january 17–23

Something to think and pray about each day this week:

Our Father, ever present

We live in an age of absent fathers. Jacques-Marie-Émile Lacan, the French psychoanalyst, saw the retreat of the father as the greatest malaise of our culture. Yet each father remains a role-model (especially for his sons) whether he wants to or not. In the child's fantasy there is no such thing as a single parent. The other one, the absent father, remains as a shadowy icon.

St. Augustine, in a memorable Latin phrase, insists that God is not like that: "Non enim fecit atque abiit" (He did not just make us and go away. *Confessions*, Book 4, Chapter 12). God works with us and for us, and we see God's hand not just in the sunshine and obvious blessings, but even in the dark times, in our sorrowful mysteries. God is always present to us. The prodigal's father stayed on at home even after the boy brought shame and sorrow on the family. His older son and neighbors—and maybe his wife, too—may have seen him as foolish and indulgent for letting the younger boy loose with money. When the prodigal returned, his father was waiting and watching. As a good father, he was there when he was needed.

The Presence of God
As I sit here, God is present,
breathing life into me and into everything around me.
For a few moments, I sit silently,
and become aware of God's loving presence.

Freedom
If God were trying to tell me something, would I know?
If God were reassuring me or challenging me, would I notice?
I ask for the grace to be free of my own preoccupations
and open to what God may be saying to me.

Consciousness
In God's loving presence I unwind the past day,
starting from now and looking back, moment by moment.
I gather in all the goodness and light, in gratitude.
I attend to the shadows and what they say to me,
seeking healing, courage, forgiveness.

The Word
I take my time to read the word of God, slowly, a few times, allowing myself to dwell on anything that strikes me. (Please turn to your scripture on the following pages. Inspiration points are there should you need them. When you are ready, return here to continue.)

Conversation
What is stirring in me as I pray?
Am I consoled, troubled, left cold?
I imagine Jesus himself standing or sitting at my side,
and share my feelings with him.

Conclusion
Glory be to the Father, and to the Son, and to the Holy Spirit,
As it was in the beginning, is now, and ever shall be,
World without end. Amen

Sunday 17th January,
Second Sunday in Ordinary Time   John 2:1–12

On the third day there was a wedding in Cana of Galilee, and the mother of Jesus was there. Jesus and his disciples had also been invited to the wedding. When the wine gave out, the mother of Jesus said to him, "They have no wine." And Jesus said to her, "Woman, what concern is that to you and to me? My hour has not yet come." His mother said to the servants, "Do whatever he tells you." Now standing there were six stone water jars for the Jewish rites of purification, each holding twenty or thirty gallons. Jesus said to them, "Fill the jars with water." And they filled them up to the brim. He said to them, "Now draw some out, and take it to the chief steward." So they took it. When the steward tasted the water that had become wine, and did not know where it came from (though the servants who had drawn the water knew), the steward called the bridegroom and said to him, "Everyone serves the good wine first, and then the inferior wine after the guests have become drunk. But you have kept the good wine until now." Jesus did this, the first of his signs, in Cana of Galilee, and revealed his glory; and his disciples believed in him. After this he went down to Capernaum with his mother, his brothers, and his disciples; and they remained there a few days.

- With a mother's instinct, Mary felt Jesus was ready. Like other young men, Jesus was reluctant to go public so he protests: "My hour has not yet come." But Mary knew it had come.
- Thank you, Lord, for the mothering that brings me to the point of taking my life in my own hands and gives me the push I need.

Monday 18th January Mark 2:18–22

Now John's disciples and the Pharisees were fasting; and people came and said to him, "Why do John's disciples and the disciples of the Pharisees fast, but your disciples do not fast?" Jesus said to them, "The wedding-guests cannot fast while the bridegroom is with them, can they? As long as they have the bridegroom with them, they cannot fast. The days will come when the bridegroom is taken away from them, and then they will fast on that day. "No one sews a piece of unshrunk cloth on an old cloak; otherwise, the patch pulls away from it, the new from the old, and a worse tear is made. And no one puts new wine into old wineskins; otherwise, the wine will burst the skins, and the wine is lost, and so are the skins; but one puts new wine into fresh wineskins."

- Jesus proclaims that the one they were waiting for has come. The time for fasting is over for now; it is time to rejoice.
- We know ourselves that life has seasons, a rhythm of death and resurrection, with times for rejoicing and times of sadness. The bridegroom has come—Jesus, the Son of God. This is for our safety when difficult times return.

Tuesday 19th January Mark 2:23–28

One sabbath Jesus was going through the grainfields; and as they made their way his disciples began to pluck heads of grain. The Pharisees said to him, "Look, why are they doing what is not lawful on the sabbath?" And he said to them, "Have you never read what David did when he and his companions were hungry and in need of food? He entered the house of God, when Abiathar was high priest, and ate the bread of the Presence, which it is not lawful for any but the priests to eat, and he gave some to his companions." Then he said to them, "The sabbath was made for humankind, and not humankind for the sabbath; so the Son of Man is lord even of the sabbath."

- Jesus' stance, that the Sabbath was for our total benefit, was a scandal to some religious people. His view of the Sabbath is the view of the one who comes to bring life to the full.
- Does my religion bring life to myself and to others? Lord, give me compassion and a balance in life where my view of religion imposes burdens on others.

Wednesday 20th January   **Mark 3:1–6**

Again he entered the synagogue, and a man was there who had a withered hand. They watched him to see whether he would cure him on the sabbath, so that they might accuse him. And he said to the man who had the withered hand, "Come forward." Then he said to them, "Is it lawful to do good or to do harm on the sabbath, to save life or to kill?" But they were silent. He looked around at them with anger; he was grieved at their hardness of heart and said to the man, "Stretch out your hand." He stretched it out, and his hand was restored. The Pharisees went out and immediately conspired with the Herodians against him, how to destroy him.

- Again, Jesus confronts those who would burden others with religious rules, and turn their backs on those who suffer. The man in question had a withered hand but a heart open to faith; the others had good health but closed and hard hearts.
- Lord, give me the energy to be compassionate in your name, even when I risk criticism from others.

Thursday 21st January   **Mark 3:7–12**

Jesus departed with his disciples to the sea, and a great multitude from Galilee followed him; hearing all that he was doing, they came to him in great numbers from Judea, Jerusalem, Idumea, beyond the Jordan, and the region around Tyre and Sidon. He told his disciples to have a boat ready for him because of the crowd, so that they would not crush him; for he had cured many, so that all who had diseases pressed upon him to touch him. Whenever the unclean spirits saw him, they fell down before him and shouted, "You are the Son of God!" But he sternly ordered them not to make him known.

- Evil was challenged by Jesus and saw him for the son of God that he was. The faith of the disciples would grow slowly, and the mystery of his message would take hold only gradually.
- Lord, lead me to an ever deeper faith, no matter how long it takes or what difficulties I confront.

Friday 22nd January　　　　　　　　　**Mark 3:13–15**

He went up the mountain and called to him those whom he wanted, and they came to him. And he appointed twelve, whom he also named apostles, to be with him, and to be sent out to proclaim the message, and to have authority to cast out demons.

- Our calling, too, is like this—to spend time in prayer, with the word of God, and to share in the work of Jesus in the world. We know from the twelve that this is not an easy journey.
- In prayer we can offer our talents to God—we want to be with him as much as he wants us to be with him.

Saturday 23rd January　　　　　　　　**Mark 3:20–21**

And the crowd came together again, so that they could not even eat. When his family heard it, they went out to restrain him, for people were saying, "He has gone out of his mind."

- Jesus broke down conventions, both religious and cultural. His family was unhappy and embarrassed by him. He drew attention to them, even putting them under suspicion or in danger.
- Am I disturbed by Christians who seem more committed than I am? Or can I be grateful for those who dare to make a difference? Lord, take away my fears, and give me faith like theirs.

Something to think and pray about each day this week:

Tuning in to the Spirit

When adults are baptized, they are sometimes confirmed at the same time. Confirmation marks the coming of the Holy Spirit, the completion of baptism. The Holy Spirit is the bond that links God the Father with his son Jesus, a link of love and communication that never tires or sleeps. We are children of God through Baptism, sisters and brothers of Jesus. When God looks on each of us, he sees in us the image of Jesus. There is an unbroken stream of love and communication binding us to the Father, and that stream, that bond, is the Holy Spirit.

It does not always seem like that. Much of the time we do not feel like temples of the Holy Spirit. It is when we feel unholy, and unable to pray, that the Holy Spirit speaks for us to the Father "with sighs too deep for words" (Rom 8: 26). As we grow older, we realize that prayer is not about finding beautiful words for our needs, or making speeches to our Lord, but rather tuning in to the Spirit of Jesus who is always linking us to our heavenly Father.

The Presence of God
As I sit here with my book, God is here.
Around me, in my sensations, in my thoughts, and deep within me.
I pause for a moment and become aware
of God's life-giving presence.

Freedom
I need to close out the noise, to rise above the noise;
The noise that interrupts, that separates,
The noise that isolates.
I need to listen to God again.

Consciousness
I remind myself that I am in the presence of the Lord.
I will take refuge in His loving heart.
He is my strength in times of weakness.
He is my comforter in times of sorrow.

The Word
God speaks to each one of us individually. I need to listen to
what he is saying to me. (Please turn to your scripture on the
following pages. Inspiration points are there should you need
them. When you are ready, return here to continue.)

Conversation
Do I notice myself reacting as I pray with the word of God?
Do I feel challenged, comforted, angry?
Imagining Jesus sitting or standing by me,
I speak out my feelings, as one trusted friend to another.

Conclusion
Glory be to the Father, and to the Son, and to the Holy Spirit,
As it was in the beginning, is now, and ever shall be,
World without end. Amen

66

Sunday 24th January,
Third Sunday in Ordinary Time   Luke 4:14–21

Then Jesus, filled with the power of the Spirit, returned to Galilee, and a report about him spread through all the surrounding country. He began to teach in their synagogues and was praised by everyone. When he came to Nazareth, where he had been brought up, he went to the synagogue on the Sabbath day, as was his custom. He stood up to read, and the scroll of the prophet Isaiah was given to him. He unrolled the scroll and found the place where it was written: "The Spirit of the Lord is upon me, because he has anointed me to bring good news to the poor. He has sent me to proclaim release to the captives and recovery of sight to the blind, to let the oppressed go free, to proclaim the year of the Lord's favor." And he rolled up the scroll, gave it back to the attendant, and sat down. The eyes of all in the synagogue were fixed on him. Then he began to say to them, "Today this scripture has been fulfilled in your hearing."

- For those few minutes, history is holding its breath. Jesus, in the synagogue of his home town, stands up to read the majestic prophecy of Isaiah. He hands back the scroll to the attendant and sits down, the posture for solemn teaching. The anointed one, the Messiah, has arrived and declared himself.
- I watch the scene unfolding, the tension in Jesus as he makes his claim, the breathless attention of the congregation, then the mixture of excitement and rejection.
- How do I react?

Monday 25th January,
Conversion of St. Paul, Apostle   Mark 16:15

Jesus said to the disciples, "Go into all the world and proclaim the good news to the whole creation."

- This is a fragile planet of which we are stewards. Our minds are constantly challenged as we learn more about this marvelous earth, our responsibilities for it, and the immeasurably huge creation of which it is part.
- Lord, open my mind to your immensity.

Tuesday 26th January   Mark 3:31–35

Then the mother and brothers of Jesus came; and standing outside, they sent to him and called him. A crowd was sitting around him; and they said to him, "Your mother and your brothers and sisters are outside, asking for you." And he replied, "Who are my mother and my brothers?" And looking at those who sat around him, he said, "Here are my mother and my brothers! Whoever does the will of God is my brother and sister and mother."

- This is an awkward moment, but Jesus is firm: the word of God is deeper than any biological tie he has. Our deepest belonging is to God; all other belongings in life flow from that. We come from God and go to God.
- Our prayer, no matter what its method and tone, with its dryness and struggles, is time given to this prime connection in our life, the relationship with God.

Wednesday 27th January   Mark 4:1–8

Again he began to teach beside the sea. Such a very large crowd gathered around him that he got into a boat on the sea and sat there, while the whole crowd was beside the sea on the land. He began to teach them many things in parables, and in his teaching he said to them: "Listen! A sower went out to sow. And as he sowed, some seed fell on the path, and the birds came and ate it up. Other seed fell on rocky ground, where it did not have much soil, and it sprang up quickly, since it had no depth of soil.

And when the sun rose, it was scorched; and since it had no root, it withered away. Other seed fell among thorns, and the thorns grew up and choked it, and it yielded no grain. Other seed fell into good soil and brought forth grain, growing up and increasing and yielding thirty and sixty and a hundredfold."

- The word of God can bear fruit in each of us or can have little effect; the sowing of the word, like the sowing of seed, may take root or be blown away.
- Take a sentence or two from the gospel today, or even a word, and allow it be your "word the today." Like a bar of music, it can echo within you all day. Let the word of God bear its fruit in you.

Thursday 28th January,
St. Thomas Aquinas   Matthew 23:8–12

Jesus said to the crowds, "But you are not to be called rabbi, for you have one teacher, and you are all students. And call no one your father on earth, for you have one Father—the one in heaven. Nor are you to be called instructors, for you have one instructor, the Messiah. The greatest among you will be your servant. All who exalt themselves will be humbled, and all who humble themselves will be exalted."

- Here Jesus contrasts titles of honor like "rabbi" and "teacher" with the real status of the disciple. The power of the disciple comes from our insertion with Jesus, who is Rabbi, Father, and Teacher. That is the humble greatness of the disciple.
- Prayer may give an awareness of where we seek our status. Is it from people who are honored and looked up to in society, church or job, rather than from our friendship with Jesus?

Friday 29th January   Mark 4:26–29, 33–34

Jesus said to the crowd, "The kingdom of God is as if someone would scatter seed on the ground, and would sleep and rise night and day, and the seed would sprout and grow, he does not know how. The earth produces of itself, first the stalk, then the head, then the full grain in the head. But when the grain is ripe, at once he goes in with his sickle, because the harvest has come." With many such parables he spoke the word to them, as they were able to hear it; he did not speak to them except in parables, but he explained everything in private to his disciples.

- Jesus thinks and speaks in parables and images which he draws from the world around him. He reaches especially for symbols of life and growth. Therein lies mystery.
- The parable draws us in, teases and entices us with their meaning so we can discover more about God. Let me take my time to do that today.

Saturday 30th January   Mark 4:35–41

On that day, when evening had come, he said to them, "Let us go across to the other side." And leaving the crowd behind, they took him with them in the boat, just as he was. Other boats were with him. A great windstorm arose, and the waves beat into the boat, so that the boat was already being swamped. But he was in the stern, asleep on the cushion; and they woke him up and said to him, "Teacher, do you not care that we are perishing?" He woke up and rebuked the wind, and said to the sea, "Peace! Be still!" Then the wind ceased, and there was a dead calm. He said to them, "Why are you afraid? Have you still no faith?" And they were filled with great awe and said to one another, "Who then is this, that even the wind and the sea obey him?"

- Lord, there are times when I need to hear your voice ordering: "Peace! Be still!" There is no basis for my fear. You are with me and I trust you. I need to turn away from the howling of the wind and disturbing noises and wait for your comforting presence.

january 31–february 6

Something to think and pray about each day this week:

The faithfulness of God

The Presentation, Candlemas, recalls the wise elders, Simeon and Anna. Aristotle wrote of the old, "We are bound to give heed to the undemonstrated sayings and opinions of the experienced and aged, not less than to demonstrations; because, from their having the eye of experience, they behold the principles of things."

"Having the eye of experience." What does that mean? Faith in a reality which does not change, and enjoyment of a reality which does. For the old, realism takes on a new meaning. What is real is the experience that things pass. You are disengaged from the daily business of life, and from ambition, and this detachment can bring wisdom, a wider perspective in which that final thing, the real thing, should become luminous. You may be tempted to capitulate to what is transitory, or even to the cynicism of hopelessness.

The true faith of old age is in direct contrast to this. It has cast aside the dreaminess of childhood, renounced the endless demands of youth, and seen how fleeting and transitory are human achievements. With this perspective the love of God, the communion of the dead and the living in Christ, can become more real than anything in this world; but not easily. It is not that those with years behind them have "the answers," but can grow to understand that faith is based on God's faithfulness.

The Presence of God
At any time of the day or night we can call on Jesus.
He is always waiting, listening for our call.
What a wonderful blessing.
No phone needed, no emails, just a whisper.

Freedom
I will ask God's help,
to be free from my own preoccupations,
to be open to God in this time of prayer,
to come to love and serve him more.

Consciousness
How am I really feeling? Light-hearted? Heavy-hearted?
I may be very much at peace, happy to be here.
Equally, I may be frustrated, worried, or angry.
I acknowledge how I really am.
It is the real me that the Lord loves.

The Word
I read the word of God slowly, a few times over, and I listen to
what God is saying to me. (Please turn to your scripture on the
following pages. Inspiration points are there should you need
them. When you are ready, return here to continue.)

Conversation
Remembering that I am still in God's presence,
I imagine Jesus himself standing or sitting beside me,
and say whatever is on my mind, whatever is in my heart,
speaking as one friend to another.

Conclusion
Glory be to the Father, and to the Son, and to the Holy Spirit,
As it was in the beginning, is now, and ever shall be,
World without end. Amen

Sunday 31st January,
Fourth Sunday in Ordinary Time   Luke 4:21–30

Then he began to say to them, "Today this scripture has been fulfilled in your hearing." All spoke well of him and were amazed at the gracious words that came from his mouth. They said, "Is not this Joseph's son?" He said to them, "Doubtless you will quote to me this proverb, 'Doctor, cure yourself!' And you will say, 'Do here also in your hometown the things that we have heard you did at Capernaum.'" And he said, "Truly I tell you, no prophet is accepted in the prophet's hometown. But the truth is, there were many widows in Israel in the time of Elijah, when the heaven was shut up three years and six months, and there was a severe famine over all the land; yet Elijah was sent to none of them except to a widow at Zarephath in Sidon. There were also many lepers in Israel in the time of the prophet Elisha, and none of them was cleansed except Naaman the Syrian." When they heard this, all in the synagogue were filled with rage. They got up, drove him out of the town, and led him to the brow of the hill on which their town was built, so that they might hurl him off the cliff. But he passed through the midst of them and went on his way.

- When they heard Jesus speak, their reaction was not to what he said but to what they knew of Jesus' foster-father Joseph. What did they know? Only that he was a village carpenter and a quiet man; they judged Jesus by association.
- Forgive me, Lord, for the times I have not listened to people with unwelcome messages and instead have judged them by association, by their families or hometown or trade or whatever.

Monday 1st February   Psalm 3:1–6

O Lord, how many are my foes! Many are rising against me; many are saying to me, "There is no help for you in God." But you, O Lord, are a shield around me, my glory, and the one who lifts up my head. I cry aloud to the Lord, and he answers me from his holy hill. I lie down and sleep; I wake again, for the Lord sustains me. I am not afraid of tens of thousands of people who have set themselves against me all around.

- "I wake again, for the Lord sustains me." For the Psalmist, the personal experience of God's loving care is the reason to hope for rescue from all the sufferings that bear down on him.
- Do I think of sleeping as an act of trust and hope? Do I base my hopes on the Lord?

Tuesday 2nd February,
Presentation of the Lord   Malachi 3:1–4

See, I am sending my messenger to prepare the way before me, and the Lord whom you seek will suddenly come to his temple. The messenger of the covenant in whom you delight—indeed, he is coming, says the Lord of hosts. But who can endure the day of his coming, and who can stand when he appears? For he is like a refiner's fire and like fullers' soap; he will sit as a refiner and purifier of silver, and he will purify the descendants of Levi and refine them like gold and silver, until they present offerings to the Lord in righteousness. Then the offering of Judah and Jerusalem will be pleasing to the Lord as in the days of old and as in former years.

- "I am sending my messenger to prepare the way before me." The name "Malachi" is usually translated as "my messenger," and his words foreshadow the role of John the Baptist.

74

- What sort of messenger do I make? Who receives the message of Jesus from me? How do they receive it? Let me think about these things and talk with the Lord about them today.

Wednesday 3rd February   Mark 6:1–3

Jesus went on to his hometown, and his disciples followed him. On the sabbath he began to teach in the synagogue, and many who heard him were astounded. They said, "Where did this man get all this? What is this wisdom that has been given to him? What deeds of power are being done by his hands! Is not this the carpenter, the son of Mary and brother of James and Joses and Judas and Simon, and are not his sisters here with us?" And they took offence at him.

- It can be hard to believe that God comes so close to me. Those in the synagogue could not believe it. How can God be speaking to me via someone I have known in my local community?
- Do I have a fixed view about where God is to be found in my life? Can I be more open to his presence?

Thursday 4th February   Mark 6:6b–11

Then he went about among the villages teaching. He called the twelve and began to send them out two by two, and gave them authority over the unclean spirits. He ordered them to take nothing for their journey except a staff; no bread, no bag, no money in their belts; but to wear sandals and not to put on two tunics. He said to them, "Wherever you enter a house, stay there until you leave the place. If any place will not welcome you and they refuse to hear you, as you leave, shake off the dust that is on your feet as a testimony against them."

- Then, as now, people judged the message of Christ by the life of his messengers. Dom Helder Camara, the saintly Brazilian bishop, told his catechists, who were speaking to illiterate people: "Sisters and brothers, watch how you live. Your lives may be the only gospel your listeners will ever read."

- Forgive me, Lord, when my actions distort your gospel.

Friday 5th February   Psalm 18:30, 46, 49–50

This God—his way is perfect; the promise of the Lord proves true; he is a shield for all who take refuge in him. The Lord lives! Blessed be my rock, and exalted be the God of my salvation. For this I will extol you, O Lord, among the nations, and sing praises to your name. Great triumphs he gives to his king, and shows steadfast love to his anointed, to David and his descendants for ever.

- The image of God as a rock is common in the Psalms; God is strong, immovable, safe, and secure. This is a God in whom we can trust and hope, who brings peace even among our turmoil.
- Do I know this God in my life? If so, how do I respond? With praise, with thanks?

Saturday 6th February   Mark 6:30–34

The apostles gathered around Jesus, and told him all that they had done and taught. He said to them, "Come away to a deserted place all by yourselves and rest a while." For many were coming and going, and they had no leisure even to eat. And they went away in the boat to a deserted place by themselves. Now many saw them going and recognized them, and they hurried there on foot from all the towns and arrived ahead of them. As he went ashore, he saw a great crowd; and he had compassion for them, because they were like sheep without a shepherd; and he began to teach them many things.

- "He had compassion on the crowd because they were like sheep without a shepherd." Jesus, son of the eternal father, sees the crowd as his sisters and brothers. His gaze spans the millennia of humankind, sees our need for direction, for compassion, and for seeking some meaning in existence.
- To his exhausted disciples, Jesus said, "Come away by yourselves to a lonely place, and rest a while." Come to a lonely place, where you can drop your public mask, reflect on your life, and rest.
- This is what I do today, in my own small way, as I sit with Sacred Space and devote some time to just God and me.

Something to think and pray about each day this week:

Community building

Why build churches? Jesus spoke of worshipping his Father not in Jerusalem or on a mountain in Samaria, but in spirit and in truth. It is true that temples of stone make no sense without temples of flesh—each of us is a temple of the Holy Spirit. We can find God anywhere, in the beauties of our locality, or in our own heart. Our children may remind us of this: "I don't need to go to a building to find God." But in every place a community needs somewhere they can call their own, somewhere to meet in prayer, especially that prayer which we offer together. There are times when our own faith is faltering, and we need the support of a believing and worshipping community, who express their faith in the works of justice and charity. We need to come together, and for that we need a place.

The Presence of God
I pause for a moment
and think of the love and the grace that God showers on me,
creating me in his image and likeness, making me his temple.

Freedom
Lord, grant me the grace to be free from the excesses of this life.
Let me not get caught up with the desire for wealth.
Keep my heart and mind free to love and serve you.

Consciousness
In the presence of my loving Creator,
I look honestly at my feelings over the last day,
the highs, the lows, and the level ground.
Can I see where the Lord has been present?

The Word
God speaks to each one of us individually. I need to listen to
what he is saying to me. (Please turn to your scripture on the
following pages. Inspiration points are there should you need
them. When you are ready, return here to continue.)

Conversation
Sometimes I wonder what I might say
if I were to meet You in person, Lord.
I might say "Thank You, Lord" for always being there for me.
I know with certainty there were times when you carried me.
When through your strength I got through the dark times in
my life.

Conclusion
Glory be to the Father, and to the Son, and to the Holy Spirit,
As it was in the beginning, is now, and ever shall be,
World without end. Amen

Sunday 7th February,
Fifth Sunday in Ordinary Time   Luke 5:4–7

When Jesus had finished speaking, he said to Simon, "Put out into the deep water and let down your nets for a catch." Simon answered, "Master, we have worked all night long but have caught nothing. Yet if you say so, I will let down the nets." When they had done this, they caught so many fish that their nets were beginning to break. So they signaled their partners in the other boat to come and help them. And they came and filled both boats, so that they began to sink.

• Simon had been fishing all night, with no catch. He and his crew were tired, and were packing up, washing their nets. It would not be easy for exhausted fishermen to respond to the instruction, "Put out into deep water." But they saw something in Jesus that moved them to hope and to do his bidding.

• Lord, this is what it comes down to: do I trust you?

Monday 8th February   Mark 6:53–56

When Jesus and the disciples had crossed over, they came to land at Gennesaret and moored the boat. When they got out of the boat, people at once recognized him, and rushed about that whole region and began to bring the sick on mats to wherever they heard he was. And wherever he went, into villages or cities or farms, they laid the sick in the marketplaces, and begged him that they might touch even the fringe of his cloak; and all who touched it were healed.

• Lord, I would not like to be thought of as a user, someone who in a selfish way exploits family, friends, church, or even God. If I feel I am being used, I resent it.

- But in this scene you are being used to the point of exhaustion, and you react without a trace of resentment as you urged us to react: The Son of Man came not to be served, but to serve.

Tuesday 9th February   Mark 7:1–2, 5–8

Now when the Pharisees and some of the scribes who had come from Jerusalem gathered around him, they noticed that some of his disciples were eating with defiled hands, that is, without washing them. So the Pharisees and the scribes asked him, "Why do your disciples not live according to the tradition of the elders, but eat with defiled hands?" He said to them, "Isaiah prophesied rightly about you hypocrites, as it is written, 'This people honors me with their lips, but their hearts are far from me; in vain do they worship me, teaching human precepts as doctrines.' You abandon the commandment of God and hold to human tradition."

- Lord, it is different for me. I do not have to face the hundreds of ritual regulations which burdened religion in your day.
- But I can still be caught by foolish scruples, which have nothing to do with love, but come from a superstitious fear of regulations. Free my heart for joy and love.

Wednesday 10th February   Mark 7:14–15

Then he called the crowd again and said to them, "Listen to me, all of you, and understand: there is nothing outside a person that by going in can defile, but the things that come out are what defile."

- Lord, I still have a lot to learn about the human heart. You point me inside, point from my behavior to the heart's intentions behind it. Yet I find myself often thinking just about my outer actions, not about the inner movements of love or envy.

- It is there, in my plans and fantasies, that your grace either moves me or meets my resistance.

Thursday 11th February   Mark 7:24–30

From there Jesus set out and went away to the region of Tyre. He entered a house and did not want anyone to know he was there. Yet he could not escape notice, but a woman whose little daughter had an unclean spirit immediately heard about him, and she came and bowed down at his feet. Now the woman was a Gentile, of Syrophoenician origin. She begged him to cast the demon out of her daughter. He said to her, "Let the children be fed first, for it is not fair to take the children's food and throw it to the dogs." But she answered him, "Sir, even the dogs under the table eat the children's crumbs." Then he said to her, "For saying that, you may go—the demon has left your daughter." So she went home, found the child lying on the bed, and the demon gone.

- Let me imagine this encounter, Lord. I believe you were smiling most of the time. You had taken what we call now a break. This demanding woman arrived and ruined your planned retreat. At first you tease her—everyone knows that Jews do not mix with Gentiles. She is unabashed and comes back hard, turning your metaphor about puppy dogs on its head.
- Lord, I would like to talk to you as the Syrophoenician did, not hesitating to bother you with my needs, and trusting in your goodness and your sense of humor.

Friday 12th February   Mark 7:31–35

Then Jesus returned from the region of Tyre, and went by way of Sidon towards the Sea of Galilee, in the region of the Decapolis. They brought to him a deaf man who had an impediment in his speech; and they begged him to lay his hand on him.

He took him aside in private, away from the crowd, and put his fingers into his ears, and he spat and touched his tongue. Then looking up to heaven, he sighed and said to him, "Ephphatha," that is, "Be opened." And immediately his ears were opened, his tongue was released, and he spoke plainly.

- You were always on the side of health, Lord. You communicated your own vigorous health to people by touching them, even sharing your saliva.
- Let me relish my senses while I have them, open my ears to music and my lips to speech. Touch me with health.

Saturday 13th February   Mark 8:1–8

In those days when there was again a great crowd without anything to eat, Jesus called his disciples and said to them, "I have compassion for the crowd, because they have been with me now for three days and have nothing to eat. If I send them away hungry to their homes, they will faint on the way—and some of them have come from a great distance." His disciples replied, "How can one feed these people with bread here in the desert?" He asked them, "How many loaves do you have?" They said, "Seven." Then he ordered the crowd to sit down on the ground; and he took the seven loaves, and after giving thanks he broke them and gave them to his disciples to distribute; and they distributed them to the crowd. They had also a few small fish; and after blessing them, he ordered that these too should be distributed. They ate and were filled; and they took up the broken pieces left over, seven baskets full.

- Lord, you were not a magician. You would not conjure loaves out of thin air, any more than you would transform mankind without engaging mankind in the mission. You started the meal with the seven loaves and the few small fish, which the disciples supplied.

- I sometimes wish, Lord, that you would manage without me. But you want my few loaves and little fishes, you want to use the inadequate contribution I can make, and transform it into something beyond my powers.

Something to think and pray about each day this week:

Reaching out

Jean Vianney, the Curé of Ars, used to see an old countryman sitting for hours in the parish church, and one day he asked him what he was doing. The man replied, "I look at the good God, and the good God looks at me." In every parish there are mystics who do not know they are mystics, people whose prayer has reached a simplicity and intimacy beyond words. You feel the aura of their prayers when you come into the church. This building has witnessed our baptism, sheltered us in sorrow, confirmed the young, celebrated committed love, and prayed over the remains of those who have gone to the Lord. It expresses the dream, the vision, the reaching out towards God, of the people of a parish and their visitors over the generations.

The Presence of God
As I sit here with my book, God is here.
Around me, in my sensations, in my thoughts and deep within me.
I pause for a moment, and become aware
of God's life-giving presence.

Freedom
A thick and shapeless tree-trunk would never believe
that it could become a statue, admired as a miracle of sculpture,
and would never submit itself to the chisel of the sculptor,
who sees by her genius what she can make of it. (St. Ignatius)
I ask for the grace to let myself be shaped by my loving Creator.

Consciousness
How am I really feeling? Light-hearted? Heavy-hearted?
I may be very much at peace, happy to be here.
Equally, I may be frustrated, worried, or angry.
I acknowledge how I really am. It is the real me that the Lord loves.

The Word
God speaks to each one of us individually. I need to listen to
what he is saying to me. (Please turn to your scripture on the
following pages. Inspiration points are there should you need
them. When you are ready, return here to continue.)

Conversation
Do I notice myself reacting as I pray with the word of God?
Do I feel challenged, comforted, angry?
Imagining Jesus sitting or standing by me,
I speak out my feelings, as one trusted friend to another.

Conclusion
Glory be to the Father, and to the Son, and to the Holy Spirit,
As it was in the beginning, is now, and ever shall be,
World without end. Amen

Sunday 14th February,
Sixth Sunday in Ordinary Time   Luke 6:17, 20–21

He came down with them and stood on a level place, with a great crowd of his disciples and a great multitude of people from all Judea, Jerusalem, and the coast of Tyre and Sidon. Then he looked up at his disciples and said: "Blessed are you who are poor, for yours is the kingdom of God. Blessed are you who are hungry now, for you will be filled. Blessed are you who weep now, for you will laugh."

- Each year we celebrate an international day of prayer for the sick. Pray for them today, and learn from them.
- Remember the words of one saint, bed-ridden for 38 years: "We are all dupes. We seek happiness, and find sorrow. We offer ourselves for suffering, and find joy."

Monday 15th February   James 1:2–8

My brothers and sisters, whenever you face trials of any kind, consider it nothing but joy, because you know that the testing of your faith produces endurance; and let endurance have its full effect, so that you may be mature and complete, lacking in nothing. If any of you is lacking in wisdom, ask God, who gives to all generously and ungrudgingly, and it will be given you. But ask in faith, never doubting, for the one who doubts is like a wave of the sea, driven and tossed by the wind; for the doubter, being double-minded and unstable in every way, must not expect to receive anything from the Lord.

- James links faith not with miracles or signs, but with loyalty and persistence. Our faith is not self-confidence, but is based on our response to God's fidelity.
- Lord, teach me to look through the darkness, to see hope and new life. Give me the gift of endurance when I begin to waver.

Tuesday 16th February   **James 1:16–18**

D
o not be deceived, my beloved. Every generous act of giving, with every perfect gift, is from above, coming down from the Father of lights, with whom there is no variation or shadow due to change. In fulfillment of his own purpose he gave us birth by the word of truth, so that we would become a kind of first fruits of his creatures.

- "The Father of lights, with whom there is no variation or shadow due to change." God is both generous and unfailingly constant, seeking our love so that we are the "first fruits" which belong to God.
- God invites me to respond: How can I do that, today?

Wednesday 17th February, Ash Wednesday   Matthew 6:1–6

"B
eware of practicing your piety before others in order to be seen by them; for then you have no reward from your Father in heaven. So whenever you give alms, do not sound a trumpet before you, as the hypocrites do in the synagogues and in the streets, so that they may be praised by others. Truly I tell you, they have received their reward. But when you give alms, do not let your left hand know what your right hand is doing, so that your alms may be done in secret; and your Father who sees in secret will reward you. And whenever you pray, do not be like the hypocrites; for they love to stand and pray in the synagogues and at the street corners, so that they may be seen by others. Truly I tell you, they have received their reward. But whenever you pray, go into your room and shut the door and pray to your Father who is in secret; and your Father who sees in secret will reward you."

- A lot of religion and faith-practice is personal, known by few others. Jesus praises that; not that religion should not be public, but

90

that it not be practiced for any reason other than for God and for
the good of others.

- We pray because we need God, and we pray because God is God.
Can I pray today for the praise and glory of God and for no other
reason?

Thursday 18th February   **Luke 9:22–25**

Jesus said to his disciples: "The Son of Man must undergo
great suffering, and be rejected by the elders, chief priests, and
scribes, and be killed, and on the third day be raised." Then he
said to them all, "If any want to become my followers, let them
deny themselves and take up their cross daily and follow me. For
those who want to save their life will lose it, and those who lose
their life for my sake will save it. What does it profit them if they
gain the whole world, but lose or forfeit themselves?"

- Jesus' life teaches us that much of what we want to hold onto in
life can be swiftly taken away—our good health, our security of
wealth, even our good name.
- What we share in love and in God cannot be taken away. Can I ask
the Lord to teach me to value love, and to offer my life now and
always in love, and for love.

Friday 19th February   **Matthew 9:14–15**

Then the disciples of John came to him, saying, "Why do we
and the Pharisees fast often, but your disciples do not fast?"
And Jesus said to them, "The wedding guests cannot mourn as
long as the bridegroom is with them, can they? The days will
come when the bridegroom is taken away from them, and then
they will fast."

- In the message of Jesus we find always the contrasts between the
joy of his presence and friendship with us, the pain that he suffers

in bringing his mission forward, and our frustration that this mission of God is not completed in the world.

- Our prayer is like this, too; sometimes we are filled with thanks and joy for the fullness of God's life; at other times with emptiness and hollowness.

Saturday 20th February   Luke 5:27–32

After this he went out and saw a tax collector named Levi, sitting at the tax booth; and he said to him, "Follow me." And he got up, left everything, and followed him. Then Levi gave a great banquet for him in his house; and there was a large crowd of tax collectors and others sitting at the table with them. The Pharisees and their scribes were complaining to his disciples, saying, "Why do you eat and drink with tax collectors and sinners?" Jesus answered, "Those who are well have no need of a physician, but those who are sick; I have come to call not the righteous but sinners to repentance."

- Jesus can enter our lives only if we know and acknowledge deep down that we really need him; otherwise he could not have come. He looks out always for the chances we offer—when we need strength, healing, forgiveness.
- In prayer let your eyes meet his, and receive the light of strength, healing, and forgiveness.

february 21–27

Something to think and pray about each day this week:

Our Father's voice

"The sheep follow the Good Shepherd because they know his voice" (Jn 10:4). How do we hear the voice of God? As a hectoring father, a nagging mother, a moralizing preacher, a didactic teacher, a calculating accountant, a roaring sergeant-major? None of these fit. We have one certainty: that God's voice is the voice of a lover, for whom I am unique, and who knows me in my health or wretchedness, my success or my disasters. I know him by the signs of his presence, in the psalm of the good shepherd, "By quiet waters he leads me, to revive my drooping spirit" (Ps 23).

The Presence of God

Jesus waits silent and unseen to come into my heart.
I will respond to His call.
He comes with His infinite power and love
May I be filled with joy in His presence.

Freedom

I ask for the grace
to let go of my own concerns
and be open to what God is asking of me,
to let myself be guided and formed by my loving Creator.

Consciousness

Knowing that God loves me unconditionally,
I can afford to be honest about how I am.
How has the last day been, and how do I feel now?
I share my feelings openly with the Lord.

The Word

I read the word of God slowly, a few times over, and I listen to
what God is saying to me. (Please turn to your scripture on the
following pages. Inspiration points are there should you need
them. When you are ready, return here to continue.)

Conversation

Remembering that I am still in God's presence,
I imagine Jesus himself standing or sitting beside me,
and say whatever is on my mind, whatever is in my heart,
speaking as one friend to another.

Conclusion

Glory be to the Father, and to the Son, and to the Holy Spirit,
As it was in the beginning, is now, and ever shall be,
World without end. Amen

Sunday 21st February,
First Sunday of Lent   **Luke 4:1–8, 13**

Jesus, full of the Holy Spirit, returned from the Jordan and was led by the Spirit in the wilderness, where for forty days he was tempted by the devil. He ate nothing at all during those days, and when they were over, he was famished. The devil said to him, "If you are the Son of God, command this stone to become a loaf of bread." Jesus answered him, "It is written, 'One does not live by bread alone.'" Then the devil led him up and showed him in an instant all the kingdoms of the world. And the devil said to him, "To you I will give their glory and all this authority; for it has been given over to me, and I give it to anyone I please. If you, then, will worship me, it will all be yours." Jesus answered him, "It is written, 'Worship the Lord your God, and serve only him.'" When the devil had finished every test, he departed from him until an opportune time.

- Lord, you deliberately told your disciples of these temptations—how else would they have known?
- Can I put words on my own temptations, the weaknesses or wickedness that I'm most attracted to?
- Can I see my temptations as you did, against the backdrop of the vocation to which you call me?

Monday 22nd February,
Chair of St. Peter, Apostle   **Matthew 16:13–19**

Now when Jesus came into the district of Caesarea Philippi, he asked his disciples, "Who do people say that the Son of Man is?" And they said, "Some say John the Baptist, but others Elijah, and still others Jeremiah or one of the prophets." He said to them, "But who do you say that I am?" Simon Peter answered, "You are the Messiah, the Son of the living God."

And Jesus answered him, "Blessed are you, Simon son of Jonah! For flesh and blood has not revealed this to you, but my Father in heaven. And I tell you, you are Peter, and on this rock I will build my church, and the gates of Hades will not prevail against it. I will give you the keys of the kingdom of heaven, and whatever you bind on earth will be bound in heaven, and whatever you loose on earth will be loosed in heaven."

- "Who do people say that I am?" The impetuous Peter confesses Jesus to be the Messiah. It is an inspired insight and an inspired confession. This uneducated fisherman is rewarded with a new name; and with a new role, as leader of the people of God.
- Lord, teach me that my strength is not in my personality or my intellect, but in the power of God.

Tuesday 23rd February   Matthew 6:7–8

"When you are praying, do not heap up empty phrases as the Gentiles do; for they think that they will be heard because of their many words. Do not be like them, for your Father knows what you need before you ask him.

- The best prayer may be silent. Jesus own prayer hints at what feeds prayer—an attitude of praising God, desiring the kingdom of love, peace, and justice to come on earth, trying to unite our desires with the desires of God for us and for the world, and to rest in our efforts to forgive others.

Wednesday 24th February   Luke 11:29–32

When the crowds were increasing, he began to say, "This generation is an evil generation; it asks for a sign, but no sign will be given to it except the sign of Jonah. For just as Jonah became a sign to the people of Nineveh, so the Son of Man will be to this generation. The queen of the South will rise at the judgment with the people of this generation and condemn them, because she came from the ends of the earth to listen to the wisdom of Solomon, and see, something greater than Solomon is here! The people of Nineveh will rise up at the judgment with this generation and condemn it, because they repented at the proclamation of Jonah, and see, something greater than Jonah is here!"

- Jonah had things to say which nobody wanted to hear: about conversion and changing some aspects of our style of life; about being faithful to God and to the best in ourselves. The gospel, too, has many sayings which are hard for us to hear.
- Jesus does not demand instant conversion, but he does ask that all his word be allowed into the mind and consciousness. Can I accept the demanding side of God's love today, and ask for help to allow the best in me to come out.

Thursday 25th February   Matthew 7:7–8

"Ask, and it will be given you; search, and you will find; knock, and the door will be opened for you. For everyone who asks receives, and everyone who searches finds, and for everyone who knocks, the door will be opened."

- In the asking is the receiving, in the searching is the finding, in the knocking is the opening. No prayer is wasted. All prayer, like all love, bears its own fruit in its own season.
- Lord, teach me to know that you are always listening and to accept that being heard is good enough in itself.

Friday 26th February   Matthew 5:23–24

So when you are offering your gift at the altar, if you remember that your brother or sister has something against you, leave your gift there before the altar and go; first be reconciled to your brother or sister, and then come and offer your gift.

- If I am at all human, I probably find feelings of hurt, resentment, and bitterness. People I wish to forget inhabit the spaces of my prayer. Jesus challenges us to reconciliation, but this is not easy.

- I can always pray for someone sincerely—that is the beginning of reconciliation. The call to us is to see the other who has hurt or damaged me as being equally loved by God. This realization works no easy miracle of healing, but is a step on the road to forgiveness.

Saturday 27th February   Matthew 5:43–48

Jesus said to the disciples, "You have heard that it was said, 'You shall love your neighbor and hate your enemy.' But I say to you, Love your enemies and pray for those who persecute you, so that you may be children of your Father in heaven; for he makes his sun rise on the evil and on the good, and sends rain on the righteous and on the unrighteous. For if you love those who love you, what reward do you have? Do not even the tax collectors do the same? And if you greet only your brothers and sisters, what more are you doing than others? Do not even the Gentiles do the same? Be perfect, therefore, as your heavenly Father is perfect."

- Jesus' sobering words about enemies come into our prayer again today. The bar is set high—love even your enemies. At other times Jesus is more gentle.

- We need to put both sides together—the comforting and the challenging. Maybe he is content with our desire to forgive, and understands with compassion when we cannot.

- We can always pray for the enemy, for the one who has done us harm. This is the beginning and may one day be forgiveness.

february 28–march 6

Something to think and pray about each day this week:

Seeking slow food

Family meals are at risk. The table can be a place where the preparation of food reflects mother's or father's care, and where parents and children can sit, enjoy, argue, joke, listen, have their voice heard, tease, attack and be attacked, but not walk out. Today couples prize a chance to enjoy a meal with their children. As work or other pressures increase, fast food and TV take over, we find families who never eat together. In some parts of the world the children grab something from the fridge and "graze," a can in one hand, junk food in the other, and their eyes fixed on a TV screen. One reckoning is that, in the USA, 40 percent of meals are eaten in cars. It is no accident that Jesus placed a meal—the Eucharist—at the centre of the Christian family. It is around a common table that a family really lives together. Don't let that disappear. Find a time, at least once a week, for slow food, not fast.

The Presence of God
For a few moments, I think of God's veiled presence in things:
in the elements, giving them existence;
in plants, giving them life; in animals, giving them sensation;
and finally, in me, giving me all this and more,
making me a temple, a dwelling-place of the Spirit.

Freedom
God is not foreign to my freedom.
Instead the Spirit breathes life into my most intimate desires,
gently nudging me towards all that is good.
I ask for the grace to let myself be enfolded by the Spirit.

Consciousness
Knowing that God loves me unconditionally,
I can afford to be honest about how I am.
How has the last day been, and how do I feel now?
I share my feelings openly with the Lord.

The Word
The word of God comes down to us through the scriptures.
May the Holy Spirit enlighten my mind and my heart to
respond to the gospel teachings. (Please turn to your scripture
on the following pages. Inspiration points are there should you
need them. When you are ready, return here to continue.)

Conversation
How has God's word moved me? Has it left me cold?
Has it consoled me or moved me to act in a new way?
I imagine Jesus standing or sitting beside me,
I turn and share my feelings with him.

Conclusion
Glory be to the Father, and to the Son, and to the Holy Spirit,
As it was in the beginning, is now, and ever shall be,
World without end. Amen

Sunday 28th February,
Second Sunday of Lent   Luke 9:28–36

Now about eight days after these sayings Jesus took with him Peter and John and James, and went up on the mountain to pray. And while he was praying, the appearance of his face changed, and his clothes became dazzling white. Suddenly they saw two men, Moses and Elijah, talking to him. They appeared in glory and were speaking of his departure, which he was about to accomplish at Jerusalem. Now Peter and his companions were weighed down with sleep; but since they had stayed awake, they saw his glory and the two men who stood with him. Just as they were leaving him, Peter said to Jesus, "Master, it is good for us to be here; let us make three dwellings, one for you, one for Moses, and one for Elijah"—not knowing what he said. While he was saying this, a cloud came and overshadowed them; and they were terrified as they entered the cloud. Then from the cloud came a voice that said, "This is my Son, my Chosen; listen to him!" When the voice had spoken, Jesus was found alone. And they kept silent and in those days told no one any of the things they had seen.

- Jesus chose Peter, James, and John to witness his glory before he faced the Passion. It woke them up, this mysterious and memorable moment on Mount Tabor.

- Thank you, Lord, for the moments when I feel you close to me. They strengthen me to face the desolate lowlands of my life.

Monday 1st March   Luke 6:36–38

"Be merciful, just as your Father is merciful. Do not judge, and you will not be judged; do not condemn, and you will not be condemned. Forgive, and you will be forgiven; give, and it will be given to you. A good measure, pressed down, shaken together, running over, will be put into your lap; for the measure you give will be the measure you get back."

- We get back from life what we put into it, is a common saying. But the challenge of Jesus is more—to be merciful is to live in a way that always makes the first move towards forgiveness.
- Mercy is the heart of God's love. Can I let mercy take hold of me, so that I will live by it?

Tuesday 2nd March   Matthew 23:9–12

Then Jesus said to the crowds and to his disciples, "And call no one your father on earth, for you have one Father—the one in heaven. Nor are you to be called instructors, for you have one instructor, the Messiah. The greatest among you will be your servant. All who exalt themselves will be humbled, and all who humble themselves will be exalted."

- "The greatest among you will be your servant." The Christian identity is servant, disciple, humble follower. Greatness is in a willingness to serve the needs of others, with love, as Jesus did.
- Can you remember a moment when you felt humbled as you served somebody, or did something important for them? Offer this memory to God in thanks.

Wednesday 3rd March   Matthew 20:25–28

But Jesus called them to him and said, "You know that the rulers of the Gentiles lord it over them, and their great ones are tyrants over them. It will not be so among you; but whoever wishes to be great among you must be your servant, and whoever wishes to be first among you must be your slave; just as the Son of Man came not to be served but to serve, and to give his life a ransom for many."

- Greatness for Jesus is in serving, engaging with the real needs of others, allowing God and the concerns of God to become the first priority in his life.
- That is what our time in prayer can do for us—it expands our concerns to include the whole world, and opens us to the Spirit of the living God.

Thursday 4th March   Luke 16:19–31

Jesus said to the Pharisees, "There was a rich man who was dressed in purple and fine linen and who feasted sumptuously every day. And at his gate lay a poor man named Lazarus, covered with sores, who longed to satisfy his hunger with what fell from the rich man's table; even the dogs would come and lick his sores. The poor man died and was carried away by the angels to be with Abraham. The rich man also died and was buried. In Hades, where he was being tormented, he looked up and saw Abraham far away with Lazarus by his side. He called out, 'Father Abraham, have mercy on me, and send Lazarus to dip the tip of his finger in water and cool my tongue; for I am in agony in these flames.' But Abraham said, 'Child, remember that during your lifetime you received your good things, and Lazarus in like manner evil things; but now he is comforted here, and you are in agony. Besides all this, between you and us a great chasm has been fixed, so that those who might want to pass from here to you cannot do so, and no one can cross from there to us.' He said, 'Then, father, I beg you to send him to my father's house— for I have five brothers—that he may warn them, so that they will not also come into this place of torment.' Abraham replied, 'They have Moses and the prophets; they should listen to them.' He said, 'No, father Abraham; but if someone goes to them from the dead, they will repent.' He said to him, 'If they do not listen to Moses and the prophets, neither will they be convinced even if someone rises from the dead.'"

- This is no ambiguity about this story. We have an obligation as Christians to feed the hungry. Every hungry man and woman in the world is on our conscience. Whether we create the problem or not, we are called to be part of the solution.
- Take some time today to enlarge your compassion for the hungry and your desire to do what you can to feed them, for in feeding them, we feed Jesus.

Friday 5th March   Matthew 21:33–43, 45–46

"Listen to another parable," Jesus said. "There was a landowner who planted a vineyard, put a fence around it, dug a wine press in it, and built a watchtower. Then he leased it to tenants and went to another country. When the harvest time had come, he sent his slaves to the tenants to collect his produce. But the tenants seized his slaves and beat one, killed another, and stoned another. Again he sent other slaves, more than the first; and they treated them in the same way. Finally he sent his son to them, saying, 'They will respect my son.' But when the tenants saw the son, they said to themselves, 'This is the heir; come, let us kill him and get his inheritance.' So they seized him, threw him out of the vineyard, and killed him. Now when the owner of the vineyard comes, what will he do to those tenants?" They said to him, "He will put those wretches to a miserable death, and lease the vineyard to other tenants who will give him the produce at the harvest time." Jesus said to them, "Have you never read in the scriptures: 'The stone that the builders rejected has become the cornerstone; this was the Lord's doing, and it is amazing in our eyes'? Therefore I tell you, the kingdom of God will be taken away from you and given to a people that produces the fruits of the kingdom. When the chief priests and the Pharisees heard his parables, they realized that he was speaking about them. They wanted to arrest him, but they feared the crowds, because they regarded him as a prophet.

- Jesus often confronts greed. Here greed causes death.
- Every hungry man or woman is having food taken from them because the food of the earth is for all.
- Again today, take time to deepen your desire that the poverty and hunger of the world become history; pray for yourself and for those who are doing their best to bring about a world of justice.

Saturday 6th March — Luke 15:22–24

But the father said to his slaves, "Quickly, bring out a robe—the best one—and put it on him; put a ring on his finger and sandals on his feet. And get the fatted calf and kill it, and let us eat and celebrate; for this son of mine was dead and is alive again; he was lost and is found!"

- Imagine yourself for a few moments clothed with a splendid robe—the treasured robe of the family. You have a ring on your finger and comfortable shoes on your feet. All these are God's gift because you have returned. He wanted you back.
- In prayer, think of anything mean in your life which you find blocks you from receiving his love, and know you are forgiven. The robe, the shoe, the ring—all signs of God's forgiveness of you.

march 7–13

Something to think and pray about each day this week:

Taking care

Jesus told us, "When you do good, your right hand should not know what your left hand is doing." That is almost a description of an experienced mother changing nappies. Her routine is so refined that her right hand barely knows what her left hand is doing as she skillfully and rapidly folds and fixes. Nobody pays parents to do this, and nobody even notices, except perhaps the baby, when things don't follow the usual routine.

This regular, repetitive task seems easy when compared with caring for the frail and incontinent. The mother is handling the precious, promising body of her baby. She is rewarded with trust and smiles. But when we are frail, our body may start to fail, and our controls slip. We are not easy to help. We are proud, ashamed, and angry at how we are reduced. Smiles may not come often or easily. Yet across any country there are wives, husbands, family, friends, and paid caregivers whose daily existence centers round cleaning up for the frail and helpless among us. "Your father who sees in secret will reward you" (Matthew 6:6).

This is unfashionable doctrine. Thomas à Kempis, author of *The Imitation of Christ*, urged us to "enjoy being unknown and regarded as nothing." Lord, give me the ability to persist through tedium, to survive without the oxygen of recognition, praise, and stroking, and to do some good things every day which are seen only by God.

The Presence of God
For a few moments, I think of God's veiled presence in things:
in the elements, giving them existence;
in plants, giving them life; in animals, giving them sensation;
and finally, in me, giving me all this and more,
making me a temple, a dwelling-place of the Spirit.

Freedom
God is not foreign to my freedom.
Instead the Spirit breathes life into my most intimate desires,
gently nudging me towards all that is good.
I ask for the grace to let myself be enfolded by the Spirit.

Consciousness
Knowing that God loves me unconditionally,
I can afford to be honest about how I am.
How has the last day been, and how do I feel now?
I share my feelings openly with the Lord.

The Word
I take my time to read the word of God, slowly, a few times,
allowing myself to dwell on anything that strikes me. (Please
turn to your scripture on the following pages. Inspiration points
are there should you need them. When you are ready, return
here to continue.)

Conversation
How has God's word moved me? Has it left me cold?
Has it consoled me or moved me to act in a new way?
I imagine Jesus standing or sitting beside me,
I turn and share my feelings with him.

Conclusion
Glory be to the Father, and to the Son, and to the Holy Spirit,
As it was in the beginning, is now, and ever shall be,
World without end. Amen

108

Sunday 7th March, Third Sunday of Lent   Luke 13:6–9

Jesus told this parable: "A man had a fig tree planted in his vineyard; and he came looking for fruit on it and found none. So he said to the gardener, "See here! For three years I have come looking for fruit on this fig tree, and still I find none. Cut it down! Why should it be wasting the soil?' He replied, 'Sir, let it alone for one more year, until I dig around it and put manure on it. If it bears fruit next year, well and good; but if not, you can cut it down.'"

- You look for fruit, Lord. We are not in this world just to absorb and take in. It is our job as your children to give something back.
- Nobody likes to be dug around and manured; but that unsought disturbance in my life can be God's way of helping me to bear fruit.

Monday 8th March   Luke 4:24–30

And he said, "Truly I tell you, no prophet is accepted in the prophet's hometown. But the truth is, there were many widows in Israel in the time of Elijah, when the heaven was shut up three years and six months, and there was a severe famine over all the land; yet Elijah was sent to none of them except to a widow at Zarephath in Sidon. There were also many lepers in Israel in the time of the prophet Elisha, and none of them was cleansed except Naaman the Syrian." When they heard this, all in the synagogue were filled with rage. They got up, drove him out of the town, and led him to the brow of the hill on which their town was built, so that they might hurl him off the cliff. But he passed through the midst of them and went on his way.

- Jesus challenges his listeners to look beyond themselves towards the outsider—those outside by nationality and by culture. Jesus'

march 2010

mission was to all, especially the outsiders, the lost sheep, and the "pagans."

- To befriend the outsider is to take the risk of being cast out by one's own group. Can I ask the Lord for the courage to risk that?

Tuesday 9th March   Psalm 24(25):4–9

Make me to know your ways, O Lord; teach me your paths. Lead me in your truth, and teach me, for you are the God of my salvation; for you I wait all day long. Be mindful of your mercy, O Lord, and of your steadfast love, for they have been from of old. Do not remember the sins of my youth or my transgressions; according to your steadfast love remember me, for your goodness' sake, O Lord! Good and upright is the Lord; therefore he instructs sinners in the way. He leads the humble in what is right, and teaches the humble his way.

- The Psalms are prayers to God, prayers that are full of human emotion whether that be despair, joy, confusion, or thanks. They are also prayers of hope in the ultimate goodness of the Lord.
- How do these words speak to me today? What word or phrase can I keep with me?

Wednesday 10th March   Matthew 5:17–19

Jesus said to his disciples, "Do not think that I have come to abolish the law or the prophets; I have come not to abolish but to fulfill. For truly I tell you, until heaven and earth pass away, not one letter, not one stroke of a letter, will pass from the law until all is accomplished. Therefore, whoever breaks one of the least of these commandments, and teaches others to do the same, will be called least in the kingdom of heaven; but whoever does them and teaches them will be called great in the kingdom of heaven."

- The fulfilment of the old religion would be a person, Jesus Christ. The law is good only because it leads to Christ. All of religion is good only insofar as it leads us to God and through Christ.
- Our prayer in the company of Jesus leads us to God our Father in the fullest way possible, the way of Jesus.

Thursday 11th March   John 4:25–29, 39–42

The Samaritan woman said to him, "I know that Messiah is coming" (who is called Christ). "When he comes, he will proclaim all things to us." Jesus said to her, "I am he, the one who is speaking to you." Just then his disciples came. They were astonished that he was speaking with a woman, but no one said, "What do you want?" or, "Why are you speaking with her?" Then the woman left her water-jar and went back to the city. She said to the people, "Come and see a man who told me everything I have ever done! He cannot be the Messiah, can he?" Many Samaritans from that city believed in him because of the woman's testimony, "He told me everything I have ever done." So when the Samaritans came to him, they asked him to stay with them; and he stayed there for two days. And many more believed because of his word. They said to the woman, "It is no longer because of what you said that we believe, for we have heard for ourselves, and we know that this is truly the Savior of the world."

- Lord, I am going about my business like the Samarian woman, I'm taken aback when you accost me at the well. You interrupt my business, my getting and spending, the routines of my day.
- Let me savor this encounter, imagine you probing my desires, showing you know the waywardness of my heart. At the end, like her, I am moved with such joy at meeting you that I cannot keep it to myself.

Friday 12th March　　　　　　　　　　**Mark 12:28–34**

One of the scribes came near and heard them disputing with one another, and seeing that he answered them well, he asked him, "Which commandment is the first of all?" Jesus answered, "The first is, 'Hear, O Israel: the Lord our God, the Lord is one; you shall love the Lord your God with all your heart, and with all your soul, and with all your mind, and with all your strength.' The second is this, 'You shall love your neighbor as yourself.' There is no other commandment greater than these." Then the scribe said to him, "You are right, Teacher; you have truly said that 'he is one, and besides him there is no other'; and 'to love him with all the heart, and with all the understanding, and with all the strength,' and 'to love one's neighbor as oneself,'—this is much more important than all whole burnt offerings and sacrifices." When Jesus saw that he answered wisely, he said to him, "You are not far from the kingdom of God." After that no one dared to ask him any question.

- Could you have an image of your heart, soul, mind, strength—maybe a picture for the feelings of your heart, or a colour for your soul; imagine the depth of your mind or the strength of your body?
- Imagine each of them in prayer, one by one; offer them to God in love. Part of prayer is bringing your whole self in love to the one who is creating you moment by moment, day by day, in love.

Saturday 13th March　　　　　　　　　**Luke 18:9–14**

He also told this parable to some who trusted in themselves that they were righteous and regarded others with contempt: "Two men went up to the temple to pray, one a Pharisee and the other a tax collector. The Pharisee, standing by himself, was praying thus, 'God, I thank you that I am not like other people: thieves, rogues, adulterers, or even like this tax collector. I fast twice a week; I give a tenth of all my income.' But the tax collector, standing far off, would not even look up to heaven, but was beating his breast and saying, 'God, be merciful to me, a sinner!' I tell you, this man went down to his home justified rather than the other; for all who exalt themselves will be humbled, but all who humble themselves will be exalted."

- There are times when we want to tell the Lord how good we are, when we look down on others' moral or spiritual life. After all, we are human.
- But that's not to be the direction of our relationship with God. Instead, we look on what is good in ourselves and know that all is gift; both our talents and what we have made of them.
- We end up with the prayer of the taxman—cover me, O Lord, with your mercy because, for all my good deeds and intentions, there is a deeply sinful side of me which needs your mercy.

march 14–20

Something to think and pray about each day this week:

Sharing hope
"I can't take any more of this. I'm at the end of my tether." You know what it is like, don't you, listening to a case that seems hopeless? While you are hearing with sympathy, part of you is wondering, "What can I say?" The mother who phoned me did not know what sort of help she needed, only that she was at the end of her resources. The household had broken apart. When she phoned it was not to ask for specific help, but rather to ask, "Is there any way we can survive?" She said, "We cannot hold this anger and frustration anymore."

Jesus spent days moving among the sick, the depressed, and the demonic, who were drawn to him because they thought, "Here is somebody who will listen to my bad news; he will not just walk away." Most of the miseries we listen to are beyond our power to change, but when we listen to friends with compassion, and avoid blaming, moralizing, or pushing solutions, we contain their miseries, share their burdens, take in their despair, and metabolize it into hope.

The Presence of God
I pause for a moment
and think of the love and the grace that God showers on me,
creating me in his image and likeness, making me his temple.

Freedom
Everything has the potential to draw forth from me a fuller love
and life.
Yet my desires are often fixed, caught, on illusions of fulfillment.
I ask that God, through my freedom, may orchestrate
my desires in a vibrant loving melody rich in harmony.

Consciousness
In the presence of my loving Creator,
I look honestly at my feelings over the last day,
the highs, the low and the level ground.
Can I see where the Lord has been present?

The Word
God speaks to each one of us individually. I need to listen to
what he is saying to me. (Please turn to your scripture on the
following pages. Inspiration points are there should you need
them. When you are ready, return here to continue.)

Conversation
What feelings are rising in me
as I pray and reflect on God's word?
I imagine Jesus himself sitting or standing beside me,
and open my heart to him.

Conclusion
Glory be to the Father, and to the Son, and to the Holy Spirit,
As it was in the beginning, is now, and ever shall be,
World without end. Amen

116

Sunday 14th March,
Fourth Sunday of Lent   **2 Corinthians 5:17–20**

So if anyone is in Christ, there is a new creation: everything old has passed away; see, everything has become new! All this is from God, who reconciled us to himself through Christ, and has given us the ministry of reconciliation; that is, in Christ God was reconciling the world to himself, not counting their trespasses against them, and entrusting the message of reconciliation to us. So we are ambassadors for Christ, since God is making his appeal through us; we entreat you on behalf of Christ, be reconciled to God.

• We are ambassadors for Christ, in a ministry of reconciliation. It is a simple mission, one that is never accomplished, but is sustained by the joy of being Jesus' ambassador.

Monday 15th March   **John 4:46–50**

Then Jesus came again to Cana in Galilee where he had changed the water into wine. Now there was a royal official whose son lay ill in Capernaum. When he heard that Jesus had come from Judea to Galilee, he went and begged him to come down and heal his son, for he was at the point of death. Then Jesus said to him, "Unless you see signs and wonders you will not believe." The official said to him, "Sir, come down before my little boy dies." Jesus said to him, "Go; your son will live." The man believed the word that Jesus spoke to him and started on his way.

• Cana is the place of self-revelation of Jesus. First he changed water into wine, and now he comes as the healer. Jesus is more than meets the eye; he is the son of Mary, and he is also the Son of God.

- Let me sit with this story, listen to what he says and watch what he does. Can I discover something new in him, and come to see Jesus as he really is?

Tuesday 16th March   John 5:1–3, 5–9

After this there was a festival of the Jews, and Jesus went up to Jerusalem. Now in Jerusalem by the Sheep Gate there is a pool, called in Hebrew Beth-zatha, which has five porticoes. In these lay many invalids—blind, lame, and paralyzed. One man was there who had been ill for thirty-eight years. When Jesus saw him lying there and knew that he had been there a long time, he said to him, "Do you want to be made well?" The sick man answered him, "Sir, I have no one to put me into the pool when the water is stirred up; and while I am making my way, someone else steps down ahead of me." Jesus said to him, "Stand up, take your mat and walk." At once the man was made well, and he took up his mat and began to walk.

- Healing is in the air. Near the temple Jesus meets people with chronic illness, the ones that the temple did not want. They just waited, and maybe this man, after 38 years, had given up.
- For Jesus, nobody is unchangeable. He has great respect for each of us, and believes we can always grow in freedom and in faith. Lord, help me to us free, and to live in the freedom of your love and healing.

Wednesday 17th March, St. Patrick   Luke 10:1–2

After this the Lord appointed seventy others and sent them on ahead of him in pairs to every town and place where he himself intended to go. He said to them, "The harvest is plentiful, but the laborers are few; therefore ask the Lord of the harvest to send out laborers into his harvest."

- Let me dip into these words from St. Patrick's Confession: "In the light of our faith in the Trinity, regardless of danger, I must make known the gift of God and everlasting consolation, without fear and frankly. I must spread everywhere the name of God so that after my decease I may leave a bequest to those whom I have baptized in the Lord—so many thousands of people."

Thursday 18th March   John 5:31–40

Jesus said to the Jews "If I testify about myself, my testimony is not true. There is another who testifies on my behalf, and I know that his testimony to me is true. You sent messengers to John, and he testified to the truth. Not that I accept such human testimony, but I say these things so that you may be saved. He was a burning and shining lamp, and you were willing to rejoice for a while in his light. But I have a testimony greater than John's. The works that the Father has given me to complete, the very works that I am doing, testify on my behalf that the Father has sent me. And the Father who sent me has himself testified on my behalf. You have never heard his voice or seen his form, and you do not have his word abiding in you, because you do not believe him whom he has sent. You search the scriptures because you think that in them you have eternal life; and it is they that testify on my behalf. Yet you refuse to come to me to have life."

- All that we know of Jesus says something about the Father—the way he lives and relates to people in compassion, open-heartedness, forgiveness, kindness. All show us the face of God.
- The challenge of faith is big—faith in God means faith in Jesus. When we enter into the presence of Jesus in prayer, we enter deeply into the presence of God.

Friday 19th March, St. Joseph   Matthew 1:18–25

Now the birth of Jesus the Messiah took place in this way. When his mother Mary had been engaged to Joseph, but before they lived together, she was found to be with child from the Holy Spirit. Her husband Joseph, being a righteous man and unwilling to expose her to public disgrace, planned to dismiss her quietly. But just when he had resolved to do this, an angel of the Lord appeared to him in a dream and said, "Joseph, son of David, do not be afraid to take Mary as your wife, for the child conceived in her is from the Holy Spirit. She will bear a son, and you are to name him Jesus, for he will save his people from their sins." All this took place to fulfill what had been spoken by the Lord through the prophet: "Look, the virgin shall conceive and bear a son, and they shall name him Emmanuel," which means, "God is with us." When Joseph awoke from sleep, he did as the angel of the Lord commanded him; he took her as his wife, but had no marital relations with her until she had borne a son; and he named him Jesus.

- We know Joseph as the man of faith. Dreams and insight gave him the impetus to know and then to do what God wanted. For Joseph, faith was both listening and doing.
- Joseph's deep faith strengthened him to do what God wanted. Prayer introduces us into the atmosphere of God's will for us. It is the space where trust can grow.

Saturday 20th March   John 7:40–43

When they heard these words, some in the crowd said, "This is really the prophet." Others said, "This is the Messiah." But some asked, "Surely the Messiah does not come from Galilee, does he? Has not the scripture said that the Messiah is descended

120

from David and comes from Bethlehem, the village where David lived?" So there was a division in the crowd because of him.

- The prejudice against Jesus is strong because of his hometown in Galilee. It is based on ignorance. They refuse to hear him and to believe he is the Christ.
- Love of God, offered and received, softens hardened prejudice. If I bring someone I don't like into the presence of the crucified Lord, my attitude will change, even if gradually.

Something to think and pray about each day this week:

Wasting words

The Bible warns against talking too much. "Is there no end to windy words?" asked Job (Job 16:3). "The more words, the more vanity . . . . There is a time to speak and a time to be silent . . ." (Ecclesiastes 6:11; RSV). Be silent, and let that be your wisdom. Jesus said of the Pharisees: "They think God will hear them for their many words" (Matthew 6:7).

What is clear in the life of Jesus is that he listened with all his senses. The Gospels often remark, "He knew what was in their hearts"—whether it was the scribes laying traps for him, or the disciples in a state of puzzlement or unease. He listened to people, watched their faces, sensed what their innermost feelings were. When they were about to stone the adulterous woman, he did not criticize them, but said just one sentence: "Let anyone among you who is without sin be the first to throw a stone" (John 8:7). After that he was silent and doodled in the sand, feeling the fury and shame of the would-be killers as they trooped out, beginning with the oldest.

When we meet Jesus in prayer, we do not need to explain. He reads our hearts, too. One of the joys of prayer is that it opens our hearts to us, so that we realize our own jealousies or resentments, our deeper feelings. To meet him in this way, we need to be still and stop making words.

The Presence of God

I reflect for a moment on God's presence around me and in me.
Creator of the universe, the sun and the moon, the earth,
every molecule, every atom, everything that is:
God is in every beat of my heart. God is with me now.

Freedom

A thick and shapeless tree-trunk would never believe
that it could become a statue, admired as a miracle of sculpture,
and would never submit itself to the chisel of the sculptor,
who sees by her genius what she can make of it. (St. Ignatius)
I ask for the grace to let myself be shaped by my loving Creator.

Consciousness

Knowing that God loves me unconditionally,
I look honestly over the last day, its events and my feelings.
Do I have something to be grateful for? Then I give thanks.
Is there something I am sorry for? Then I ask forgiveness.

The Word

I read the word of God slowly, a few times over, and I listen to
what God is saying to me. (Please turn to your scripture on the
following pages. Inspiration points are there should you need
them. When you are ready, return here to continue.)

Conversation

What is stirring in me as I pray?
Am I consoled, troubled, left cold?
I imagine Jesus himself standing or sitting at my side,
and share my feelings with him.

Conclusion

Glory be to the Father, and to the Son, and to the Holy Spirit,
As it was in the beginning, is now, and ever shall be,
World without end. Amen

124

Sunday 21st March, Fifth Sunday of Lent   John 8:2–11

Early in the morning Jesus came again to the temple. All the people came to him and he sat down and began to teach them. The scribes and the Pharisees brought a woman who had been caught in adultery; and making her stand before all of them, they said to him, "Teacher, this woman was caught in the very act of committing adultery. Now in the law Moses commanded us to stone such women. Now what do you say?" They said this to test him, so that they might have some charge to bring against him. Jesus bent down and wrote with his finger on the ground. When they kept on questioning him, he straightened up and said to them, "Let anyone among you who is without sin be the first to throw a stone at her." And once again he bent down and wrote on the ground. When they heard it, they went away, one by one, beginning with the elders; and Jesus was left alone with the woman standing before him. Jesus straightened up and said to her, "Woman, where are they? Has no one condemned you?" She said, "No one, sir." And Jesus said, "Neither do I condemn you. Go your way, and from now on do not sin again."

- Where do I stand in this scene? Like the woman standing before her accusers? Like a silent sympathizer hoping that something will happen to save her? Like the skulking male adulterer who got her into this trouble? Like the bystanders already collecting the best stones with a view to a killing? Like one of the elders who slink away, unable to cast the first stone?
- What goes through my head as Jesus is doodling in the sand?

Monday 22nd March   John 8:12

Again Jesus spoke to them, saying, "I am the light of the world. Whoever follows me will never walk in darkness but will have the light of life."

- "I am the light of the world." Jesus, whose light shines to reveal his Father, speaks the words of God.
- Those who follow Jesus also receive this light and are called to be "the light of the world," and not to hide the good news of Jesus.
- How can I reveal the light of Jesus today?

Tuesday 23rd March   John 8:28–30

So Jesus said "When you have lifted up the Son of Man, then you will realize that I am he, and that I do nothing on my own, but I speak these things as the Father instructed me. And the one who sent me is with me; he has not left me alone, for I always do what is pleasing to him." As he was saying these things, many believed in him.

- If we look at the cross of Jesus, we see love. The wood of the cross is alive with love; Jesus on the cross looks at each of us with love.
- Saint Ignatius, looking at the one who is "lifted up" in the love of the father for us, asked "What have I done for Christ? What am I doing for Christ? What ought I to do for Christ?"
- Allow yourself to accept this look of Jesus; his dying look is one of love for each of us, personally and as a vast multitude. How do you respond?

Wednesday 24th March   John 8:31–32

Then Jesus said to the Jews who had believed in him, "If you continue in my word, you are truly my disciples; and you will know the truth, and the truth will make you free."

- The word of God is like a space of welcome and a house where we belong. There we hear the best of God's message—that we are immensely loved. We are called into the service of God and in the home of the word of God we become disciples.

- Let me listen, learn, and commit myself to partnership with Jesus in God's work in the world.

Thursday 25th March,
Annunciation of the Lord   Luke 1:26–29

In the sixth month the angel Gabriel was sent by God to a town in Galilee called Nazareth, to a virgin whose name was Mary. And he came to her and said, "Greetings, favored one! The Lord is with you." But she was much perplexed by his words and pondered what sort of greeting this might be.

- You might find it helpful to contemplate an icon or one of the many great paintings or frescos of this scene. Imagine what Mary felt as she was given this awesome news.
- Mary is concerned and confused, she has questions, and she voices them, but she says "yes" to God's will for her.
- Can I learn from her example?

Friday 26th March   John 10:31–42

The Jews took up stones again to stone him. Jesus replied, "I have shown you many good works from the Father. For which of these are you going to stone me?" The Jews answered, "It is not for a good work that we are going to stone you, but for blasphemy, because you, though only a human being, are making yourself God." Jesus answered, "Is it not written in your law, 'I said, you are gods'? If those to whom the word of God came were called 'gods'—and the scripture cannot be annulled—can you say that the one whom the Father has sanctified and sent into the world is blaspheming because I said, 'I am God's Son'? If I am not doing the works of my Father, then do not believe me. But if I do them, even though you do not believe me, believe the works, so that you may know and understand that the Father is in me and I am in the Father." Then they tried to arrest him again, but he escaped from their hands. He went away again across the Jordan to the place where John had been baptizing earlier, and he remained there. Many came to him, and they were saying, "John performed no sign, but everything that John said about this man was true." And many believed in him there.

- "Then they tried to arrest him again, but he escaped from their hands." This is the last Friday before Jesus' death; his time is close, but it is not yet come.
- How can I use these last few days of Lent? Are there "stones" that I throw at others—perhaps harsh words or rash judgments—that I should lay aside? Can I forgive those who throw such "stones" at me?

Saturday 27th March   John 11:47–52

So the chief priests and the Pharisees called a meeting of the council, and said, "What are we to do? This man is performing many signs. If we let him go on like this, everyone will believe in him, and the Romans will come and destroy both our holy place and our nation." But one of them, Caiaphas, who was high priest that year, said to them, "You know nothing at all! You do not understand that it is better for you to have one man die for the people than to have the whole nation destroyed." He did not say this on his own, but being high priest that year he prophesied that Jesus was about to die for the nation, and not for the nation only, but to gather into one the dispersed children of God.

- Caiaphas was a Sadducee, ruthless, political, and determined to buttress the status quo and the privileges of his wealthy class. He uses the argument of the powerful: we must eliminate the trouble-maker in the name of the common good—in this case, the comfort of the Sadducees.
- But he spoke wiser than he knew. One man, Jesus, was to die for the people, and for me.

march 28–april 3

Something to think and pray about each day this week:

In the face of evil

Why do the wicked prosper? The Psalmist complained to God about it, and the question still haunts us. It haunted Jesus, "My God, why have you forsaken me?" Before his passion when he looked down on Jerusalem, his religious capital, he had the same sickness of heart, "Why did you not use your opportunities while you had them?" He foresaw the destruction of Jerusalem by the Romans, and knew that he could nothing to stop it. If Jesus felt impotent in face of evil, so do we.

Such impotence is part of the human condition. It means being passive, unable to act. It is the central suffering of the passion, whether the passion of Jesus or of any of us. It can lead to a particular sort of prayer. King David in the psalms is constantly crying to God, in a mood that blends anger and frustration with childlike trust:

> Why, O God, have you cast us off for ever?
> How long, O God, is the enemy to scoff?
> Is the foe to insult your name for ever?
> Why, O Lord, do you hold back your hand?
> Why do you keep your right hand hidden? (Psalm 74)

Prayer is the raising of the mind and heart to God, and if it is a heart heavy with anger, impotence, or anguish, that too can find expression.

The Presence of God

In the silence of my innermost being,
in the fragments of my yearned-for wholeness,
can I hear the whispers of God's presence?
Can I remember when I felt God's nearness?
When we walked together and I let myself be embraced by
God's love.

Freedom

There are very few people
who realize what God would make of them
if they abandoned themselves into his hands,
and let themselves be formed by his grace. (St. Ignatius)
I ask for the grace to trust myself totally to God's love.

Consciousness

How do I find myself today?
Where am I with God? With others?
Do I have something to be grateful for? Then I give thanks.
Is there something I am sorry for? Then I ask forgiveness.

The Word

I take my time to read the word of God, slowly, a few times,
allowing myself to dwell on anything that strikes me. (Please
turn to your scripture on the following pages. Inspiration points
are there should you need them. When you are ready, return
here to continue.)

Conversation

Do I notice myself reacting as I pray with the word of God?
Do I feel challenged, comforted, angry?
Imagining Jesus sitting or standing by me,
I speak out my feelings, as one trusted friend to another.

Conclusion

Glory be to the Father, and to the Son, and to the Holy Spirit,
As it was in the beginning, is now, and ever shall be,
World without end. Amen

Sunday 28th March,
Palm Sunday of the Lord's Passion   Philippians 2:5–11

Let the same mind be in you that was in Christ Jesus, who, though he was in the form of God, did not regard equality with God as something to be exploited, but emptied himself, taking the form of a slave, being born in human likeness. And being found in human form, he humbled himself and became obedient to the point of death—even death on a cross. Therefore God also highly exalted him and gave him the name that is above every name, so that at the name of Jesus every knee should bend, in heaven and on earth and under the earth, and every tongue should confess that Jesus Christ is Lord, to the glory of God the Father.

- This hymn expresses the depth of the mystery—that Jesus' inmost nature was divine, but still he emptied himself and took on a human form. He entered our humanity completely.
- Lord, lead me further into this mystery: today and in this week to come.

Monday 29th March   John 12:1–6

Six days before the Passover Jesus came to Bethany, the home of Lazarus, whom he had raised from the dead. There they gave a dinner for him. Martha served, and Lazarus was one of those at the table with him. Mary took a pound of costly perfume made of pure nard, anointed Jesus' feet, and wiped them with her hair. The house was filled with the fragrance of the perfume. But Judas Iscariot, one of his disciples (the one who was about to betray him), said, "Why was this perfume not sold for three hundred denarii and the money given to the poor?" (He said this not because he cared about the poor, but because he was a thief; he kept the common purse and used to steal what was put into it.)

- We join the dinner party and are struck by the surpassing generosity of Mary's gesture and then by the bitter stinginess with which Judas interpreted the gift.
- Lord, when I find myself critical of others, it may be my own warped vision that needs to be corrected.

Tuesday 30th March   **John 13:21–30**

Afer saying this Jesus was troubled in spirit, and declared, "Very truly, I tell you, one of you will betray me." The disciples looked at one another, uncertain of whom he was speaking. One of his disciples—the one whom Jesus loved—was reclining next to him; Simon Peter therefore motioned to him to ask Jesus of whom he was speaking. So while reclining next to Jesus, he asked him, "Lord, who is it?" Jesus answered, "It is the one to whom I give this piece of bread when I have dipped it in the dish." So when he had dipped the piece of bread, he gave it to Judas son of Simon Iscariot. After he received the piece of bread, Satan entered into him. Jesus said to him, "Do quickly what you are going to do." Now no one at the table knew why he said this to him. Some thought that, because Judas had the common purse, Jesus was telling him, "Buy what we need for the festival"; or, that he should give something to the poor. So, after receiving the piece of bread, he immediately went out. And it was night.

- The drama here is centered on Judas. Just two apostles were close enough to Jesus to hear him speak quietly: the beloved disciple (was it John?) reclining on his right, and Judas, reclining on his left, the place of honor. In placing Judas there, and offering him a special morsel, Jesus was making a last appeal to the traitor's heart.
- He would invite him, but not force him; just as he invites us.
- Lord, may I never be so wrapped up in my own plans that I miss your appeals and invitations.

Wednesday 31st March   **Matthew 26:14–16, 20–25**

Then one of the twelve, who was called Judas Iscariot, went to the chief priests and said, "What will you give me if I betray him to you?" They paid him thirty pieces of silver. And from that moment he began to look for an opportunity to betray him. When it was evening, he took his place with the twelve; and while they were eating, he said, "Truly I tell you, one of you will betray me." And they became greatly distressed and began to say to him one after another, "Surely not I, Lord?" He answered, "The one who has dipped his hand into the bowl with me will betray me. The Son of Man goes as it is written of him, but woe to that one by whom the Son of Man is betrayed! It would have been better for that one not to have been born." Judas, who betrayed him, said, "Surely not I, Rabbi?" He replied, "You have said so."

* Why does the treachery of a friend hurt me more than hostility from strangers? It seems like a judgment on me from someone who knows and once loved me.
* Judas succeeded in planning the betrayal unknown to the other apostles. Jesus, however, knew what was in his heart, and could have denounced or prevented him. Instead, he responded with the same love he had shown to Judas from his first calling.
* Again, he never deviated from his respect for human free will. He would appeal, but not force.

Thursday 1st April, Holy Thursday   **John 13:2–15**

During supper Jesus, knowing that the Father had given all things into his hands, and that he had come from God and was going to God, got up from the table, took off his outer robe, and tied a towel around himself. Then he poured water into a basin and began to wash the disciples' feet and to wipe them with the towel that was tied around him. He came to Simon Peter, who said to him, "Lord, are you going to wash my feet?" Jesus answered, "You do not know now what I am doing, but later you will understand." Peter said to him, "You will never wash my feet." Jesus answered, "Unless I wash you, you have no share with me." Simon Peter said to him, "Lord, not my feet only but also my hands and my head!" Jesus said to him, "One who has bathed does not need to wash, except for the feet, but is entirely clean. And you are clean, though not all of you." For he knew who was to betray him; for this reason he said, "Not all of you are clean." After Jesus had washed their feet, had put on his robe, and had returned to the table, he said to them, "Do you know what I have done to you? You call me Teacher and Lord—and you are right, for that is what I am. So if I, your Lord and Teacher, have washed your feet, you also ought to wash one another's feet. For I have set you an example, that you also should do as I have done to you."

- It is not just that Jesus takes the role of a slave. Significantly, the fourth gospel places this incident where other gospels describe the Eucharist, and where St. Luke tells of a dispute between the apostles as to which of them was the greatest.
- Lord, ambition, rivalry, and self-promotion enter even into the holiest moments. I imagine myself sitting like Peter, with you handling my dirty feet. If I want a share with you, then I, too, belong on my knees, in service.

Friday 2nd April, Good Friday — John 18:3–11

So Judas brought a detachment of soldiers together with police from the chief priests and the Pharisees, and they came there with lanterns and torches and weapons. Then Jesus, knowing all that was to happen to him, came forward and asked them, "Whom are you looking for?" They answered, "Jesus of Nazareth." Jesus replied, "I am he." Judas, who betrayed him, was standing with them. When Jesus said to them, "I am he," they stepped back and fell to the ground. Again he asked them, "Whom are you looking for?" And they said, "Jesus of Nazareth." Jesus answered, "I told you that I am he. So if you are looking for me, let these men go." This was to fulfill the word that he had spoken, "I did not lose a single one of those whom you gave me." Then Simon Peter, who had a sword, drew it, struck the high priest's slave, and cut off his right ear. The slave's name was Malchus. Jesus said to Peter, "Put your sword back into its sheath. Am I not to drink the cup that the Father has given me?"

- This is not easy, Lord. Peter drew his sword because he wanted to fight, to "rage, rage against the dying of the light." It is not that Jesus went "gentle into that good night." Rather he accepted the cup from his Father with sorrow and courage, and love for all of us who suffer like him.

- Help me to come to terms with my mortality, Lord. I do not wish for death, but I find in you the only model of facing what I dread.

Saturday 3rd April, Holy Saturday   Luke 24:1–12

But on the first day of the week, at early dawn, they came to the tomb, taking the spices that they had prepared. They found the stone rolled away from the tomb, but when they went in, they did not find the body. While they were perplexed about this, suddenly two men in dazzling clothes stood beside them. The women were terrified and bowed their faces to the ground, but the men said to them, "Why do you look for the living among the dead? He is not here, but has risen. Remember how he told you, while he was still in Galilee, that the Son of Man must be handed over to sinners, and be crucified, and on the third day rise again." Then they remembered his words, and returning from the tomb, they told all this to the eleven and to all the rest. Now it was Mary Magdalene, Joanna, Mary the mother of James, and the other women with them who told this to the apostles. But these words seemed to them an idle tale, and they did not believe them. But Peter got up and ran to the tomb; stooping and looking in, he saw the linen cloths by themselves; then he went home, amazed at what had happened.

- "Why do you look for the living among the dead?" You are not in any tomb, Lord. The tomb is empty. You are not a dead hero to be studied in retrospect. You are alive, and meeting me, at my side, in my heart, feeding me in the Eucharist.
- The report brought by the women, dismissed by the apostles as an idle tale, is the creed by which I live.

april 4–10

Something to think and pray about each day this week:

The seeds of new life

If we have suffered with Jesus, we shall rise with him. At Easter, the church describes that new life, using symbols of fertility and life: light, birth, song, and the great candle plunging into the baptismal font. In the Northern Hemisphere, the signs of new life are around—in the heat of the sun, birds singing and building nests, daffodils in bloom, buds on the chestnuts, lambs, calves, and young of every sort.

Even if we are no longer young, no longer feel the pulse of energy in springtime, this season of Easter assures us that the best part of us will not die. We have never met a mere mortal. In each of us, deeper than our weakness, our weariness, or our badness, lies the true Frank or Kate or Helen or Phil, the part of us that is one with Jesus in his suffering, and that like him longs for a fuller, less threatened life. The seeds of the resurrection lie buried in each of us, and they are nourished at Easter by the body of the risen Lord.

The Presence of God
God is with me, but more,
God is within me, giving me existence.
Let me dwell for a moment on God's life-giving presence
in my body, my mind, my heart,
and in the whole of my life.

Freedom
Many countries are at this moment suffering
the agonies of war.
I bow my head in thanksgiving for my freedom.
I pray for all prisoners and captives.

Consciousness
I remind myself that I am in the presence of the Lord.
I will take refuge in His loving heart.
He is my strength in times of weakness.
He is my comforter in times of sorrow.

The Word
I read the word of God slowly, a few times over, and I listen to what God is saying to me. (Please turn to your scripture on the following pages. Inspiration points are there should you need them. When you are ready, return here to continue.)

Conversation
How has God's word moved me? Has it left me cold?
Has it consoled me or moved me to act in a new way?
I imagine Jesus standing or sitting beside me,
I turn and share my feelings with him.

Conclusion
Glory be to the Father, and to the Son, and to the Holy Spirit,
As it was in the beginning, is now, and ever shall be,
World without end. Amen

Sunday 4th April, Easter Sunday   John 20:1–9

Early on the first day of the week, while it was still dark, Mary Magdalene came to the tomb and saw that the stone had been removed from the tomb. So she ran and went to Simon Peter and the other disciple, the one whom Jesus loved, and said to them, "They have taken the Lord out of the tomb, and we do not know where they have laid him." Then Peter and the other disciple set out and went toward the tomb. The two were running together, but the other disciple outran Peter and reached the tomb first. He bent down to look in and saw the linen wrappings lying there, but he did not go in. Then Simon Peter came, following him, and went into the tomb. He saw the linen wrappings lying there, and the cloth that had been on Jesus' head, not lying with the linen wrappings but rolled up in a place by itself. Then the other disciple, who reached the tomb first, also went in, and he saw and believed; for as yet they did not understand the scripture, that he must rise from the dead.

- Mary Magdalene waited patiently throughout the Sabbath, but before even the sun rose on the first day of the week, she was at the tomb, driven by love.
- Let me recapture the enormity of her shock, as she saw the stone rolled back, the burial wrappings laid aside, the tomb empty. Death, man's oldest enemy, had found its master. A mortal body had found a new life.

Monday 5th April   Matthew 28:8–10

So the women left the tomb quickly with fear and great joy, and ran to tell his disciples. Suddenly Jesus met them and said, "Greetings!" And they came to him, took hold of his feet, and worshiped him. Then Jesus said to them, "Do not be afraid; go and tell my brothers to go to Galilee; there they will see me." Jesus' invitation is to go to Galilee and there "they will see him."

- It's the same invitation he gives to us. "Galilee" can be the neighborhood, the family, the prayer space, the poor, and the many moments we find ourselves aware of Jesus' presence.
- Go back in your own memory to when God was close, and give thanks. In prayer, allow the Lord to tell you to "go and see."

Tuesday 6th April　　　　　　　　　　　John 20:11–17

As Mary wept, she bent over to look into the tomb; and she saw two angels in white, sitting where the body of Jesus had been lying, one at the head and the other at the feet. They said to her, "Woman, why are you weeping?" She said to them, "They have taken away my Lord, and I do not know where they have laid him." When she had said this, she turned around and saw Jesus standing there, but she did not know that it was Jesus. Jesus said to her, "Woman, why are you weeping? Whom are you looking for?" Supposing him to be the gardener, she said to him, "Sir, if you have carried him away, tell me where you have laid him, and I will take him away." Jesus said to her, "Mary!" She turned and said to him in Hebrew, "Rabbouni!" (which means Teacher). Jesus said to her, "Do not hold on to me, because I have not yet ascended to the Father. But go to my brothers and say to them, 'I am ascending to my Father and your Father, to my God and your God.'"

- "Do not hold on to me." Jesus gives Mary little time to express her joy at finding him; instead, he turns her attention towards the future, towards the mission that she and "the brothers" now face.
- Let me meditate a moment on how unlimited the Lord Jesus is now. His risen body embraces the whole world and me.

Wednesday 7th April　　　　　　　　　　Luke 24:13–27

Now on that same day two of them were going to a village called Emmaus, about seven miles from Jerusalem, and talking with each other about all these things that had happened. While they were talking and discussing, Jesus himself came near and went with them, but their eyes were kept from recognizing him. And he said to them, "What are you discussing with each other while you walk along?" They stood still, looking sad. Then one of them, whose name was Cleopas, answered him, "Are you the only stranger in Jerusalem who does not know the things that have taken place there in these days?" He asked them, "What things?" They replied, "The things about Jesus of Nazareth, who was a prophet mighty in deed and word before God and all the people, and how our chief priests and leaders handed him over to be condemned to death and crucified him. But we had hoped that he was the one to redeem Israel. Yes, and besides all this, it is now the third day since these things took place. Moreover, some women of our group astounded us. They were at the tomb early this morning, and when they did not find his body there, they came back and told us that they had indeed seen a vision of angels who said that he was alive. Some of those who were with us went to the tomb and found it just as the women had said; but they did not see him." Then he said to them, "Oh, how foolish you are, and how slow of heart to believe all that the prophets have declared! Was it not necessary that the Messiah should suffer these things and then enter into his glory?" Then beginning with Moses and all the prophets, he interpreted to them the things about himself in all the scriptures.

- Did you ever meet someone while on a journey—in a public place, on a train or bus, while hitchhiking, on a Sunday walk, in a queue at the hospital, at the dentist—and then had a personal chat? People in these situations may share all sorts of personal details about themselves and their children.

- It was the same for the disciples on this Sunday walk. The disciples on the road at a bad time in their lives met a stranger who made some sense of their troubles. Jesus made sense of their distress by his presence and his word. A good chat can heal a bad day. Prayer can do the same.

Thursday 8th April   Luke 24:35–45

Then the disciples told what had happened on the road, and how he had been made known to them in the breaking of the bread. While they were talking about this, Jesus himself stood among them and said to them, "Peace be with you." They were startled and terrified, and thought that they were seeing a ghost. He said to them, "Why are you frightened, and why do doubts arise in your hearts? Look at my hands and my feet; see that it is I myself. Touch me and see; for a ghost does not have flesh and bones as you see that I have." And when he had said this, he showed them his hands and his feet. While in their joy they were disbelieving and still wondering, he said to them, "Have you anything here to eat?" They gave him a piece of broiled fish, and he took it and ate in their presence. Then he said to them, "These are my words that I spoke to you while I was still with you—that everything written about me in the law of Moses, the prophets, and the psalms must be fulfilled." Then he opened their minds to understand the scriptures.

- In simple ways, like eating a piece of fish, the disciples saw with the eyes of faith. Jesus is showing them in simple ways that it is the same Lord they knew in earlier days.
- The Lord of Easter is called the Christ of faith. We are blessed because we believe, even though we cannot see. Lord, I believe; strengthen my belief.

Friday 9th April   John 21:4–14

Just after daybreak, Jesus stood on the beach; but the disciples did not know that it was Jesus. Jesus said to them, "Children, you have no fish, have you?" They answered him, "No." He said to them, "Cast the net to the right side of the boat, and you will find some." So they cast it, and now they were not able to haul it in because there were so many fish. That disciple whom Jesus loved said to Peter, "It is the Lord!" When Simon Peter heard that it was the Lord, he put on some clothes, for he was naked, and jumped into the sea. But the other disciples came in the boat, dragging the net full of fish, for they were not far from the land, only about a hundred yards off. When they had gone ashore, they saw a charcoal fire there, with fish on it, and bread. Jesus said to them, "Bring some of the fish that you have just caught." So Simon Peter went aboard and hauled the net ashore, full of large fish, a hundred fifty-three of them; and though there were so many, the net was not torn. Jesus said to them, "Come and have breakfast." Now none of the disciples dared to ask him, "Who are you?" because they knew it was the Lord. Jesus came and took the bread and gave it to them, and did the same with the fish. This was now the third time that Jesus appeared to the disciples after he was raised from the dead.

- "It is the Lord," "The Lord is near," "Come Lord Jesus": many of the mantra sentences of prayer can deepen our times of prayer. Peter's heart must have jumped when he realized that Jesus was alive, and once again inviting them to follow him.
- Choose your mantra and practice it often!

Saturday 10th April   Acts 4:13–21

Now when they saw the boldness of Peter and John and realized that they were uneducated and ordinary men, they were amazed and recognized them as companions of Jesus. When they saw the man who had been cured standing beside them, they had nothing to say in opposition. So they ordered them to leave the council while they discussed the matter with one another. They said, "What will we do with them? For it is obvious to all who live in Jerusalem that a notable sign has been done through them; we cannot deny it. But to keep it from spreading further among the people, let us warn them to speak no more to anyone in this name." So they called Peter and John and ordered them not to speak or teach at all in the name of Jesus. But Peter and John answered them, "Whether it is right in God's sight to listen to you rather than to God, you must judge; for we cannot keep from speaking about what we have seen and heard." After threatening them again, they let them go, finding no way to punish them because of the people, for all of them praised God for what had happened.

- "We cannot keep from speaking about what we have seen and heard." For Peter and John, there is no alternative—they must preach the risen Jesus, everywhere they can, no matter what the authorities say.
- Can I think of someone who has accepted God's love and been changed profoundly? Am I open to that in my life?

april 11–17

Something to think and pray about each day this week:

Lighting the way
When Jesus said "Let your light shine before all," did he mean that we should be haranguing people in the street? It would not work. There was a time when street-preaching might have made an impact on people. Nowadays everyone who has a radio or TV is bombarded with messages from another sort of street-preacher, the advertiser. They beguile, hector, amuse, and titillate in order to seduce you into buying. As Christians, we are not expected to rival them. We could not. Our Lord's words are not about coercing other people into religion, but about doing good in a visible way, "so that others, seeing your good works, may glorify your father in heaven." In Recife, Brazil, where great numbers of poor people were illiterate, Bishop Helder Camara used to instruct his catechists, "Sisters and brothers, watch how you live. Your lives may be the only gospel your neighbors will ever read." We are all witnesses, at every moment of the day. That does not mean shouting the Creed from the rooftops. It means living in such a way that our lives would not make sense if God did not exist.

The Presence of God

To be present is to arrive as one is and open up to the other.
At this instant, as I arrive here, God is present waiting for me.
God always arrives before me, desiring to connect with me
even more than my most intimate friend.
I take a moment and greet my loving God.

Freedom

"In these days, God taught me
as a schoolteacher teaches a pupil" (St. Ignatius).
I remind myself that there are things God has to teach me yet,
and ask for the grace to hear them and let them change me.

Consciousness

How am I really feeling? Light-hearted? Heavy-hearted?
I may be very much at peace, happy to be here.
Equally, I may be frustrated, worried, or angry.
I acknowledge how I really am. It is the real me that the
Lord loves.

The Word

I take my time to read the word of God, slowly, a few times,
allowing myself to dwell on anything that strikes me. (Please
turn to your scripture on the following pages. Inspiration points
are there should you need them. When you are ready, return
here to continue.)

Conversation

What feelings are rising in me
as I pray and reflect on God's word?
I imagine Jesus himself sitting or standing beside me,
and open my heart to him.

Conclusion

Glory be to the Father, and to the Son, and to the Holy Spirit,
As it was in the beginning, is now and ever shall be,
World without end. Amen

Sunday 11th April,
Second Sunday of Easter   **John 20:19–29**

When it was evening on that day, the first day of the week, and the doors of the house where the disciples had met were locked for fear of the Jews, Jesus came and stood among them and said, "Peace be with you." After he said this, he showed them his hands and his side. Then the disciples rejoiced when they saw the Lord. Jesus said to them again, "Peace be with you. As the Father has sent me, so I send you." When he had said this, he breathed on them and said to them, "Receive the Holy Spirit. If you forgive the sins of any, they are forgiven them; if you retain the sins of any, they are retained." But Thomas (who was called the Twin), one of the twelve, was not with them when Jesus came. So the other disciples told him, "We have seen the Lord." But he said to them, "Unless I see the mark of the nails in his hands, and put my finger in the mark of the nails and my hand in his side, I will not believe." A week later his disciples were again in the house, and Thomas was with them. Although the doors were shut, Jesus came and stood among them and said, "Peace be with you." Then he said to Thomas, "Put your finger here and see my hands. Reach out your hand and put it in my side. Do not doubt but believe." Thomas answered him, "My Lord and my God!" Jesus said to him, "Have you believed because you have seen me? Blessed are those who have not seen and yet have come to believe."

- "Unless I see . . . I will not believe." You can sense some of Thomas' deep feelings of isolation, defiance, and even resentment because he missed out on Jesus' visit.
- Have I suffered in this way when I isolated myself from the community of faith, when I felt slighted or taken for granted? It is

when I am stunned by sorrow that I most need the company of friends and the support of faith.

Monday 12th April   Acts 4:27–31

Peter and John said to their friends, "For in this city, in fact, both Herod and Pontius Pilate, with the Gentiles and the peoples of Israel, gathered together against your holy servant Jesus, whom you anointed, to do whatever your hand and your plan had predestined to take place. And now, Lord, look at their threats, and grant to your servants to speak your word with all boldness, while you stretch out your hand to heal, and signs and wonders are performed through the name of your holy servant Jesus." When they had prayed, the place in which they were gathered together was shaken; and they were all filled with the Holy Spirit and spoke the word of God with boldness.

- Such is the power of this experience for the new community, filled with the Spirit, that "when they had prayed, the place in which they were gathered together was shaken."
- Lord, fill me with the Spirit, that I may live and speak boldly, in your name.

Tuesday 13th April   Acts 4:32–35

Now the whole group of those who believed were of one heart and soul, and no one claimed private ownership of any possessions, but everything they owned was held in common. With great power the apostles gave their testimony to the resurrection of the Lord Jesus, and great grace was upon them all. There was not a needy person among them, for as many as owned lands or houses sold them and brought the proceeds of what was sold. They laid it at the apostles' feet, and it was distributed to each as any had need.

- Luke gives us a lovely summary, a snapshot of this first, small community of believers. It is almost idyllic—pure, joyful, and tranquil, yet vigorous in its testimony to the risen Jesus.
- Lord, teach me to strive for the best that I can do, in your name.

Wednesday 14th April   Acts 5:17–26

Then the high priest took action; he and all who were with him (that is, the sect of the Sadducees), being filled with jealousy, arrested the apostles and put them in the public prison. But during the night an angel of the Lord opened the prison doors, brought them out, and said, "Go, stand in the temple and tell the people the whole message about this life." When they heard this, they entered the temple at daybreak and went on with their teaching. When the high priest and those with him arrived, they called together the council and the whole body of the elders of Israel, and sent to the prison to have them brought. But when the temple police went there, they did not find them in the prison; so they returned and reported, "We found the prison securely locked and the guards standing at the doors, but when we opened them, we found no one inside." Now when the captain of the temple and the chief priests heard these words, they were perplexed about them, wondering what might be going on. Then someone arrived and announced, "Look, the men whom you put in prison are standing in the temple and teaching the people!" Then the captain went with the temple police and brought them, but without violence, for they were afraid of being stoned by the people.

- The apostles were locked up by the Sadducees, but they were not to be stopped; with great irony they were released by "an angel of the Lord"—the Sadducees did not believe in angels.
- Lord, you give us the freedom to be your followers and to tell others "the whole message about this life."

Thursday 15th April   Acts 5:27–33

W hen they had brought them, they had them stand before the council. The high priest questioned them, saying, "We gave you strict orders not to teach in this name, yet here you have filled Jerusalem with your teaching and you are determined to bring this man's blood on us." But Peter and the apostles answered, "We must obey God rather than any human authority. The God of our ancestors raised up Jesus, whom you had killed by hanging him on a tree. God exalted him at his right hand as Leader and Savior, so that he might give repentance to Israel and forgiveness of sins. And we are witnesses to these things, and so is the Holy Spirit whom God has given to those who obey him." When they heard this, they were enraged and wanted to kill them.

- Despite further arrests and harassment, Peter and the others all remain resolute: "We must obey God rather than any human authority . . . we are witnesses to these things."
- How do my beliefs affect my actions, my words, my thoughts, my plans, and my intentions? Is my faith resolute, or do I waver? Let me talk with the Lord about this.

Friday 16th April   Acts 5:34–35, 38–42

B ut a Pharisee in the council named Gamaliel, a teacher of the law, respected by all the people, stood up and ordered the men to be put outside for a short time. Then he said to them, "Fellow Israelites, consider carefully what you propose to do to these men. . . .I tell you, keep away from these men and let them alone; because if this plan or this undertaking is of human origin, it will fail; but if it is of God, you will not be able to overthrow them—in that case you may even be found fighting against God!" They were convinced by him, and when they had called in the apostles, they had them flogged. Then they ordered them not to speak in the name of Jesus, and let them go. As they left the council, they rejoiced that they were considered worthy to suffer dishonor for the sake of the name. And every day in the temple and at home they did not cease to teach and proclaim Jesus as the Messiah.

- "They rejoiced that they were considered worthy to suffer dishonor for the sake of the name." They suffer, but with joy.
- To bear suffering with joy? Can I do that? Who will help me?
- Lord, teach me to know "Christ's joy in spite of sorrow" (Gerard Manley Hopkins).

Saturday 17th April   Acts 6:1–7

Now during those days, when the disciples were increasing in number, the Hellenists complained against the Hebrews because their widows were being neglected in the daily distribution of food. And the twelve called together the whole community of the disciples and said, "It is not right that we should neglect the word of God in order to wait at tables. Therefore, friends, select from among yourselves seven men of good standing, full of the Spirit and of wisdom, whom we may appoint to this task, while we, for our part, will devote ourselves to prayer and to serving the word." What they said pleased the whole community, and they chose Stephen, a man full of faith and the Holy Spirit, together with Philip, Prochorus, Nicanor, Timon, Parmenas, and Nicolaus, a proselyte of Antioch. They had these men stand before the apostles, who prayed and laid their hands on them. The word of God continued to spread; the number of the disciples increased greatly in Jerusalem, and a great many of the priests became obedient to the faith.

- The new community needed to expand, to reach out to others. That can be difficult and may bring changes that disturb some people. But it must be done if the word of God is to spread.
- Let me take some time to imagine myself part of this community as numbers increase. How do I respond to these changes?

april 18–24

Something to think and pray about each day this week:

The new world of Jesus

If Jesus were to appear in our world, he (or she—let us allow scope to possibilities) would be born unnoticed, to a good, struggling family in Ecuador, Uzbekistan, or some place out of the news. People would be puzzled: "Where is that place?" He would not be on television, nor would he occupy a centre of power or wealth. He would be pushed around, slandered, and criticized. He would speak simple truths, and some would listen to him and recognize the voice of God. The good news would spread slowly, as it did two thousand years ago. It would graft on to whatever was good in the world he found. The brokers of power and wealth would not notice it, nor offer their sponsorship. The happy irony of today is that after the first 2000 years, the good news is so widespread that whether they knew it or not, the whole human race joined in celebrating Jesus' millennium birthday.

The Presence of God
What is present to me is what has a hold on my becoming.
I reflect on the presence of God always there in love,
amidst the many things that have a hold on me.
I pause and pray that I may let God
affect my becoming in this precise moment.

Freedom
If God were trying to tell me something, would I know?
If God were reassuring me or challenging me, would I notice?
I ask for the grace to be free of my own preoccupations
and open to what God may be saying to me.

Consciousness
Knowing that God loves me unconditionally,
I can afford to be honest about how I am.
How has the last day been, and how do I feel now?
I share my feelings openly with the Lord.

The Word
God speaks to each one of us individually. I need to listen to
what he is saying to me. (Please turn to your scripture on the
following pages. Inspiration points are there should you need
them. When you are ready, return here to continue.)

Conversation
What is stirring in me as I pray?
Am I consoled, troubled, left cold?
I imagine Jesus himself standing or sitting at my side,
and share my feelings with him.

Conclusion
Glory be to the Father, and to the Son, and to the Holy Spirit,
As it was in the beginning, is now, and ever shall be,
World without end. Amen

Sunday 18th April,
Third Sunday of Easter   John 21:15–17

When they had finished breakfast, Jesus said to Simon Peter, "Simon son of John, do you love me more than these?" He said to him, "Yes, Lord; you know that I love you." Jesus said to him, "Feed my lambs." A second time he said to him, "Simon son of John, do you love me?" He said to him, "Yes, Lord; you know that I love you." Jesus said to him, "Tend my sheep." He said to him the third time, "Simon son of John, do you love me?" Peter felt hurt because he said to him the third time, "Do you love me?" And he said to him, "Lord, you know everything; you know that I love you." Jesus said to him, "Feed my sheep."

- Peter has denied Jesus three times, so three times Jesus tests his love. Through this test of love, he appoints Peter shepherd of his flock. Peter's past is now his past; his commitment to Jesus leads him into God's future.

- Lord, you teach me that true service requires me always to be open to your ways. Sometimes, this can be painful; it may mean that, like Peter, I will be broken open.

Monday 19th April   John 6:26–27a

Jesus answered them, "Very truly, I tell you, you are looking for me, not because you saw signs, but because you ate your fill of the loaves. Do not work for the food that perishes, but for the food that endures for eternal life, which the Son of Man will give you."

- The big sign of God is in the life, works, and words of Jesus Christ. The people wanted more bread, more miracles. The bread of Capernaum is not just flour and water—it is the word and love of God in Jesus.

- This work is in each of us, too—God's work is our faith. Let our prayer be a desire to believe more deeply: "Lord I believe; strengthen my belief."

Tuesday 20th April   John 6:30–35

So they said to him, "What sign are you going to give us then, so that we may see it and believe you? What work are you performing? Our ancestors ate the manna in the wilderness; as it is written, 'He gave them bread from heaven to eat.'" Then Jesus said to them, "Very truly, I tell you, it was not Moses who gave you the bread from heaven, but it is my Father who gives you the true bread from heaven. For the bread of God is that which comes down from heaven and gives life to the world." They said to him, "Sir, give us this bread always." Jesus said to them, "I am the bread of life. Whoever comes to me will never be hungry, and whoever believes in me will never be thirsty."

- The bread from heaven is the word of God and the Eucharist. With the food of this teaching, nothing else is needed for living in the truth.
- Prayer can be a time of being grateful to God for this word of life, and for this bread which means that God is never far away from us. The word and the bread nourish us all the days of life.

Wednesday 21st April   John 6:35

Jesus said to them, "I am the bread of life. No one who comes to me will ever hunger. No one who believes in me will ever thirst."

- The bread of life exists within the community of Jesus Christ. We, his people, are his bread. We are to be this bread for each other. The mystery of the Eucharist is of God being close to God's people, and of God's people being the body of Christ. We are baptized into Christ.

- Think in prayer this day of those close to us who need the nourishment and the comfort of the love of God and his care.
- Can we give it to them?

Thursday 22nd April   John 6:45–51

Jesus said to the people: "It is written in the prophets: 'And they shall all be taught by God.' Everyone who has heard and learned from the Father comes to me. Not that anyone has seen the Father except the one who is from God; he has seen the Father. Very truly, I tell you, whoever believes has eternal life. I am the bread of life. Your ancestors ate the manna in the wilderness, and they died. This is the bread that comes down from heaven, so that one may eat of it and not die. I am the living bread that came down from heaven. Whoever eats of this bread will live forever; and the bread that I will give for the life of the world is my flesh."

- We live two lives—the flesh and the spirit, earthly and eternal. Faith in God is life-giving. It gives energy to the everyday, to the commonplace. The struggle to do good and to live a gospel-centered life is nourished by our faith.
- Prayer is a time to be aware of the life which is eternal. Moments of prayer bring us in touch with the eternal within us, and the eternal around us, the atmosphere of the risen Christ.

Friday 23rd April   John 6:52–53, 56–59

The Jews then disputed among themselves, saying, "How can this man give us his flesh to eat?" So Jesus said to them, "Very truly, I tell you, unless you eat the flesh of the Son of Man and drink his blood, you have no life in you. Those who eat my flesh and drink my blood abide in me, and I in them. Just as the living Father sent me, and I live because of the Father, so whoever eats me will live because of me."

- This chapter of John's gospel presents Jesus as the giver of divine life. He possesses the fullness of godly life. This is what he leaves to us in his flesh and blood, the Eucharist.
- Prayer unites us to the sacrifice of Jesus who, all through his life, gave himself to us as teacher, healer, protector—always as loving friend. What is your favorite title for Jesus? Keep that in mind and bring it through the day like a lingering line of a song or a tune.

Saturday 24th April   John 6:66–69

Because of his teaching many of his disciples turned back and no longer went about with him. So Jesus asked the twelve, "Do you also wish to go away?" Simon Peter answered him, "Lord, to whom can we go? You have the words of eternal life. We have come to believe and know that you are the Holy One of God."

- Maybe Peter repeated these words often to himself: "You have the words of eternal life."
- It can be a mantra of prayer for us, as can other favorite lines from the scriptures. The word of God is a personal gift; let me sit quietly with the words of scripture I enjoy, the words that take me through my day.

april 25–may 1

Something to think and pray about each day this week:

Clothed in Christ

Again and again in the Spiritual Exercises Ignatius Loyola returns to the theme that the "uniform" of Jesus' followers is like that of Jesus himself—poverty, humility, false accusation, maybe prison, and death. In the Exercises, you try to put yourself in the person of Christ when he was resisted, abused, accused falsely, and finally tortured and killed. You learn not to be shocked by hardship, and to recognize there the "livery" of Jesus. You don't look for it, but if it hits you, you don't think it is the end of the world. You meet insults and hardship with as much love and patience as you can muster. You show your mettle more in the bad times than in the good.

The Presence of God

At any time of the day or night, we can call on Jesus.
He is always waiting, listening for our call.
What a wonderful blessing.
No phone needed, no emails, just a whisper.

Freedom

I need to close out the noise, to rise above the noise;
The noise that interrupts, that separates,
The noise that isolates.
I need to listen to God again.

Consciousness

Help me, Lord, to be more conscious of your presence.
Teach me to recognize your presence in others.
Fill my heart with gratitude for the times your love
has been shown to me through the care of others.

The Word

I read the Word of God slowly, a few times over, and I listen to
what God is saying to me. (Please turn to your scripture on the
following pages. Inspiration points are there should you need
them. When you are ready, return here to continue.)

Conversation

Do I notice myself reacting as I pray with the Word of God?
Do I feel challenged, comforted, angry?
Imagining Jesus sitting or standing by me,
I speak out my feelings, as one trusted friend to another.

Conclusion

Glory be to the Father, and to the Son, and to the Holy Spirit,
As it was in the beginning, is now, and ever shall be,
World without end. Amen

Sunday 25th April,
Fourth Sunday of Easter   Revelation 7:9

After this I looked, and there was a great multitude that no one could count, from every nation, from all tribes and peoples and languages, standing before the throne and before the Lamb, robed in white, with palm branches in their hands.

* Dare I let myself hope for such a finale, the unity of all mankind, nations, tribes, peoples, languages?
* Lord, you longed for the unity of God's children. What can I do to bring it closer?

Monday 26th April   Psalms 41(42):1–2

Like the deer that yearns for running streams so my soul is yearning for you, my God. My soul is thirsting for God, the God of my life; When can I enter and see the face of God?

* Do I know the feeling of wanting God in my life, of yearning for and thirsting for "the God of my life"?
* God is waiting to slake my thirst, but I must first turn towards him, with mouth open to receive the refreshing waters.

Tuesday 27th April   Acts 11:25–26

Then Barnabas went to Tarsus to look for Saul, and when he had found him, he brought him to Antioch. So it was that for an entire year they met with the church and taught a great many people, and it was in Antioch that the disciples were first called "Christians."

* The early community continued to grow and grow, despite persecution. In Antioch the number of Gentile converts grew so that it became the hub of further missionary activity.
* Do others know me as "Christian"? How do I feel about that? Do I seek the name, or do I shrink from it sometimes?
* Let me talk with the Lord about this, in our silence.

Wednesday 28th April · John 12:44–46

Then Jesus cried aloud: "Whoever believes in me believes not in me but in him who sent me. And whoever sees me sees him who sent me. I have come as light into the world, so that everyone who believes in me should not remain in the darkness."

- Humanity is lit up by Jesus, enlightened by its creator, so that we know that within our human personality is the spark of divinity. Jesus became like us so that we might become like him.
- God's light shines through all creation, bringing life, compassion, and justice. What role do I have in this? How can I help?

Thursday 29th April, St. Catherine of Siena · 1 John 1:5–7

This is the message we have heard from him and proclaim to you, that God is light and in him there is no darkness at all. If we say that we have fellowship with him while we are walking in darkness, we lie and do not do what is true; but if we walk in the light as he himself is in the light, we have fellowship with one another, and the blood of Jesus his Son cleanses us from all sin.

- Catherine of Siena said, "Where we see sins, God sees weakness." Her words point to the reality that many people try to do their best but find that their faults and failings often overcome them.
- God sees the heart and sees our efforts to do good, even though these efforts do not always succeed. God's Spirit, given with many gifts and energies, also brings the gift of forgiveness.
- Lord, teach me to walk away from darkness and keep to the well-lit path.

Friday 30th April · John 14:1–6

Jesus said to his disciples, "Do not let your hearts be troubled. Believe in God, believe also in me. In my Father's house there are many dwelling places. If it were not so, would I have told you that I go to prepare a place for you? And if I go and prepare a place for you, I will come again and will take you to myself, so that where I am, there you may be also. And you know the way to the place where I am going." Thomas said to him, "Lord, we do not know where you are going. How can we know the way?" Jesus said to him, "I am the way, and the truth, and the life. No one comes to the Father except through me."

- "I am the way, and the truth, and the life." Jesus leaves us in no doubt—God is accessible through him because he is God.
- These words are a gift: that with and in Jesus we have the deepest personal security in life, knowing that all can be found in him.

Saturday 1st May   John 14:10b–11

Jesus said to his disciples, "The words that I say to you I do not speak on my own; but the Father who dwells in me does his works. Believe me that I am in the Father and the Father is in me; but if you do not, then believe me because of the works themselves."

- When we pray, something goes on deep inside us. Without being able to articulate it, we get to know God. Everyone who prays knows God.
- The people who just know in their heart that God is near, that God is caring and that God is love, and that everything in life can make sense, are people of deep faith.
- Do I try too hard to reach God? Can I let God reach out to me, and receive him? Let me give thanks for this great gift.

may 2–8

Something to think and pray about each day this week:

Living through faith

My friend Karl served God as a Jesuit for fifty years. Instead of celebrating his jubilee, he was just one of the thousands murdered in East Timor during 1999. Deaths like his acutely pose the Psalmist's question, "Why do the wicked prosper?" They make Christ's death on the cross more central than any other mystery of our faith. Whatever else we know about the Father of Jesus, it is clear that he does not protect his loved ones from wickedness, but rather gives them the grace to bring good out of evil, provided they do not follow the example of those who do them wrong.

We can say, in a spirit of faith, that Karl celebrates his jubilee in heaven, and this is a comforting thought. But it does no justice to the mix of feelings that his life and death leaves us. As long-married couples and long-serving religious know only too well, the taste of a jubilee, look back over the years, is not so much a long draught of sweet wine, as a cocktail of different flavors, sweet and sour. We have lived through a lot, and we are blessed if the experience has not left us bitter. It was St. Paul who said, "Do not be defeated by evil, but overcome evil with good." That was the faith of Karl and of the peace-makers. It is a faith for the strong, not the weak.

The Presence of God
As I sit here, the beating of my heart,
the ebb and flow of my breathing, the movements of my mind
are all signs of God's ongoing creation of me.
I pause for a moment and become aware
of this presence of God within me.

Freedom
I will ask God's help,
to be free from my own preoccupations,
to be open to God in this time of prayer,
to come to love and serve him more.

Consciousness
Knowing that God loves me unconditionally,
I look honestly over the last day, its events, and my feelings.
Do I have something to be grateful for? Then I give thanks.
Is there something I am sorry for? Then I ask forgiveness.

The Word
I take my time to read the word of God, slowly, a few times,
allowing myself to dwell on anything that strikes me. (Please
turn to your scripture on the following pages. Inspiration points
are there should you need them. When you are ready, return
here to continue.)

Conversation
Remembering that I am still in God's presence,
I imagine Jesus himself standing or sitting beside me,
and say whatever is on my mind, whatever is in my heart,
speaking as one friend to another.

Conclusion
Glory be to the Father, and to the Son, and to the Holy Spirit,
As it was in the beginning, is now, and ever shall be,
World without end. Amen

Sunday 2nd May,
Fifth Sunday of Easter   John 13:31a, 34–35

When Judas had gone out, Jesus said, "I give you a new commandment, that you love one another. Just as I have loved you, you also should love one another. By this everyone will know that you are my disciples, if you have love for one another."

- "Love one another." This was not an easy, sentimental invitation. Jesus had just seen his friend Judas go out into the night, with a view to betraying him. He had loved Judas with an unselfish love, but had lost him.
- Lord, you know me, you know that I could act as Judas did. You know that I do not want to go that way, but rather to live in such a way that everyone would know me as your disciple.

Monday 3rd May,
Sts. Philip and James, Apostles   John 14:8–10a

Philip said to Jesus, "Lord, show us the Father, and we will be satisfied." Jesus said to him, "Have I been with you all this time, Philip, and you still do not know me? Whoever has seen me has seen the Father. How can you say, 'Show us the Father'? Do you not believe that I am in the Father and the Father is in me?"

- Let me stand in Philip's shoes, and hear Jesus' words. What do I really know of Jesus and his Father's relationship? Am I confused, too, like Philip?
- Lord, I can know you through your words, but also through what you are. Let me enter more deeply into that mystery.

Tuesday 4th May   John 14:27, 31b

Jesus said to his disciples, "Peace I leave with you; my peace I give to you. I do not give to you as the world gives. Do not let your hearts be troubled, and do not let them be afraid. Rise, let us be on our way."

- It has been said that the most common phrase in scripture is "do not be afraid." At each moment God walks with us, hand in hand, with deep care, wanting us to be safe.
- Even when in fear or anxiety, we are safe because we belong to God. In that is our peace.

Wednesday 5th May   John 15:1–8

Jesus said to his disciples, "I am the true vine, and my Father is the vine-grower. He removes every branch in me that bears no fruit. Every branch that bears fruit he prunes to make it bear more fruit. You have already been cleansed by the word that I have spoken to you. Abide in me as I abide in you. Just as the branch cannot bear fruit by itself unless it abides in the vine, neither can you unless you abide in me. I am the vine, you are the branches. Those who abide in me and I in them bear much fruit, because apart from me you can do nothing. Whoever does not abide in me is thrown away like a branch and withers; such branches are gathered, thrown into the fire, and burned. If you abide in me, and my words abide in you, ask for whatever you wish, and it will be done for you. My Father is glorified by this, that you bear much fruit and become my disciples."

- Each of us can see the life and work of God in others—in ministry, in love, in courage and endurance, in ordinary human care and compassion. Each of us is gifted in some unique way.
- Each of us can bear fruit for God in a way nobody else can; the tone of the gospel is different in everyone who spreads it.
- Can I think about the special gifts of someone I know? Do they see in themselves what I see? What gifts might others see in me?

Thursday 6th May   **John 15:9–11**

Jesus said to his disciples, "As the Father has loved me, so I have loved you; abide in my love. If you keep my commandments, you will abide in my love, just as I have kept my Father's commandments and abide in his love. I have said these things to you so that my joy may be in you, and that your joy may be complete."

- The deepest joys and satisfactions of life have to do with our experience of loving and being loved: the love parents have for their children; the love of friends that is strong and lasting.
- Love enables us to die for others, love spends itself for another. Only love lasts as a motive for any good we want to do. It is the greatest of God's gifts. Let us give thanks for this gift.

Friday 7th May   **John 15:15**

Jesus said to his disciples: "I do not call you servants any longer, because the servant does not know what the master is doing; but I have called you friends, because I have made known to you everything that I have heard from my Father.

- Jesus, my friend; the person I can relax with, be quiet or talk at length, complain or rejoice, be serious or humorous.
- Can I allow myself to be friends with Jesus?

Saturday 8th May   **John 15:18–21**

Jesus said to his disciples: "If the world hates you, be aware that it hated me before it hated you. If you belonged to the world, the world would love you as its own. Because you do not belong to the world, but I have chosen you out of the world—therefore the world hates you. Remember the word that I said to you, 'Servants are not greater than their master.' If they persecuted me, they will persecute you; if they kept my word, they will keep yours also. But they will do all these things to you on account of my name, because they do not know him who sent me."

- Jesus wants our faith and our presence with him. The coming of the Trinity among us arises from the desire of God to invite us into belonging with them, and to know the mystery of God from the inside.
- We can say "yes" or "no" to that invitation. Prayer is one way of saying "yes" and of opening ourselves to the divine energy in the world and inside each of us.

Something to think and pray about each day this week:

Death's victory

You may know this story from the siege of Toledo in the Spanish Civil war. The starving garrison inside the fortress was commanded by Colonel Moscardó. The besieging army him telephoned the Colonel, "We have captured your son. We will shoot him unless you surrender." Moscardó asked to speak to his son on the phone. When the boy came, his father spoke only two words, "Muere bien (Die well)."

Of all we have to do in this life, here is the hardest task, to die well. The thousands of deaths we see on television do not prepare us to see it as a task at all. Death is often presented as the ultimate failure in dramas that flood our screens. But the most comforting memories of my years as a priest are of the people who showed me what it was to die well. In a New York hospital I was called to an old Irishman. He was worn out by a life of hard work on the docks, and he knew he was dying. Alone in the harsh city, he had drifted, rather than moved, away from the church. He was so overwhelmed at finding an Irish priest, and receiving the last sacraments, that both of us were weeping. He could remember the Hail Mary, and as his strength ebbed away, he kept repeating with total contentment, "Pray for us sinners, now and at the hour of our death." Many of his generation saw death in Ireland ('bás in Éireann') as a blessing. He had the next best thing.

The Presence of God
I pause for a moment
and reflect on God's life-giving presence
in every part of my body, in everything around me,
in the whole of my life.

Freedom
God is not foreign to my freedom.
Instead the Spirit breathes life into my most intimate desires,
gently nudging me towards all that is good.
I ask for the grace to let myself be enfolded by the Spirit.

Consciousness
How do I find myself today?
Where am I with God? With others?
Do I have something to be grateful for? Then I give thanks.
Is there something I am sorry for? Then I ask forgiveness.

The Word
God speaks to each one of us individually. I need to listen to
what he is saying to me. (Please turn to your scripture on the
following pages. Inspiration points are there should you need
them. When you are ready, return here to continue.)

Conversation
How has God's word moved me? Has it left me cold?
Has it consoled me or moved me to act in a new way?
I imagine Jesus standing or sitting beside me,
I turn and share my feelings with him.

Conclusion
Glory be to the Father, and to the Son, and to the Holy Spirit,
As it was in the beginning, is now, and ever shall be,
World without end. Amen

Sunday 9th May,
Sixth Sunday of Easter   John 14:25–27

Jesus answered: "I have said these things to you while I am still with you. But the Advocate, the Holy Spirit, whom the Father will send in my name, will teach you everything, and remind you of all that I have said to you. Peace I leave with you; my peace I give to you. I do not give to you as the world gives. Do not let your hearts be troubled, and do not let them be afraid."

* What a prospect of learning you open up for me, Lord! The Holy Spirit is to go on teaching me all my days, reminding me of your words, and unwrapping their meaning in all my circumstances.
* And the sign of his work in me with be peace. My heart will be untroubled, unafraid.

Monday 10th May   John 15:26–16:4

Jesus said to his disciples, "When the Advocate comes, whom I will send to you from the Father, the Spirit of truth who comes from the Father, he will testify on my behalf. You also are to testify because you have been with me from the beginning. I have said these things to you to keep you from stumbling. They will put you out of the synagogues. Indeed, an hour is coming when those who kill you will think that by doing so they are offering worship to God. And they will do this because they have not known the Father or me. But I have said these things to you so that when their hour comes you may remember that I told you about them. I did not say these things to you from the beginning, because I was with you."

* There's an atmosphere in these chapters of John's gospel that Jesus wants to be with us, that he likes being with us, and cares about his friendships with us. Each of us is invited.

- Can I hand over my cares, joys, and sorrows into the care of the loving God?

Tuesday 11th May   John 16:5–7

Jesus said to his disciples, "But now I am going to him who sent me; yet none of you asks me, 'Where are you going?' But because I have said these things to you, sorrow has filled your hearts. Nevertheless I tell you the truth: it is to your advantage that I go away, for if I do not go away, the Advocate will not come to you; but if I go, I will send him to you."

- As we approach pentecost, the scripture leads us to focus on the future—the risen Christ in no longer physically present in a place. Now, the Spirit is present, always and in every place.
- Can I sit with that for a moment or two? The Spirit, my Advocate, is always present.

Wednesday 12th May   John 16:12–15

Jesus said to his disciples, "I still have many things to say to you, but you cannot bear them now. When the Spirit of truth comes, he will guide you into all the truth; for he will not speak on his own, but will speak whatever he hears, and he will declare to you the things that are to come. He will glorify me, because he will take what is mine and declare it to you. All that the Father has is mine. For this reason I said that he will take what is mine and declare it to you."

- The mystery of the Trinity is difficult for us. One important word that helps us approach the Trinity is "sharing." The three persons live in the love of sharing their truth and all they are.
- Prayer introduces us to the mystery of God, the mystery of truth and of gift. All of God is gift; prayer is our time of allowing the gift of Father, Son, and Spirit reach deeply into our lives.

Thursday 13th May   **John 16:19–20**

Jesus knew that they wanted to ask him, so he said to them, "Are you discussing among yourselves what I meant when I said, 'A little while, and you will no longer see me, and again a little while, and you will see me'? Very truly, I tell you, you will weep and mourn, but the world will rejoice; you will have pain, but your pain will turn into joy."

- The turning of pain into joy is often a focus of Jesus' words; it is based on his conviction of his resurrection from death.
- The resurrection of Jesus means that there is always a future for us—a future of fullness of life and of freedom in the joy of his friendship, now and in eternal life.

Friday 14th May, St. Mathias, Apostle   **John 15:12–14**

Jesus said to his disciples, "This is my commandment, that you love one another as I have loved you. No one has greater love than this, to lay down one's life for one's friends. You are my friends if you do what I command you."

- We know little of Mathias except that scripture tells us he was a witness to the great events of Jesus' life, and was chosen, by election, to replace Judas, the great betrayer.
- In the face of failure from others, especially from those in whom great trust was placed, am I prepared to step forward? Or do I want to retreat, to withdraw, to hold back a little longer?

Saturday 15th May   **John 16:23–28**

Jesus said to his disciples, "Very truly, I tell you, if you ask anything of the Father in my name, he will give it to you. Until now you have not asked for anything in my name. Ask and you will receive, so that your joy may be complete. I have said these things to you in figures of speech. The hour is coming when I will no longer speak to you in figures, but will tell you plainly of the Father. On that day you will ask in my name. I do not say to you that I will ask the Father on your behalf; for the Father himself loves you, because you have loved me and have believed that I came from God. I came from the Father and have come into the world; again, I am leaving the world and am going to the Father."

- We may struggle with or even lose the conviction that it is worthwhile asking for what we want in prayer.
- "If you ask anything of the Father in my name, he will give it to you." Jesus awaits our asking. Full-hearted asking of God always brings a gift in return; it may be a specific grace or petition we ask for, or it may be simply the deep support from God that enables us to cope and to grow even when life is difficult.

may 16–22

Something to think and pray about each day this week:

Moving on

The strange story of Jesus' transfiguration on Mount Tabor describes what we could call a peak experience. The three witnesses, Peter, James and John, are bowled over by the sense of exaltation, light, and happiness. Peter is for building a tent there. He wants to keep things as they are. Not so, says Jesus. It can never be so. Down the mountain they must slide. The transfiguration is a reminder that nothing in this world is static or permanent. Living beings change and move. We are forever in the business, not of holding on, but of letting go. We may think that, by owning or capturing or tent-building, we can make the party last forever. Not so. Our God can never be held or locked in a tent. Our God lives with us and lovingly moves through time with us. That is why moments like birthdays, or times of togetherness, remind us that God's light shines from within us all. They are moments to remember with joy.

The Presence of God
I pause for a moment
and think of the love and the grace that God showers on me,
creating me in his image and likeness, making me his temple.

Freedom
Lord, grant me the grace to be free from the excesses of this life.
Let me not get caught up with the desire for wealth.
Keep my heart and mind free to love and serve you.

Consciousness
In the presence of my loving Creator,
I look honestly at my feelings over the last day,
the highs, the lows, and the level ground.
Can I see where the Lord has been present?

The Word
God speaks to each one of us individually. I need to listen to
what he is saying to me. (Please turn to your scripture on the
following pages. Inspiration points are there should you need
them. When you are ready, return here to continue.)

Conversation
Sometimes I wonder what I might say
if I were to meet You in person, Lord.
I might say "Thank You, Lord" for always being there for me.
I know with certainty there were times when you carried me.
When through your strength I got through the dark times in
my life.

Conclusion
Glory be to the Father, and to the Son, and to the Holy Spirit,
As it was in the beginning, is now, and ever shall be,
World without end. Amen

Sunday 16th May,
Ascension of the Lord   Luke 24:46–53

Jesus said to the disciples: "Thus it is written, that the Messiah is to suffer and to rise from the dead on the third day, and that repentance and forgiveness of sins is to be proclaimed in his name to all nations, beginning from Jerusalem. You are witnesses of these things. And see, I am sending upon you what my Father promised; so stay here in the city until you have been clothed with power from on high." Then he led them out as far as Bethany, and, lifting up his hands, he blessed them. While he was blessing them, he withdrew from them and was carried up into heaven. And they worshipped him, and returned to Jerusalem with great joy; and they were continually in the temple blessing God.

- I'm walking out to Bethany with Jesus and the disciples. He seems to be giving us final instructions. We are filled with love, but also with foreboding. He constantly comes back to the promise of help, of the Holy Spirit, of the Comforter, of power from on high.
- He raises his hand in a familiar blessing—and suddenly he is gone. Astonishingly I feel, in my companions and myself, not desolation, but joy.

Monday 17th May   John 16:29–33

The disciples said to Jesus, "Yes, now you are speaking plainly, not in any figure of speech! Now we know that you know all things, and do not need to have anyone question you; by this we believe that you came from God. Jesus answered them, "Do you now believe? The hour is coming, indeed it has come, when you will be scattered, each one to his home, and you will leave me alone. Yet I am not alone because the Father is with me. I have said this to you, so that in me you may have peace. In the world you face persecution. But take courage; I have conquered the world!"

- These words of Jesus are the foundation and basis for Christian hope, built on the victory of Jesus over death, and his presence in our lives. He has conquered anything that can make for despair and discouragement.
- As Pope Benedict XVI has written, "A first essential setting for learning hope is prayer. When no one listens to me any more, God listens to me."

Tuesday 18th May   John 17:1–3

After Jesus had spoken these words, he looked up to heaven and said, "Father, the hour has come; glorify your Son so that the Son may glorify you, since you have given him authority over all people, to give eternal life to all whom you have given him. And this is eternal life, that they may know you, the only true God, and Jesus Christ whom you have sent."

- Eternal life is not just for the future; it is a gift partly given now in our faith. To be in touch with Jesus is to be in touch with a rich and full eternal life, the mysterious life of God.
- We tap into that life in prayer. It is like living water, new sight. We are enlightened by the Light of the World.

Wednesday 19th May   John 17:11

Jesus said to the disciples, "And now I am no longer in the world, but they are in the world, and I am coming to you. Holy Father, protect them in your name that you have given me, so that they may be one, as we are one."

- Jesus is like a good friend. He wants to keep us with him, just as none of us want to lose a friend. Friendship with Jesus is being with him and being sent in his name.

- Our mission as his followers is in the midst of and in the depths of the world. He wants his love and message inserted in the center of our world. This is how we deepen our friendship.

Thursday 20th May   John 17:20–23

Jesus looked up to heaven and said, "Father, I ask not only on behalf of these, but also on behalf of those who will believe in me through their word, that they may all be one. As you, Father, are in me and I am in you, may they also be in us, so that the world may believe that you have sent me. The glory that you have given me I have given them, so that they may be one, as we are one, I in them and you in me, that they may become completely one, so that the world may know that you have sent me and have loved them even as you have loved me."

- This is the prayer of Jesus for his followers through the ages. Jesus prays for each of us.
- Can we imagine him at prayer, as he names his apostles, his friends, and all he wants to pray for? Prayer is our naming of God; it is also Jesus' naming of us to his Father.
- Can I hear Jesus say my name?

Friday 21st May   John 21:15–17

When they had finished breakfast, Jesus said to Simon Peter, "Simon son of John, do you love me more than these?" He said to him, "Yes, Lord; you know that I love you." Jesus said to him, "Feed my lambs." A second time he said to him, "Simon son of John, do you love me?" He said to him, "Yes, Lord; you know that I love you." Jesus said to him, "Tend my sheep." He said to him the third time, "Simon son of John, do you love me?" Peter felt hurt because he said to him the third time, "Do you love me?" And he said to him, "Lord, you know everything; you know that I love you." Jesus said to him, "Feed my sheep."

- "Lord you know I love you." It's a humble prayer because often we feel we don't live up to our call from God or to the goodness of love we receive in life. We may feel shame, as Peter felt when he denied his friend, Jesus.

- God looks into the heart and sees what we would like to be, as well as seeing what we have done in life. Let me become aware that God is looking into my heart and loving me.

Saturday 22nd May — John 21:20–25

Peter turned and saw the disciple whom Jesus loved following them; he was the one who had reclined next to Jesus at the supper and had said, "Lord, who is it that is going to betray you?" When Peter saw him, he said to Jesus, "Lord, what about him?" Jesus said to him, "If it is my will that he remain until I come, what is that to you? Follow me!" So the rumor spread in the community that this disciple would not die. Yet Jesus did not say to him that he would not die, but, "If it is my will that he remain until I come, what is that to you?" This is the disciple who is testifying to these things and has written them, and we know that his testimony is true. But there are also many other things that Jesus did; if every one of them were written down, I suppose that the world itself could not contain the books that would be written.

- Can you note where and when your life with Jesus began? Like John, we don't know where it will end. Where is Jesus now writing his gospel in your life so that others will know his love, his call, and his identity?

- Can I speak with the Lord about this?

may 23–29

Something to think and pray about each day this week:

Living together
I once lived beside a field where Brent geese came in the winter to graze. Watching them closely, you could see families and other relationships. The gander is larger than the goose, and is a jealous guardian of his mate and goslings. He keeps them in a cluster; any encroaching male is chased by the home bird, who charges at the invader with a straight, swollen neck, honking and furious. It never comes to blows or blood. The intruder retires and grazing resumes. If you look at a flock feeding on the grass, the first impression of kindly, peaceful birds changes to something much more like a human family at table. There are squabbles going on all the time, mostly about territory. Geese, like people, cannot share a patch for long without finding something to argue about. They differ from us—and can teach us a lesson—in that they have ritual and harmless ways of settling their arguments. Rows are never serious enough to interrupt a meal, and they never lead to bloodshed or serious breakdown of relationships. When they find an angry gander defending his territory with loud honks, they give him space. There is no blood on the carpet, no expelling or separation, simply an adjustment to the other. We could learn from them.

The Presence of God
Jesus waits silent and unseen to come into my heart.
I will respond to His call.
He comes with His infinite power and love.
May I be filled with joy in His presence.

Freedom
A thick and shapeless tree-trunk would never believe
that it could become a statue, admired as a miracle of sculpture,
and would never submit itself to the chisel of the sculptor,
who sees by her genius what she can make of it. (St. Ignatius)
I ask for the grace to let myself be shaped by my loving Creator.

Consciousness
Knowing that God loves me unconditionally,
I look honestly over the last day, its events, and my feelings.
Do I have something to be grateful for? Then I give thanks.
Is there something I am sorry for? Then I ask forgiveness.

The Word
I read the word of God slowly, a few times over, and I listen to
what God is saying to me. (Please turn to your scripture on the
following pages. Inspiration points are there should you need
them. When you are ready, return here to continue.)

Conversation
Do I notice myself reacting as I pray with the word of God?
Do I feel challenged, comforted, angry?
Imagining Jesus sitting or standing by me,
I speak out my feelings, as one trusted friend to another.

Conclusion
Glory be to the Father, and to the Son, and to the Holy Spirit,
As it was in the beginning, is now, and ever shall be,
World without end. Amen

184

Sunday 23rd May, Pentecost   John 20:19

When it was evening on that day, the first day of the week, and the doors of the house where the disciples had met were locked for fear of the Jews, Jesus came and stood among them and said, "Peace be with you."

- St. Teresa of Avila reflected on Jesus' capacity to bring peace: "You find yourself in pain, in trouble, and these few words, 'Do not be troubled' calm you, fill you with light, and dissipate all your troubles—troubles from which, a few moments before, you would not have believed the wisest in the world could have delivered you."
- Let me think about the wisdom of her words.

Monday 24th May   Mark 10:17–23

As he was setting out on a journey, a man ran up and knelt before him, and asked him, "Good Teacher, what must I do to inherit eternal life?" Jesus said to him, "Why do you call me good? No one is good but God alone. You know the commandments: 'You shall not murder; You shall not commit adultery; You shall not steal; You shall not bear false witness; You shall not defraud; Honor your father and mother.'" He said to him, "Teacher, I have kept all these since my youth." Jesus, looking at him, loved him and said, "You lack one thing; go, sell what you own, and give the money to the poor, and you will have treasure in heaven; then come, follow me." When he heard this, he was shocked and went away grieving, for he had many possessions. Then Jesus looked around and said to his disciples, "How hard it will be for those who have wealth to enter the kingdom of God!"

- This is an encounter to savor. Here is a well-heeled man of considerable good will, wanting to deepen his spiritual life. He is glad to be able to tell Jesus that he has kept the commandments. Jesus loves him for it and asks him to make the next leap: not into more commandments, but into the following of Jesus with all the uncertainties that entails.

- As Machado wrote: "Traveler, there is no path. Paths are made by walking." We should not use the commandments as an excuse for not stepping out in faith.

Tuesday 25th May   Mark 10:28–30

Peter began to say to him, "Look, we have left everything and followed you." Jesus said, "Truly I tell you, there is no one who has left house or brothers or sisters or mother or father or children or fields, for my sake and for the sake of the good news, who will not receive a hundredfold now in this age—houses, brothers and sisters, mothers and children, and fields, with persecutions—and in the age to come eternal life."

- Peter watched the rich young man ponder and then decline the invitation of Jesus. It brings home to him the extraordinary move he himself made on the shore of the lake, when he left his boat and home to follow Jesus; and as so often, he has the gift of blurting out what is on the mind of the other disciples.
- I sense the warmth of Jesus' reply and promise. What does this mean for me?

Wednesday 26th May   Mark 10:32, 35–40

They were on the road, going up to Jerusalem, and Jesus was walking ahead of them … James and John, the sons of Zebedee, came forward to him and said to him, "Teacher, we want you to do for us whatever we ask of you." And he said to them, "What is it you want me to do for you?" And they said to him, "Grant us to sit, one at your right hand and one at your left, in your glory." But Jesus said to them, "You do not know what you are asking. Are you able to drink the cup that I drink, or be baptized with the baptism that I am baptized with?" They replied, "We are able." Then Jesus said to them, "The cup that I drink you will drink; and with the baptism with which I am baptized, you will be baptized; but to sit at my right hand or at my left is not mine to grant, but it is for those for whom it has been prepared."

- The dynamics of this story are intriguing. James and John are trying for some self-promotion: an instance of individuals using religion for their own selfish and worldly purposes. We have seen the same in public and church life, among parents seeking school places, in people's hunger for respectability and status.
- Lord save me from the temptation to use religion for anything else except as a path to you.

Thursday 27th May   **Mark 10:46–52**

They came to Jericho. As he and his disciples and a large crowd were leaving Jericho, Bartimaeus son of Timaeus, a blind beggar, was sitting by the roadside. When he heard that it was Jesus of Nazareth, he began to shout out and say, "Jesus, Son of David, have mercy on me!" Many sternly ordered him to be quiet, but he cried out even more loudly, "Son of David, have mercy on me!" Jesus stood still and said, "Call him here." And they called the blind man, saying to him, "Take heart; get up, he is calling you." So throwing off his cloak, he sprang up and came to Jesus. Then Jesus said to him, "What do you want me to do for you?" The blind man said to him, "My teacher, let me see again." Jesus said to him, "Go; your faith has made you well." Immediately he regained his sight and followed him on the way.

- Bartimaeus' cloak was his uniform by day and his blanket by night. Leaving it behind was to throw off of his security.
- Jesus welcomes us without our securities. Stripped of everything we come to him. Prayer is a time to leave off pretence and short-term

securities, a time just to be ourselves with the one who knows us through and through.

Friday 28th May   Mark 11:15–17

Then they came to Jerusalem. Jesus entered the temple and began to drive out those who were selling and those who were buying in the temple, and he overturned the tables of the money-changers and the seats of those who sold doves; and he would not allow anyone to carry anything through the temple. He was teaching and saying, "Is it not written, 'My house shall be called a house of prayer for all the nations'? But you have made it a den of robbers."

- What aroused anger in Jesus was that commerce and caste had ousted reverence. The moneychangers and sellers of doves used their privilege and license to extort high prices from poor pilgrims. People had created barriers and divisions between the courts to exclude gentiles and women from some areas.
- Do I always respect what a church should be? A house of prayer, not of commerce; and for all nations, without compartments; a place where all can seek God.

Saturday 29th May   Jude 17, 20–21

But you, beloved, must remember the predictions of the apos-tles of our Lord Jesus Christ; . . . build yourselves up on your most holy faith; pray in the Holy Spirit; keep yourselves in the love of God; look forward to the mercy of our Lord Jesus Christ that leads to eternal life.

- "Build yourselves up." In our age, fitness and looking physically impressive are part of a new religion. Scripture reminds us of what we need to do to stay spiritually fit. The instructions are clearly set out for us.
- Can I do improve my spiritual fitness, to deepen my faith? What can I work on today?

may 30–june 5

Something to think and pray about each day this week:

God of relationship

When we speak of the Blessed Trinity, we circle around it and wonder how it touches us. It is about relationships—one God in three persons. We do not understand the Trinity, but we experience it, as Patrick Kavanagh put it:

That through the hole in reason's ceiling
We can fly to knowledge
Without ever going to college.

The Holy Spirit was the bond of love and communion between Jesus and his father. As sisters and brothers of Jesus, we are joined to God by the same Spirit. As we grow older, we may feel lost and lonely. We can temper our loneliness by remembering our bond with the Trinity, every time we bless ourselves in the name of our Father who created us, our brother Jesus who redeemed us, and the Holy Spirit who binds into the godhead.

The Presence of God
As I sit here with my book, God is here.
Around me, in my sensations, in my thoughts, and deep within me.
I pause for a moment and become aware
of God's life-giving presence.

Freedom
A thick and shapeless tree-trunk would never believe
that it could become a statue, admired as a miracle of sculpture,
and would never submit itself to the chisel of the sculptor,
who sees by her genius what she can make of it. (St. Ignatius)
I ask for the grace to let myself be shaped by my loving Creator.

Consciousness
How am I really feeling? Light-hearted? Heavy-hearted?
I may be very much at peace, happy to be here.
Equally, I may be frustrated, worried, or angry.
I acknowledge how I really am. It is the real me that the Lord loves.

The Word
The word of God comes down to us through the scriptures.
May the Holy Spirit enlighten my mind and my heart to respond to the gospel teachings. (Please turn to your scripture
on the following pages. Inspiration points are there should you
need them. When you are ready, return here to continue.)

Conversation
Do I notice myself reacting as I pray with the word of God?
Do I feel challenged, comforted, angry?
Imagining Jesus sitting or standing by me,
I speak out my feelings, as one trusted friend to another.

Conclusion
Glory be to the Father, and to the Son, and to the Holy Spirit,
As it was in the beginning, is now, and ever shall be,
World without end. Amen

Sunday 30th May, The Holy Trinity — John 16:12–14

"I still have many things to say to you, but you cannot bear them now. When the Spirit of truth comes, he will guide you into all the truth; for he will not speak on his own, but will speak whatever he hears, and he will declare to you the things that are to come. He will glorify me, because he will take what is mine and declare it to you."

- "You cannot bear them now," you said. Lord, you time your interventions for my readiness.
- They that wait upon you shall renew their strength, says Isaiah. May I learn how to wait upon you.

Monday 31st May, Visitation of the Virgin Mary — Luke 1:39–47

In those days Mary set out and went with haste to a Judean town in the hill country, where she entered the house of Zechariah and greeted Elizabeth. When Elizabeth heard Mary's greeting, the child leaped in her womb. And Elizabeth was filled with the Holy Spirit and exclaimed with a loud cry, "Blessed are you among women, and blessed is the fruit of your womb. And why has this happened to me, that the mother of my Lord comes to me? For as soon as I heard the sound of your greeting, the child in my womb leaped for joy. And blessed is she who believed that there would be a fulfillment of what was spoken to her by the Lord." And Mary said, "My soul magnifies the Lord, and my spirit rejoices in God my Savior."

- The Magnificat was a daily prayer of Mary, in good times and bad. We can imagine that she often prayed in words like that. Even at times like the passion and death of her son, her faith remained strong that God would care of her and of him.

- In prayer we can pray our own Magnificat, thanking God for blessings, for good times, for bad times through which God protected us, and for the ways in which we have grown up—in good times and bad.

Tuesday 1st June   Mark 12:13–17

Then they sent to Jesus some Pharisees and some Herodians to trap him in what he said. And they came and said to him, "Teacher, we know that you are sincere, and show deference to no one; for you do not regard people with partiality, but teach the way of God in accordance with truth. Is it lawful to pay taxes to the emperor, or not? Should we pay them, or should we not?" But knowing their hypocrisy, he said to them, "Why are you putting me to the test? Bring me a denarius and let me see it." And they brought one. Then he said to them, "Whose head is this, and whose title?" They answered, "The emperor's." Jesus said to them, "Give to the emperor the things that are the emperor's, and to God the things that are God's." And they were utterly amazed at him.

- Only give divinity to God—is that the meaning of the text today? The Pharisees and Herodians got a lot from being under Roman rule, and Jesus has as much as told them they owe something in return.
- But life and truth and religion are more than political. To people who saw the emperor as almost divine, Jesus asserted that only God is divine and only to God is worship due.
- In my prayer and worship, let me render what is due to God.

Wednesday 2nd June   Mark 12:18–27

Some Sadducees, who say there is no resurrection, came to Jesus and asked him a question, saying, "Teacher, Moses wrote for us that 'if a man's brother dies, leaving a wife but no child, the man shall marry the widow and raise up children for his brother.' There were seven brothers; the first married and, when he died, left no children; and the second married her and died, leaving no children; and the third likewise; none of the seven left children. Last of all the woman herself died. In the resurrection whose wife will she be? For the seven had married her." Jesus said to them, "Is not this the reason you are wrong, that you know neither the scriptures nor the power of God? For when they rise from the dead, they neither marry nor are given in marriage, but are like angels in heaven. And as for the dead being raised, have you not read in the book of Moses, in the story about the bush, how God said to him, 'I am the God of Abraham, the God of Isaac, and the God of Jacob'? He is God not of the dead, but of the living; you are quite wrong."

- The strange questions lead to a good answer about God—God is the God of life, of living beings. We are to leave what comes after this life to God, knowing that the answers we seek will not be easily forthcoming.

- In prayer we can grapple with big religious questions knowing that they get some sort of a context at the feet of Jesus, or at the cross. Our questions are not always answered in prayer, but prayer gives them a context in which they can be lived. "Live the questions," said Rainer Maria Rilke, "and one day you will find the answers."

Thursday 3rd June   **Mark 12:28–34**

One of the scribes came near and heard them disputing with one another, and seeing that Jesus answered them well, he asked him, "Which commandment is the first of all?" Jesus answered, "The first is, 'Hear, O Israel: the Lord our God, the Lord is one; you shall love the Lord your God with all your heart, and with all your soul, and with all your mind, and with all your strength.' The second is this, 'You shall love your neighbor as yourself.' There is no other commandment greater than these." Then the scribe said to him, "You are right, Teacher; you have truly said that 'he is one, and besides him there is no other'; and 'to love him with all the heart, and with all the understanding, and with all the strength,' and 'to love one's neighbor as oneself,'—this is much more important than all whole burnt offerings and sacrifices." When Jesus saw that he answered wisely, he said to him, "You are not far from the kingdom of God." After that no one dared to ask him any question.

- At the heart of our openness to God and our desire to do God's will, we hear that there is one great commandment of love—to love God and to love our neighbor. Long believed by the Jewish people but often clouded in regulations and minute laws, Jesus is offering his path to true faith in God, through love.
- We touch here the heart of religion, and in prayer we enter into that space and listen.

Friday 4th June   Mark 12:35–37

While Jesus was teaching in the temple, he said, "How can the scribes say that the Messiah is the son of David? David himself, by the Holy Spirit, declared, 'The Lord said to my Lord, "Sit at my right hand, until I put your enemies under your feet."' David himself calls him Lord; so how can he be his son?" And the large crowd was listening to him with delight.

- Jesus is more than the son of David. He is Jesus the Lord, the beloved son "in whom the Father was well pleased." He is Son of God, human and divine.
- In his love and to him we pray.

194

Saturday 5th June **Mark 12:41–44**

Jesus sat down opposite the treasury, and watched the crowd putting money into the treasury. Many rich people put in large sums. A poor widow came and put in two small copper coins, which are worth a penny. Then he called his disciples and said to them, "Truly I tell you, this poor widow has put in more than all those who are contributing to the treasury. For all of them have contributed out of their abundance; but she out of her poverty has put in everything she had, all she had to live on."

- Nobody would even know that the widow put anything into the collection box. The coins were small and would make no noise— the large sums were easily heard! Jesus recognized her offering, her gift, and her sacrifice.
- Our work for the Lord may be simple and unknown to all but a few. It is known to God and in God's sight; this is enough reward.

june 6–12

Something to think and pray about each day this week:

Wisdom of the cross
Jesus said, "Take up your cross" (Mk 8:34–35). It is not something you go looking for in faraway places. Sooner or later the Lord hands us a cross, and our job is to recognize it. For each of us there are events that made a difference. Our sorrowful mysteries will be different for each reader. Maybe it was a meeting with a friend, a lover or an enemy. Maybe it was a sickness, or a triumph. We try to see our life through the eyes of faith, with a confidence that God in his Providence can draw good out of the most awful and unwelcome happenings.

This is true wisdom, to find a faith that can carry us through darkness, doubt, and suffering. They call it the mystical phase of religious development, and many of you who form the Sacred Space community are there.

The Presence of God

For a few moments, I think of God's veiled presence in things:
in the elements, giving them existence;
in plants, giving them life; in animals, giving them sensation;
and finally, in me, giving me all this and more,
making me a temple, a dwelling-place of the Spirit.

Freedom

I ask for the grace to believe
in what I could be and do
if I only allowed God, my loving Creator,
to continue to create me, guide me, and shape me.

Consciousness

In the presence of my loving Creator,
I look honestly at my feelings over the last day,
the highs, the lows, and the level ground.
Can I see where the Lord has been present?

The Word

I take my time to read the word of God, slowly, a few times,
allowing myself to dwell on anything that strikes me. (Please
turn to your scripture on the following pages. Inspiration points
are there should you need them. When you are ready, return
here to continue.)

Conversation

How has God's word moved me? Has it left me cold?
Has it consoled me or moved me to act in a new way?
I imagine Jesus standing or sitting beside me,
I turn and share my feelings with him.

Conclusion

Glory be to the Father, and to the Son, and to the Holy Spirit,
As it was in the beginning, is now, and ever shall be,
World without end. Amen

Sunday 6th June,
Feast of the Body and Blood of Christ Luke 9:11–17

When the crowds found out about it, they followed him; and he welcomed them, and spoke to them about the kingdom of God, and healed those who needed to be cured. The day was drawing to a close, and the twelve came to him and said, "Send the crowd away, so that they may go into the surrounding villages and countryside, to lodge and get provisions; for we are here in a deserted place." But he said to them, "You give them something to eat." They said, "We have no more than five loaves and two fish—unless we are to go and buy food for all these people." For there were about five thousand men. And he said to his disciples, "Make them sit down in groups of about fifty each." They did so and made them all sit down. And taking the five loaves and the two fish, he looked up to heaven, and blessed and broke them, and gave them to the disciples to set before the crowd. And all ate and were filled. What was left over was gathered up, twelve baskets of broken pieces.

- "You give them something to eat." Lord, what did you mean by that? One reading is that many people had brought food with them, but did not want to share it out until the apostles led the way with their five loaves and two fish. So Jesus' miracle was to turn selfish, wary people into generous people, happy to share.
- Lord, transform me in this same way.

Monday 7th June Matthew 5:1–12

When Jesus saw the crowds, he went up the mountain; and after he sat down, his disciples came to him. Then he began to speak, and taught them, saying: "Blessed are the poor in spirit, for theirs is the kingdom of heaven. Blessed are those who mourn, for they will be comforted. Blessed are the meek, for they will inherit the earth. Blessed are those who hunger and thirst for righteousness, for they will be filled. Blessed are the merciful, for they will receive mercy. Blessed are the pure in heart, for they will see God. Blessed are the peacemakers, for they will be called children of God. Blessed are those who are persecuted for righteousness' sake, for theirs is the kingdom of heaven. Blessed are you when people revile you and persecute you and utter all kinds of evil against you falsely on my account. Rejoice and be glad, for your reward is great in heaven, for in the same way they persecuted the prophets who were before you."

• Jesus lived every one of the "Blesseds." As you list them, notice how he might have lived them himself: he was merciful, pure in heart (single-minded), a peacemaker, etc.

• Note them as you read the gospel and in your prayer. Jesus knew each of the Beatitudes from the inside out. He knew just where the blessing and presence of God may be found.

Tuesday 8th June   Matthew 5:14–16

Jesus said to the disciples, "You are the light of the world. A city built on a hill cannot be hidden. No one after lighting a lamp puts it under the bushel basket, but on the lampstand, and it gives light to all in the house. In the same way, let your light shine before others, so that they may see your good works and give glory to your Father in heaven."

• Each of us is a light for the world because we are enlightened by Jesus, the light of the world. The light within us is not our own, but is a reflection of his light, the light of God.

• Prayer exposes us to this. Lord, enlighten me.

Wednesday 9th June   Matthew 5:17–19

Jesus said to the crowds, "Do not think that I have come to abolish the law or the prophets; I have come not to abolish but to fulfill. For truly I tell you, until heaven and earth pass away, not one letter, not one stroke of a letter, will pass from the law until all is accomplished. Therefore, whoever breaks one of the least of these commandments, and teaches others to do the same, will be called least in the kingdom of heaven; but whoever does them and teaches them will be called great in the kingdom of heaven."

- When I read these words, I am troubled, Lord. Some scholars deny the authenticity of these verses. After all, Jesus nowhere insists on observance of all 613 precepts of Old Testament law, much of it ceremonial.

- What sense have these words for me? That the meaning of the law is love of God and of my neighbor?

Thursday 10th June   Matthew 5:21–24

Jesus said to the crowds, "You have heard that it was said to those of ancient times, 'You shall not murder'; and 'whoever murders shall be liable to judgment.' But I say to you that if you are angry with a brother or sister, you will be liable to judgment; and if you insult a brother or sister, you will be liable to the council; and if you say, 'You fool,' you will be liable to the hell of fire. So when you are offering your gift at the altar, if you remember that your brother or sister has something against you, leave your gift there before the altar and go; first be reconciled to your brother or sister, and then come and offer your gift."

- What we have against others, or another has against us, comes to the surface in our prayer. This is a good space for hurts, grudges, bitterness, and anger to be in. The space of prayer is a space of love, and the healing of life's hurts is rooted in the love of God for everyone.

- In times of hurt, pray for the other—it will not magically heal hurts or change things, but it does make a big difference.

Friday 11th June, Feast of the Sacred Heart   Luke 15:3–7

So he told them this parable: "Which one of you, having a hundred sheep and losing one of them, does not leave the ninety-nine in the wilderness and go after the one that is lost until he finds it? When he has found it, he lays it on his shoulders and rejoices. And when he comes home, he calls together his friends and neighbors, saying to them, 'Rejoice with me, for I have found my sheep that was lost.' Just so, I tell you, there will be more joy in heaven over one sinner who repents than over ninety-nine righteous people who need no repentance."

- Lord, I find comfort in contemplating your heart.
- As you reveal yourself through the gospels, I find that the basic attitude of your heart is one of unconditional love, not hatred or ambivalence. The first and last message of the gospel is that God loves this world and every person in it.

Saturday 12th June   Matthew 5:33–37

Jesus said to the crowds, "Again, you have heard that it was said to those of ancient times, 'You shall not swear falsely, but carry out the vows you have made to the Lord.' But I say to you, Do not swear at all, either by heaven, for it is the throne of God, or by the earth, for it is his footstool, or by Jerusalem, for it is the city of the great King. And do not swear by your head, for you cannot make one hair white or black. Let your word be 'Yes, Yes' or 'No, No'; anything more than this comes from the evil one."

- Jesus shows us that calling on God as witness is something of great importance. It is truly sacred.
- Do I need to review my attitude on this? Do I need to look to how I speak? Do I resort to speaking powerfully when I should speak plainly?

june 13–19

Something to think and pray about each day this week:

Building the kingdom

In the kingdom of God, it is deeds that count, not words. I once lived with two old Jesuits, one passionate about Irish and the other passionate about exercise. They had warm hearts concealed behind exteriors that seemed crotchety to others; indeed, they seemed crotchety to one another. After years of increasingly cross exchanges, they lapsed into silence, and stopped talking to each other. They could get away with it in a large community. Willie, who loved the Irish language, spent part of his morning collecting firewood to bring it to his fireplace. But in his late eighties, as he grew more frail, this became too hard. It was as much as he could do to walk outside, much less collect and carry.

One morning he came back from his walk to find his fire made up, and a stack of dry wood beside it. The pattern was repeated, day after day. His old sparring partner, Piaras, had noticed Willie's plight, and every day gathered a bundle for him. No words were exchanged. Instead, Willie would use his morning walk, once a week, to visit the corner shop and buy a bag of Piaras' favorite sweets. Every Friday Willie would leave them at his door, without a word. So the exchange went on, firewood for sweets, week by week, till Willie lapsed into his final illness. Piaras came to make peace with him, but talk was unnecessary. They had made up long before, without words.

The Presence of God

I remind myself that, as I sit here now,
God is gazing on me with love and holding me in being.
I pause for a moment and think of this.

Freedom

I need to close out the noise, to rise above the noise;
The noise that interrupts, that separates,
The noise that isolates.
I need to listen to God again.

Consciousness

In God's loving presence I unwind the past day,
starting from now and looking back, moment by moment.
I gather in all the goodness and light, in gratitude.
I attend to the shadows and what they say to me,
seeking healing, courage, forgiveness.

The Word

I take my time to read the word of God, slowly, a few times,
allowing myself to dwell on anything that strikes me. (Please
turn to your scripture on the following pages. Inspiration points
are there should you need them. When you are ready, return
here to continue.)

Conversation

Do I notice myself reacting as I pray with the word of God?
Do I feel challenged, comforted, angry?
Imagining Jesus sitting or standing by me,
I speak out my feelings, as one trusted friend to another.

Conclusion

Glory be to the Father, and to the Son, and to the Holy Spirit,
As it was in the beginning, is now, and ever shall be,
World without end. Amen

Sunday 13th June,
Eleventh Sunday in Ordinary Time   Luke 7:36–39

One of the Pharisees asked Jesus to eat with him, and he went into the Pharisee's house and took his place at the table. And a woman in the city, who was a sinner, having learned that he was eating in the Pharisee's house, brought an alabaster jar of ointment. She stood behind him at his feet, weeping, and began to bathe his feet with her tears and to dry them with her hair. Then she continued kissing his feet and anointing them with the ointment. Now when the Pharisee who had invited him saw it, he said to himself, "If this man were a prophet, he would have known who and what kind of woman this is who is touching him—that she is a sinner."

- This is a story of extravagance and generosity. The ointment was expensive and so was the alabaster jar. The woman whom nobody wanted near the feast was extravagant in love.
- Somehow Jesus' forgiving love had got through to her, and she responded as best she knew, by giving something really expensive, by giving her all. Jesus saw beyond the sin and behind the oil to the love. That would conquer all in the end.

Monday 14th June   Matthew 5:38–42

Jesus said to the crowds, "You have heard that it was said, 'An eye for an eye and a tooth for a tooth.' But I say to you, Do not resist an evildoer. But if anyone strikes you on the right cheek, turn the other also; and if anyone wants to sue you and take your coat, give your cloak as well; and if anyone forces you to go one mile, go also the second mile. Give to everyone who begs from you, and do not refuse anyone who wants to borrow from you."

- "Go the extra mile," to do more than is expected, is a saying which encourages us really to give of ourselves for others. This happens regularly in friendship, in marriage, in parenting, in the workplace, and the household.

- Let me recall those who have gone the extra mile for me; and those who do it each day in their work or in their home. Lord, I give thanks for the generosity people show each day.

Tuesday 15th June   Matthew 5:43–48

Jesus said to the crowds, "You have heard that it was said, 'You shall love your neighbor and hate your enemy.' But I say to you, Love your enemies and pray for those who persecute you, so that you may be children of your Father in heaven; for he makes his sun rise on the evil and on the good, and sends rain on the righteous and on the unrighteous. For if you love those who love you, what reward do you have? Do not even the tax collectors do the same? And if you greet only your brothers and sisters, what more are you doing than others? Do not even the Gentiles do the same? Be perfect, therefore, as your heavenly Father is perfect."

- The command to "be perfect" may be translated as "be complete," to be merciful and compassionate to the fullest, to be at one with God, to be holy.
- Fulfilment in Jesus Christ is not attained only through our own efforts. It happens when we open ourselves to the action of Jesus in our lives and try to model and shape our lives on his, to be people who strive to live for others.

Wednesday 16th June   Matthew 6:1, 5–6

Jesus said to the disciples, "Beware of practising your piety before others in order to be seen by them; for then you have no reward from your Father in heaven." "Whenever you pray, do not be like the hypocrites; for they love to stand and pray in the synagogues and at the street corners, so that they may be seen by others. Truly I tell you, they have received their reward. But whenever you pray, go into your room and shut the door and pray to your Father who is in secret; and your Father who sees in secret will reward you."

- Jesus reminds us of Isaiah's words, "This people honors me with their lips, but their hearts are far from me" (Mt 15:8). Echoing the words of the prophets, Jesus reminds us that religion can sometimes be ostentatious.
- God wants the love of our hearts and our care for others. Public religion must be done for God and the love of God.
- How do I measure up on this?

Thursday 17th June — Matthew 6:7–13

Jesus said to the crowds, "When you are praying, do not heap up empty phrases as the Gentiles do; for they think that they will be heard because of their many words. Do not be like them, for your Father knows what you need before you ask him. "Pray then in this way: Our Father in heaven, hallowed be your name. Your kingdom come. Your will be done, on earth as it is in heaven. Give us this day our daily bread. And forgive us our debts, as we also have forgiven our debtors. And do not bring us to the time of trial, but rescue us from the evil one."

- Say the Our Father slowly today, pondering a word here and there. Say it aloud to yourself if you are in a suitable place. Each word, each phrase can be a way of deepening our awareness of God in our lives.
- Let the words echo so that their tone and meaning become a sort of mantra you can often return to.

Friday 18th June — Matthew 6:19–21

Jesus said to his disciples, "Do not store up for yourselves treasures on earth, where moth and rust consume and where thieves break in and steal; but store up for yourselves treasures in heaven, where neither moth nor rust consumes and where thieves do not break in and steal. For where your treasure is, there your heart will be also.

- These wisdom sayings of Jesus that Matthew recorded focus on a big theme of Jesus' preaching: that true security and happiness are found in the kingdom of heaven, and in doing our best to live the values of this kingdom.
- Today, let me ask God to enlighten me, to see the "big picture," and to know where I need to apply this message in my life.

Saturday 19th June   Matthew 6:25–29

Jesus said, "Therefore I tell you, do not worry about your life, what you will eat or what you will drink, or about your body, what you will wear. Is not life more than food, and the body more than clothing? Look at the birds of the air; they neither sow nor reap nor gather into barns, and yet your heavenly Father feeds them. Are you not of more value than they? And can any of you by worrying add a single hour to your span of life? And why do you worry about clothing? Consider the lilies of the field, how they grow; they neither toil nor spin, yet I tell you, even Solomon in all his glory was not clothed like one of these."

- God alone is worth our total trust, and God is totally faithful to us. Worries about fashions and menus and diets and money take us away from being concerned with the things of God.
- Can I take a walk in a park today or look out a window, see grass or flowers, observe birds in the trees and in the air, or listen to birdsong?
- Lord, help me to recognize what's really important in life.

june 20–26

Something to think and pray about each day this week:

God's children

Children are deprived not because we do not give them things, but because we do not sufficiently value what they give us. We need to be alert to welcome what children have to offer. You remember how Kahlil Gibran wrote about children:

> You may give them your love but not your thoughts, for they have their own thoughts. You may house their bodies but not their souls, for their souls dwell in the house of tomorrow, which you cannot visit, not even in your dreams. You may strive to be like them, but seek not to make them like you. For life goes not backward nor tarries with yesterday. You are the bows from which your children as living arrows are sent forth.

Our children are flying forward into areas we have not charted ourselves. What is asked of us is in Kahlil's last phrase, "Even as the Archer loves the arrow that flies, so He loves also the bow that is stable." We are expected to be calm, reliable, showing a steady love in our own lives, and to offer our children what Jesus offered: time, love, stability, and a readiness to bless.

The Presence of God
At any time of the day or night we can call on Jesus.
He is always waiting, listening for our call.
What a wonderful blessing.
No phone needed, no emails, just a whisper.

Freedom
Lord, grant me the grace to be free from the excesses of this life.
Let me not get caught up with the desire for wealth.
Keep my heart and mind free to love and serve you.

Consciousness
I exist in a web of relationships—links to nature, people, God.
I trace out these links, giving thanks for the life that flows
through them.
Some links are twisted or broken: I may feel regret, anger,
disappointment.
I pray for the gift of acceptance and forgiveness.

The Word
God speaks to each one of us individually. I need to listen to
what he is saying to me. (Please turn to your scripture on the
following pages. Inspiration points are there should you need
them. When you are ready, return here to continue.)

Conversation
Remembering that I am still in God's presence,
I imagine Jesus himself standing or sitting beside me,
and say whatever is on my mind, whatever is in my heart,
speaking as one friend to another.

Conclusion
Glory be to the Father, and to the Son, and to the Holy Spirit,
As it was in the beginning, is now, and ever shall be,
World without end. Amen

Sunday 20th June,
Twelfth Sunday in Ordinary Time   Galatians 3:26–29

In Christ Jesus you are all children of God through faith. As many of you as were baptized into Christ have clothed yourselves with Christ. There is no longer Jew or Greek, there is no longer slave or free, there is no longer male and female; for all of you are one in Christ Jesus. And if you belong to Christ, then you are Abraham's offspring, heirs according to the promise.

- "All of you are one in Christ Jesus." This is the new Christian life and reality: being baptized into the crucified and risen Christ and welcomed into a new community. It is the same path for all of us, no matter how different we are from each other.

- In what ways does this challenge me? Do I live this out in my family, in my community, in my workplace?

Monday 21st June, St. Aloysius Gonzaga   Mark 10:23–27

Then Jesus looked around and said to his disciples, "How hard it will be for those who have wealth to enter the kingdom of God!" And the disciples were perplexed at these words. But Jesus said to them again, "Children, how hard it is to enter the kingdom of God! It is easier for a camel to go through the eye of a needle than for someone who is rich to enter the kingdom of God." They were greatly astounded and said to one another, "Then who can be saved?" Jesus looked at them and said, "For mortals it is impossible, but not for God; for God all things are possible."

- Many people live in societies which assume without question that wealth equals worth, that price trumps value every time. Jesus radically contradicts that assumption, so radically that the disciples are overwhelmed. God alone saves.

- How do I block God's saving grace? By seeking power, wealth, status, entertainment, special friendships?

Tuesday 22nd June   **Matthew 7:12–14**

J esus said to the crowds, "In everything do to others as you
  would have them do to you; for this is the law and the prophets. Enter through the narrow gate; for the gate is wide and the
road is easy that leads to destruction, and there are many who
take it. For the gate is narrow and the road is hard that leads to
life, and there are few who find it."

- "Do to others as you would have them do to you." This phrase has
  passed into common usage, so our response to it may be dulled.
- But what do I really want from another person? Is it tolerance,
  forgiveness, compassion? Am I responding in the same way?

Wednesday 23rd June   **Matthew 7:15–20**

J esus told the crowds, "Beware of false prophets, who come to
  you in sheep's clothing but inwardly are ravenous wolves. You
will know them by their fruits. Are grapes gathered from thorns,
or figs from thistles? In the same way, every good tree bears good
fruit, but the bad tree bears bad fruit. A good tree cannot bear
bad fruit, nor can a bad tree bear good fruit. Every tree that does
not bear good fruit is cut down and thrown into the fire. Thus
you will know them by their fruits."

- We grow if we are well tended—in education, in family, in love.
  We grow when we mind and nourish ourselves with the food and
  drink that do not ruin the body, and produce "good fruit."
- What are my "outputs"? Can I do better here? What do I need to
  change today?

Thursday 24th June,
Birth of St. John the Baptist   **Luke 1:57–66**

N ow the time came for Elizabeth to give birth, and she bore
  a son. Her neighbors and relatives heard that the Lord had

shown his great mercy to her, and they rejoiced with her. On the eighth day they came to circumcise the child, and they were going to name him Zechariah after his father. But his mother said, "No; he is to be called John." They said to her, "None of your relatives has this name." Then they began motioning to his father to find out what name he wanted to give him. He asked for a writing tablet and wrote, "His name is John." And all of them were amazed. Immediately his mouth was opened and his tongue freed, and he began to speak, praising God. Fear came over all their neighbors, and all these things were talked about throughout the entire hill country of Judea. All who heard them pondered them and said, 'What then will this child become?' For, indeed, the hand of the Lord was with him.

- No doubt Elizabeth had wanted this birth and prayed for it for many years. Instead, she had her son in God's time.
- Much of what we want and pray for may happen in God's time. John the Baptist would learn that himself, as he searched out God's path for him.
- Can we trust God in this?

Friday 25th June   **Matthew 8:1–3**

When Jesus had come down from the mountain, great crowds followed him; and there was a leper who came to him and knelt before him, saying, "Lord, if you choose, you can make me clean." He stretched out his hand and touched him, saying, "I do choose. Be made clean!" Immediately his leprosy was cleansed.

- Jesus' welcome to this man was a complete reversal of what was expected: the leper was an outcast, contagious and shunned. That someone would even come near him was highly unusual.

- Jesus highlights the fact that nobody is unwelcome in his house, at his table, in his presence. All are welcome, anytime.
- Lord, I know I can talk with you at any time, in any place.

Saturday 26th June   Matthew 8:5–13

When he entered Capernaum, a centurion came to him, appealing to him and saying, "Lord, my servant is lying at home paralyzed, in terrible distress." And he said to him, "I will come and cure him." The centurion answered, "Lord, I am not worthy to have you come under my roof; but only speak the word, and my servant will be healed. For I also am a man under authority, with soldiers under me; and I say to one, 'Go,' and he goes, and to another, 'Come,' and he comes, and to my slave, 'Do this,' and the slave does it." When Jesus heard him, he was amazed and said to those who followed him, "Truly I tell you, in no one in Israel have I found such faith. I tell you, many will come from east and west and will eat with Abraham and Isaac and Jacob in the kingdom of heaven, while the heirs of the kingdom will be thrown into the outer darkness, where there will be weeping and gnashing of teeth." And to the centurion Jesus said, "Go; let it be done for you according to your faith." And the servant was healed in that hour.

- Again, Jesus confronts "correct" social behaviour. He offers to go to the house of a Gentile, which would make him unclean in the eyes of the disciples and the crowd following him.
- Jesus' life and prayer showed him that the narrow definitions of race, gender, and holiness were false. One eye went to those who welcomed him, and the other eye looked to whoever might be called the "outsider."
- Do I feel like an "outsider" to God sometimes, not worthy of being close? Can I bring that honestly before God?

june 27–july 3

Something to think and pray about each day this week:

Managing our pain

You could see Jesus' life as a struggle against sickness and death. He was a healer, and reached out to cure the pains that disable people. He wanted them to forget about their bodies and feel fit to serve, like Simon Peter's mother-in-law, whom Jesus cured of a fever. Once her temperature dropped, she got up to make a meal. I have known people who would feel a headache coming on, speak of "offering up" the pain but then continue talking about it. That is not the Christian way: better to take some medicine, forget about the headache and get on with the job. I knew an Ethiopian who had a sore shoulder and was urged to go to a doctor. Knowing the sort of medical care he might receive, he said, "Now I am a healthy man with a sore shoulder. If I go to a doctor I will be a sick man with a sore shoulder. No thank you."

Pain and sickness are obviously bad, something to be fought and resisted, yet the Lord touches us through them. A time comes when we can no longer feel God's touch in prayer, but we sense how God is shaping us through our suffering. It is remarkable how many people find the grace to seek whatever help medicine can offer, and then to accept the remaining pain as the background of a peaceful existence—and without talking about it.

The Presence of God

God is with me, but more,
God is within me, giving me existence.
Let me dwell for a moment on God's life-giving presence
in my body, my mind, my heart,
and in the whole of my life.

Freedom

God is not foreign to my freedom.
Instead the Spirit breathes life into my most intimate desires,
gently nudging me towards all that is good.
I ask for the grace to let myself be enfolded by the Spirit.

Consciousness

How am I really feeling? Light-hearted? Heavy-hearted?
I may be very much at peace, happy to be here.
Equally, I may be frustrated, worried, or angry.
I acknowledge how I really am. It is the real me that the Lord
loves.

The Word

I read the word of God slowly, a few times over, and I listen to
what God is saying to me. (Please turn to your scripture on the
following pages. Inspiration points are there should you need
them. When you are ready, return here to continue.)

Conversation

How has God's word moved me? Has it left me cold?
Has it consoled me or moved me to act in a new way?
I imagine Jesus standing or sitting beside me,
I turn and share my feelings with him.

Conclusion

Glory be to the Father, and to the Son, and to the Holy Spirit,
As it was in the beginning, is now, and ever shall be,
World without end. Amen

Sunday 27th June,
Thirteenth Sunday in Ordinary Time — Luke 9:51–56

When the days drew near for him to be taken up, he set his face to go to Jerusalem. And he sent messengers ahead of him. On their way they entered a village of the Samaritans to make ready for him; but they did not receive him, because his face was set towards Jerusalem. When his disciples James and John saw it, they said, "Lord, do you want us to command fire to come down from heaven and consume them?" But he turned and rebuked them.

- James and John are restless, asking "what is the use of having power if you do not use it on those who reject you?" The gentle tolerance of Jesus demands greater strength than the spirit of revenge and furious retaliation.
- When Abraham Lincoln was criticized for being too courteous to his enemies, he replied: "Do I not destroy my enemies when I make them my friends?"

Monday 28th June — Matthew 8:18–22

Now when Jesus saw great crowds around him, he gave orders to go over to the other side. A scribe then approached and said, "Teacher, I will follow you wherever you go." And Jesus said to him, "Foxes have holes, and birds of the air have nests; but the Son of Man has nowhere to lay his head." Another of his disciples said to him, "Lord, first let me go and bury my father." But Jesus said to him, "Follow me, and let the dead bury their own dead."

- Jesus emphasized that, for him, there are even stronger securities than home and family. The work of God comes first.
- Following Jesus means that nothing else should cut across his gospel in the principal relationships of our lives.
- How does that fit with my actions and priorities today?

Tuesday 29th June,
Sts. Peter & Paul, Apostles   Matthew 16:13–19

Now when Jesus came into the district of Caesarea Philippi, he asked his disciples, "Who do people say that the Son of Man is?" And they said, "Some say John the Baptist, but others Elijah, and still others Jeremiah or one of the prophets." He said to them, "But who do you say that I am?" Simon Peter answered, "You are the Messiah, the Son of the living God." And Jesus answered him, "Blessed are you, Simon son of Jonah! For flesh and blood has not revealed this to you, but my Father in heaven. And I tell you, you are Peter, and on this rock I will build my church, and the gates of Hades will not prevail against it. I will give you the keys of the kingdom of heaven, and whatever you bind on earth will be bound in heaven, and whatever you loose on earth will be loosed in heaven."

- How different these two men were! One, a simple but impetuous fisherman; the other, well-educated and with deep emotions. They did not always agree, but we celebrate them together, as each had a role in founding the early community of believers.

- Do I struggle with those who want to debate questions of belief? Or am I annoyed by those whose faith seems based on emotion? Lord, teach me that my heart and my head are both important.

Wednesday 30th June   Matthew 8:28–34

When he came to the other side, to the country of the Gadarenes, two demoniacs coming out of the tombs met him. They were so fierce that no one could pass that way. Suddenly they shouted, "What have you to do with us, Son of God? Have you come here to torment us before the time?" Now a large herd of swine was feeding at some distance from them. The demons begged him, "If you cast us out, send us into the herd of swine."

And he said to them, "Go!" So they came out and entered the swine; and suddenly, the whole herd rushed down the steep bank into the lake and perished in the water. The swineherds ran off, and on going into the town, they told the whole story about what had happened to the demoniacs. Then the whole town came out to meet Jesus; and when they saw him, they begged him to leave their neighborhood.

- The location of this story says a lot about Jesus. It is in Gentile territory, where Jews would not normally go. Even after this miracle, the local people ask Jesus to leave.
- Jesus is always the man for the "other," for the stranger, the ones nobody wants to know. His life goes back and forth, from one side of the lake to the other, from one people to another.

Thursday 1st July   Matthew 9:1–8

And after getting into a boat he crossed the water and came to his own town. And just then some people were carrying a paralyzed man lying on a bed. When Jesus saw their faith, he said to the paralytic, "Take heart, son; your sins are forgiven." Then some of the scribes said to themselves, "This man is blaspheming." But Jesus, perceiving their thoughts, said, "Why do you think evil in your hearts? For which is easier, to say, 'Your sins are forgiven,' or to say, 'Stand up and walk'? But so that you may know that the Son of Man has authority on earth to forgive sins"—he then said to the paralytic—"Stand up, take your bed and go to your home." And he stood up and went to his home. When the crowds saw it, they were filled with awe, and they glorified God, who had given such authority to human beings.

- The paralyzed man was brought to Jesus by friends or neighbors. Forgiveness for his sins came to him in the company of others, without whom he would not have got near Jesus.

- It is the same for us. We go to God in the community of the church and of many others. Our faith is personal, not private.

Friday 2nd July   Matthew 9:9–13

As Jesus was walking along, he saw a man called Matthew sitting at the tax booth; and he said to him, "Follow me." And he got up and followed him. And as he sat at dinner in the house, many tax collectors and sinners came and were sitting with him and his disciples. When the Pharisees saw this, they said to his disciples, "Why does your teacher eat with tax collectors and sinners?" But when he heard this, he said, "Those who are well have no need of a physician, but those who are sick. Go and learn what this means, 'I desire mercy, not sacrifice.' For I have come to call not the righteous but sinners."

- "I desire mercy, not sacrifice." Mercy covers over sin and faults; it sees beyond what a person does to who a person is. We need the mercy of God for sins and faults and failings; we need also the mercy of others.
- We don't show mercy when we mock others or spread gossip. Lord, teach me to be merciful in word and in deed.

Saturday 3rd July, St. Thomas, Apostle   John 20:24–29

But Thomas (who was called the Twin), one of the twelve, was not with them when Jesus came. So the other disciples told him, "We have seen the Lord." But he said to them, "Unless I see the mark of the nails in his hands, and put my finger in the mark of the nails and my hand in his side, I will not believe." A week later his disciples were again in the house, and Thomas was with them. Although the doors were shut, Jesus came and stood among them and said, "Peace be with you." Then he said to Thomas, "Put your finger here and see my hands. Reach out your hand and put it in my side. Do not doubt but believe."

Thomas answered him, "My Lord and my God!" Jesus said to him, "Have you believed because you have seen me? Blessed are those who have not seen and yet have come to believe."

- "My Lord and my God!" Pope Benedict XVI has written that this is the most splendid profession of faith in the New Testament.
- St. Augustine wrote that Thomas "saw and touched the man, and acknowledged the God whom he neither saw nor touched." In this way, he put away doubt and believed.
- Lord, lead me towards a ever deeper faith in you.

july 4–10

Something to think and pray about each day this week:

Safe conversations
Being a grandparent has many bonuses. It is more agreeable than being in charge. You shed the power of authority, and also shed the distance which it imposes. Children use their grandparents in a particular way. They can be very direct and contemporary in their comments. A friend was telling his granddaughter a story when she interrupted him with, "Fast forward, please, grandpa." Grandparents can be safe people to talk to. Children know they can count on affection, and need not fear retribution if they tell things the way they are. In return, children give their grandparents a joy that compares with that of parenthood.

The Presence of God

To be present is to arrive as one is and open up to the other.
At this instant, as I arrive here, God is present waiting for me.
God always arrives before me, desiring to connect with me
even more than my most intimate friend.
I take a moment and greet my loving God.

Freedom

Everything has the potential to draw forth from me a fuller love
and life,
Yet my desires are often fixed, caught, on illusions of fulfillment.
I ask that God, through my freedom, may orchestrate
my desires in a vibrant loving melody rich in harmony.

Consciousness

Knowing that God loves me unconditionally,
I can afford to be honest about how I am.
How has the last day been, and how do I feel now?
I share my feelings openly with the Lord.

The Word

I take my time to read the word of God, slowly, a few times,
allowing myself to dwell on anything that strikes me. (Please
turn to your scripture on the following pages. Inspiration points
are there should you need them. When you are ready, return
here to continue.)

Conversation

What feelings are rising in me
as I pray and reflect on God's word?
I imagine Jesus himself sitting or standing beside me,
and I open my heart to him.

Conclusion

Glory be to the Father, and to the Son, and to the Holy Spirit,
As it was in the beginning, is now, and ever shall be,
World without end. Amen

Sunday 4th July,
Fourteenth Sunday in Ordinary Time   Luke 10:3–6

" See, I am sending you out like lambs into the midst of wolves. Carry no purse, no bag, no sandals; and greet no one on the road. Whatever house you enter, first say, 'Peace to this house!' And if anyone is there who shares in peace, your peace will rest on that person; but if not, it will return to you."

* A lamb among wolves—am I ready for that role?
* Lord, you bid me travel light and bring a blessing of peace wherever I go. I beg you to calm the worries in my own heart so that I may be truly a carrier of your peace.

Monday 5th July   Matt 9:18–19, 23–26

While he was saying these things to them, suddenly a leader of the synagogue came in and knelt before him, saying, "My daughter has just died; but come and lay your hand on her, and she will live." And Jesus got up and followed him, with his disciples. When Jesus came to the leader's house and saw the flute players and the crowd making a commotion, he said, "Go away; for the girl is not dead but sleeping." And they laughed at him. But when the crowd had been put outside, he went in and took her by the hand, and the girl got up. And the report of this spread throughout that district.

* We find that physical touch is common in Jesus relationships with other people. A touch means people are near to each other, that nothing like sin or fear or shame is a barrier. Touch is a sacramental moment when God and the individual share what is deepest in each other.
* Prayer is like Jesus touching us. It is like Jesus taking the dead girl by the hand and raising her.

- Prayer is close intimacy with God: the intimacy of holding a hand, stroking a brow, touching a person's clothing.

Tuesday 6th July   Matthew 9:36–38

When Jesus saw the crowds, he had compassion for them, because they were harassed and helpless, like sheep without a shepherd. Then he said to his disciples, "The harvest is plentiful, but the laborers are few; therefore ask the Lord of the harvest to send out laborers into his harvest."

- The heart of Jesus is characterised by compassion. He could enter into the lives of others, particularly the lost and the needy, and they knew he cared.
- Sheep without a shepherd roam in circles, and they may even be led off by a false shepherd. Thus it is with us.

Wednesday 7th July   Matthew 10:1–7

Then Jesus summoned his twelve disciples and gave them authority over unclean spirits, to cast them out, and to cure every disease and every sickness. These are the names of the twelve apostles: first, Simon, also known as Peter, and his brother Andrew; James son of Zebedee, and his brother John; Philip and Bartholomew; Thomas and Matthew the tax collector; James son of Alphaeus, and Thaddaeus; Simon the Cananaean, and Judas Iscariot, the one who betrayed him. These twelve Jesus sent out with the following instructions: "Go nowhere among the Gentiles, and enter no town of the Samaritans, but go rather to the lost sheep of the house of Israel. As you go, proclaim the good news, 'The kingdom of heaven has come near.'"

- Their names are still known—some of the most ordinary people of Galilee, a small place itself in a small country.

228

- Our names are in that list, in the mind of God and in the Book of Life. Called like them, we are partners with Jesus in the salvation of the world, in whatever corner of the globe we may find ourselves. In word and life, we must try to let others know that the kingdom of heaven and the love of God are very near.

Thursday 8th July   **Matthew 10:7–14**

"As you go, proclaim the good news, 'The kingdom of heaven has come near.' Cure the sick, raise the dead, cleanse the lepers, cast out demons. You received without payment; give without payment. Take no gold, or silver, or copper in your belts, no bag for your journey, or two tunics, or sandals, or a staff; for laborers deserve their food. Whatever town or village you enter, find out who in it is worthy, and stay there until you leave. As you enter the house, greet it. If the house is worthy, let your peace come upon it; but if it is not worthy, let your peace return to you. If anyone will not welcome you or listen to your words, shake off the dust from your feet as you leave that house or town."

- There's something quite single-minded about this gospel passage. When we work for the Lord, we stop worrying about clothing, money, and shelter. We are concerned but not anxious.
- Day-to-day practicalities aside, it asks us to be open-minded and open-hearted in how we follow Christ. Can I do that today?

Friday 9th July   **Matthew 10:16–23**

"See, I am sending you out like sheep into the midst of wolves; so be wise as serpents and innocent as doves. Beware of them, for they will hand you over to councils and flog you in their synagogues; and you will be dragged before governors and kings because of me, as a testimony to them and the Gentiles. When they hand you over, do not worry about how you are to speak or what you are to say; for what you are to say will be given to you at that time; for it is not you who speak, but the Spirit of your Father speaking through you. Brother will betray brother to death, and a father his child, and children will rise against parents and have them put to death; and you will be hated by all because of my name. But the one who endures to the end will be saved. When they persecute you in one town, flee to the next; for truly I tell you, you will not have gone through all the towns of Israel before the Son of Man comes."

- The God of heaven and earth is to be "handed over," a term which indicates suffering, mockery, helplessness, and injustice.
- It has a humiliating meaning, as when families betray each other. This will be a regular occurrence for the disciples; even if they flee one place, it may happen in the next. When this occurs to us, we are following in the footsteps of the Master.

Saturday 10th July   Matthew 10:24–25a

Jesus said to the Twelve: "A disciple is not above the teacher, nor a slave above the master; it is enough for the disciple to be like the teacher, and the slave like the master."

- Jesus often tells the disciples to be like him. He knows that they will suffer like he did.
- Our following of him as best we can is enough for fulfillment and wholeness in our lives. He is the best of teachers, the most compassionate of masters. His relationship with us is divine and human.
- As he works in the Father's name, we work in his name.

july 11–17

Something to think and pray about each day this week:

Pricking the clerical balloon

There was a strong vein of anti-clericalism in Jesus to which he was not afraid to give utterance. He denounced the scribes and Pharisees who laid heavy burdens on others but did not move a finger to lift them themselves. He spoke of hypocrites, of blind guides, of teachers who cleaned the outside of the cup but left the inside filthy, worrying more about external observance of the law than about the movements in people's hearts. The clerical establishment of the Jews were furious, and in the end, on Calvary, they had their revenge.

So we have to learn to combine reverence and love for the Church with a cool appraisal of its officials. We, the people of God, are the church. As the Spanish proverb has it. "We are the people, and wisdom will die with us." The clergy, religious, bishops, have their part to play, and we need to keep them up to the mark. We ought not be astonished when we find evidence of the seven deadly sins in those who profess greater piety. All through the centuries the church has had this job of criticizing and reforming itself. But the critics in any age, like the Jews who surrounded the adulterous woman, also need to heed Jesus' warning, "Let the one who is without sin among you cast the first stone."

The Presence of God

What is present to me is what has a hold on my becoming.
I reflect on the presence of God always there in love,
amidst the many things that have a hold on me.
I pause and pray that I may let God
affect my becoming in this precise moment.

Freedom

There are very few people
who realize what God would make of them
if they abandoned themselves into his hands,
and let themselves be formed by his grace. (St. Ignatius)
I ask for the grace to trust myself totally to God's love.

Consciousness

In the presence of my loving Creator,
I look honestly at my feelings over the last day,
the highs, the lows, and the level ground.
Can I see where the Lord has been present?

The Word

God speaks to each one of us individually. I need to listen to
what he is saying to me. (Please turn to your scripture on the
following pages. Inspiration points are there should you need
them. When you are ready, return here to continue.)

Conversation

What is stirring in me as I pray?
Am I consoled, troubled, left cold?
I imagine Jesus himself standing or sitting at my side,
and share my feelings with him.

Conclusion

Glory be to the Father, and to the Son, and to the Holy Spirit,
As it was in the beginning, is now, and ever shall be,
World without end. Amen

232

Sunday 11th July,
Fifteenth Sunday in Ordinary Time   Luke 10:25–37

J ust then a lawyer stood up to test Jesus. "Teacher," he said, "what must I do to inherit eternal life?" He said to him, "What is written in the law? What do you read there?" He answered, "You shall love the Lord your God with all your heart, and with all your soul, and with all your strength, and with all your mind; and your neighbor as yourself." And he said to him, "You have given the right answer; do this, and you will live." But wanting to justify himself, he asked Jesus, "And who is my neighbor?" Jesus replied, "A man was going down from Jerusalem to Jericho, and fell into the hands of robbers, who stripped him, beat him, and went away, leaving him half dead. Now by chance a priest was going down that road; and when he saw him, he passed by on the other side. So likewise a Levite, when he came to the place and saw him, passed by on the other side. But a Samaritan while traveling came near him; and when he saw him, he was moved with pity. He went to him and bandaged his wounds, having poured oil and wine on them. Then he put him on his own animal, brought him to an inn, and took care of him. The next day he took out two denarii, gave them to the innkeeper, and said, 'Take care of him; and when I come back, I will repay you whatever more you spend.' Which of these three, do you think, was a neighbor to the man who fell into the hands of the robbers?" He said, "The one who showed him mercy." Jesus said to him, "Go and do likewise."

* How well do I know that temptation to pass by on the other side of the road!
* Lord, when you mention the priest and the Levite, you are pointing at those who value orthodoxy—the priest would have been

contaminated, and disqualified from serving in the Temple, if he had touched a dead body.

- Your words are aimed at us, for the times when we put our own activities before the obvious needs of others. Lord, teach me to be worthy of the title of Good Samaritan.

Monday 12th July   Matthew 10:34–39

Jesus said to his disciples, "Do not think that I have come to bring peace to the earth; I have not come to bring peace, but a sword. For I have come to set a man against his father, and a daughter against her mother, and a daughter-in-law against her mother-in-law; and one's foes will be members of one's own household. Whoever loves father or mother more than me is not worthy of me; and whoever loves son or daughter more than me is not worthy of me; and whoever does not take up the cross and follow me is not worthy of me. Those who find their life will lose it, and those who lose their life for my sake will find it."

- Isn't it strange that we save our life by losing it? But we know that when we put our energy into helping others, rather than just looking out for ourselves, we can receive great reward.
- The self-centered person is the one who is caught up in controlling and preserving all for the self. Jesus is the opposite—he makes the best of himself, to give to others. I am called to follow.

Tuesday 13th July   Matthew 11:20–24

Then Jesus began to reproach the cities in which most of his deeds of power had been done, because they did not repent. "Woe to you, Chorazin! Woe to you, Bethsaida! For if the deeds of power done in you had been done in Tyre and Sidon, they would have repented long ago in sackcloth and ashes. But I tell you, on the day of judgment it will be more tolerable for Tyre and Sidon than for you. And you, Capernaum, will you be exalted to heaven? No, you will be brought down to Hades. For if the deeds of power done in you had been done in Sodom, it would have remained until this day. But I tell you that on the day of judgment it will be more tolerable for the land of Sodom than for you."

- Jesus seems to expect some sort of change to happen in us when we meet him, when we pray. Prayer is meant to have its fruits.
- Are there "fruits" from my prayer? How does it affect my life?

Wednesday 14th July   Matthew 11:25–27

At that time Jesus said, "I thank you, Father, Lord of heaven and earth, because you have hidden these things from the wise and the intelligent and have revealed them to infants; yes, Father, for such was your gracious will. All things have been handed over to me by my Father; and no one knows the Son except the Father, and no one knows the Father except the Son and anyone to whom the Son chooses to reveal him."

- One of Jesus' principal missions was to make God his Father known. People then, as now, suffered from having God portrayed as harsh or punitive. Jesus emphasizes here that he knows the Father intimately and that he wants his followers also to know God in this way.
- Can we pray to the Father as to an intimate parent? Our prayer could be simply saying, "Lord, show us the Father."

Thursday 15th July   Matthew 11:28–30

Jesus said, "Come to me, all you that are weary and are carrying heavy burdens, and I will give you rest. Take my yoke upon you, and learn from me; for I am gentle and humble in heart, and you will find rest for your souls. For my yoke is easy, and my burden is light."

- A woman said that she always offered a glass of water to people running the marathon as they passed her house. The gracious hostess was offering refreshment.
- Jesus in a simple way is saying that in his house, in his space, we will find a spot to breathe fresh air, to become refreshed. He is the gentle host into whose company we are invited. This is the invitation to sit in prayer on the journey of life.

Friday 16th July   Matthew 12:1–8

A t that time Jesus went through the grainfields on the sabbath; his disciples were hungry, and they began to pluck heads of grain and to eat. When the Pharisees saw it, they said to him, "Look, your disciples are doing what is not lawful to do on the sabbath." He said to them, "Have you not read what David did when he and his companions were hungry? He entered the house of God and ate the bread of the Presence, which it was not lawful for him or his companions to eat, but only for the priests. Or have you not read in the law that on the sabbath the priests in the temple break the sabbath and yet are guiltless? I tell you, something greater than the temple is here. But if you had known what this means, 'I desire mercy and not sacrifice,' you would not have condemned the guiltless. For the Son of Man is lord of the sabbath."

- Nothing is more central to the Christian life than Jesus Christ, his words, his life, death, and resurrection. Regulations about the Sabbath—all religious regulations—are put into perspective.
- Our faith is about a person who is both God and human, whose life touches all the important times of our life—birth, ministry, suffering, and death.
- How do I put my religious belief into practice?

Saturday 17th July   **Matthew 12:14–21**

But the Pharisees went out and conspired against him, how to destroy him. When Jesus became aware of this, he departed. Many crowds followed him, and he cured all of them, and he ordered them not to make him known. This was to fulfill what had been spoken through the prophet Isaiah: "Here is my servant, whom I have chosen, my beloved, with whom my soul is well pleased. I will put my Spirit upon him, and he will proclaim justice to the Gentiles. He will not wrangle or cry aloud, nor will anyone hear his voice in the streets. He will not break a bruised reed or quench a smoldering wick until he brings justice to victory. And in his name the Gentiles will hope."

- Jesus is on the side of the weak. His message, though demanding an active response, does not crush people. Justice comes through compassion—like care for the bruised reed—not through the exercise of power and violence.
- In this way Jesus is pleasing to his Father. Prayer strengthens the soul and personality, making us ever-more pleasing to God.

july 18–24

Something to think and pray about each day this week:

Personal commitment

It was in a recent July that I celebrated fifty years as a priest. All those years ago, we talked of ordination as an offering of one's life. It was easy to idealize. The many happy weddings I have witnessed shared the same atmosphere and aspiration. The commitment of priesthood, like that of marriage, is a solemn and free act that touches us as deeply as any act can. This gift, of all that we are and may become, suggests the image of a silver chalice, filled with all that is precious. Alas, it does not work that way.

All of us who live by vows, whether in marriage or religion, know that a goblet of precious wine is an inadequate image for a personal commitment. Our lives and relationships are inevitably a mixed drink, bitter-sweet. As we look back, over ten, or thirty, or sixty years, we can see what a mixture it was, at once richer and more painful than when we took our vows. Only a jubilee shows what a complicated and unexpected mixture is there. The God we serve is a God of surprises, and as we look back, it becomes clear that it is his plans, not ours, that counted. He does not call us to help him out of a jam. He calls us because he loves us.

The Presence of God
Jesus waits silent and unseen to come into my heart.
I will respond to His call.
He comes with His infinite power and love
May I be filled with joy in His presence.

Freedom
A thick and shapeless tree-trunk would never believe
that it could become a statue, admired as a miracle of sculpture,
and would never submit itself to the chisel of the sculptor,
who sees by her genius what she can make of it. (St. Ignatius)
I ask for the grace to let myself be shaped by my loving Creator.

Consciousness
Knowing that God loves me unconditionally,
I look honestly over the last day, its events, and my feelings.
Do I have something to be grateful for? Then I give thanks.
Is there something I am sorry for? Then I ask forgiveness.

The Word
I read the word of God slowly, a few times over, and I listen to
what God is saying to me. (Please turn to your scripture on the
following pages. Inspiration points are there should you need
them. When you are ready, return here to continue.)

Conversation
Do I notice myself reacting as I pray with the word of God?
Do I feel challenged, comforted, angry?
Imagining Jesus sitting or standing by me,
I speak out my feelings, as one trusted friend to another.

Conclusion
Glory be to the Father, and to the Son, and to the Holy Spirit,
As it was in the beginning, is now, and ever shall be,
World without end. Amen

Sunday 18th July,
Sixteenth Sunday in Ordinary Time   Luke 10:38–42

Now as they went on their way, he entered a certain village, where a woman named Martha welcomed him into her home. She had a sister named Mary, who sat at the Lord's feet and listened to what he was saying. But Martha was distracted by her many tasks; so she came to him and asked, "Lord, do you not care that my sister has left me to do all the work by myself? Tell her then to help me." But the Lord answered her, "Martha, Martha, you are worried and distracted by many things; there is need of only one thing. Mary has chosen the better part, which will not be taken away from her."

• Here are contrasting ways of showing kindness: Martha's was to focus on preparing a meal; Mary's was to listen and heed her sense that Jesus, facing Jerusalem and his passion, needed friendly company more than food.

• Lord, teach me the sort of kindness that takes cues from other people's needs, not from my own plans.

Monday 19th July   Matthew 12:38–42

Then some of the scribes and Pharisees said to him, "Teacher, we wish to see a sign from you." But he answered them, "An evil and adulterous generation asks for a sign, but no sign will be given to it except the sign of the prophet Jonah. For just as Jonah was three days and three nights in the belly of the sea monster, so for three days and three nights the Son of Man will be in the heart of the earth. The people of Nineveh will rise up at the judgment with this generation and condemn it, because they repented at the proclamation of Jonah, and see, something greater than Jonah is here! The queen of the South will rise up at the judgment with this generation and condemn it, because she came from the ends of the earth to listen to the wisdom of Solomon, and see, something greater than Solomon is here!"

- While opponents are looking for divine signs from Jesus he slides away from these demands. The divine signs he puts forward are God's compassion and forgiveness. For saying he was equal to God he would be killed.
- Do I look for signs of God's presence in my life? What do I see?

Tuesday 20th July   Matthew 12:46–50

While he was still speaking to the crowds, his mother and his brothers were standing outside, wanting to speak to him. Someone told him, "Look, your mother and your brothers are standing outside, wanting to speak to you." But to the one who had told him this, Jesus replied, "Who is my mother, and who are my brothers?" And pointing to his disciples, he said, "Here are my mother and my brothers! For whoever does the will of my Father in heaven is my brother and sister and mother."

- We came from God before we came from father and mother, so there are times when family comes second to God.
- How would Mary have taken this statement? Was she being diminished? How do I take this statement? What might it mean in my life?

Wednesday 21st July   Matthew 13:1–9

That same day Jesus went out of the house and sat beside the sea. Such great crowds gathered around him that he got into a boat and sat there, while the whole crowd stood on the beach. And he told them many things in parables, saying: "Listen! A sower went out to sow. And as he sowed, some seeds fell on the path, and the birds came and ate them up. Other seeds fell on rocky ground, where they did not have much soil, and they sprang up quickly, since they had no depth of soil. But when the sun rose, they were scorched; and since they had no root, they withered away. Other seeds fell among thorns, and the thorns grew up and choked them. Other seeds fell on good soil and brought forth grain, some a hundredfold, some sixty, some thirty. Let anyone with ears listen!"

- Just as a river flows from the source and may water lands many miles away, our love and goodness can influence people in future generations.
- We are content to do what we can, and leave the fruits of our goodness to God. Let me put this in God's hands, today.

Thursday 22nd July, St. Mary Magdalene   John 20:11–18

But Mary stood weeping outside the tomb. As she wept, she bent over to look into the tomb; and she saw two angels in white, sitting where the body of Jesus had been lying, one at the head and the other at the feet. They said to her, "Woman, why are you weeping?" She said to them, "They have taken away my Lord, and I do not know where they have laid him." When she had said this, she turned around and saw Jesus standing there, but she did not know that it was Jesus. Jesus said to her, "Woman, why are you weeping? Whom are you looking for?" Supposing him to be the gardener, she said to him, "Sir, if you have carried him away, tell me where you have laid him, and I will take him away." Jesus said to her, "Mary!" She turned and said to him in Hebrew, "Rabbouni!" (which means Teacher). Jesus said to her, "Do not hold on to me, because I have not yet ascended to the Father. But go to my brothers and say to them, 'I am ascending to my Father and your Father, to my God and your God.'" Mary Magdalene went and announced to the disciples, "I have seen the Lord"; and she told them that he had said these things to her.

- Allow yourself to see Mary in great distress. The one she longs to see is there, but she can't recognize him.
- The sound of her own name breaks through the cloud of her unknowing.
- Can I imagine Jesus calling me by my name? How does it sound?

Friday 23rd July   Jeremiah 3:14–17

Return, O faithless children, says the Lord, for I am your master; I will take you, one from a city and two from a family, and I will bring you to Zion. I will give you shepherds after my own heart, who will feed you with knowledge and understanding. And when you have multiplied and increased in the land, in those days, says the Lord, they shall no longer say, "The ark of the covenant of the Lord." It shall not come to mind, or be remembered, or missed; nor shall another one be made. At that time Jerusalem shall be called the throne of the Lord, and all nations shall gather to it, to the presence of the Lord in Jerusalem, and they shall no longer stubbornly follow their own evil will.

- Jeremiah was called to be a prophet at a difficult time, and he struggled and suffered greatly. Yet he held firm to the "word," to the mission he was called to, and remained a man of hope.
- "I will give you shepherds after my own heart." Lord, when we struggle with the invitation to be your disciples, to take up the cross, lead us to seek out those who can show us the way.

Saturday 24th July   Jeremiah 7:1–7

The word that came to Jeremiah from the Lord: Stand in the gate of the Lord's house, and proclaim there this word, and say, Hear the word of the Lord, all you people of Judah, you that enter these gates to worship the Lord. Thus says the Lord of hosts, the God of Israel: Amend your ways and your doings, and let me dwell with you in this place. Do not trust in these deceptive words: "This is the temple of the Lord, the temple of the Lord, the temple of the Lord." For if you truly amend your ways and your doings, if you truly act justly one with another, if you do not oppress the alien, the orphan, and the widow, or shed innocent blood in this place, and if you do not go after other gods to your own hurt, then I will dwell with you in this place, in the land that I gave of old to your ancestors for ever and ever.

- Can I listen to the fiery Jeremiah speaking to me, reminding me that having access to the temple—going to church on Sundays?—is not some sort of magic formula for salvation.
- "Amend your ways and your doings." This is a call to action, to actually change my ways. Jeremiah suggests some actions and attitudes I can start with. Perhaps I can add a few more, and set to work.

july 25–31

Something to think and pray about each day this week:

A picture of God
Of all the words that Jesus spoke, the ones most commonly re-peated by his followers begin the prayer, "Our Father." Jesus took a big gamble when he spoke of our father in heaven. God is be-yond gender, beyond our imagination. God is spirit, with no hu-man body, so in calling God male or female we are projecting our own mortal notions onto the immortal and invisible. Moreover, if we have bad associations or memories of either father or moth-er, we risk contaminating our idea of God with them.

That is where Jesus took the gamble. Those who have known a father as a tyrant or drunk, will have strange overtones to "Our father in heaven." If Jesus had spoken of "Our mother in heav-en," he would have run a similar risk. No human words are as heavily laden with emotional overtones as "father" and "mother." It is only when we move away from home, and reflect on our his-tory, that we begin to see what mother and father did to us, for better or worse. And when we do, some of our religious attitudes and feelings start to make sense.

All through life we try to sort out our sense of our heavenly father/mother. Jesus always speaks of his father. We see what he meant in the parable of the Prodigal Son, in which the central figure is the merciful father. In that extraordinary and moving story, Jesus comes nearest to giving us a picture of God.

The Presence of God

As I sit here, the beating of my heart,
the ebb and flow of my breathing, the movements of my mind
are all signs of God's ongoing creation of me.
I pause for a moment and become aware
of this presence of God within me.

Freedom

I ask for the grace
to let go of my own concerns
and be open to what God is asking of me,
to let myself be guided and formed by my loving Creator.

Consciousness

How do I find myself today?
Where am I with God? With others?
Do I have something to be grateful for? Then I give thanks.
Is there something I am sorry for? Then I ask forgiveness.

The Word

I take my time to read the word of God, slowly, a few times,
allowing myself to dwell on anything that strikes me. (Please
turn to your scripture on the following pages. Inspiration points
are there should you need them. When you are ready, return
here to continue.)

Conversation

Remembering that I am still in God's presence,
I imagine Jesus himself standing or sitting beside me,
and say whatever is on my mind, whatever is in my heart,
speaking as one friend to another.

Conclusion

Glory be to the Father, and to the Son, and to the Holy Spirit,
As it was in the beginning, is now, and ever shall be,
World without end. Amen

Sunday 25th July,
Seventeenth Sunday in Ordinary Time   Luke 11:1–4

He was praying in a certain place, and after he had finished, one of his disciples said to him, "Lord, teach us to pray, as John taught his disciples." He said to them, "When you pray, say: Father, hallowed be your name. Your kingdom come. Give us each day our daily bread. And forgive us our sins, for we ourselves forgive everyone indebted to us. And do not bring us to the time of trial."

• Thank you, Lord, for answering that disciple so briefly yet so generously. If I linger on this prayer, savoring it phrase by phrase, I have everything I need from prayer: raising my heart and mind to God, begging and giving forgiveness, asking for what I need, and being safe from trials beyond my strength.

Monday 26th July   Matthew 13:31–32

Jesus put before them another parable: "The kingdom of heaven is like a mustard seed that someone took and sowed in his field; it is the smallest of all the seeds, but when it has grown it is the greatest of shrubs and becomes a tree, so that the birds of the air come and make nests in its branches."

• God sows small seeds in deep soil and lets them grow at their own pace. God does not look for the maturity of an adult from a teenager, nor the wisdom of the elderly from younger ones.

• We depend on each other for growth in faith and in prayer, and we find that God "grows" us in the soil of love, mercy, compassion, and friendship.

Tuesday 27th July   Matthew 13:36–43

His disciples approached Jesus, saying, "Explain to us the parable of the weeds of the field." He answered, "The one who sows the good seed is the Son of Man; the field is the world, and the good seed are the children of the kingdom; the weeds are the children of the evil one, and the enemy who sowed them is the devil; the harvest is the end of the age, and the reapers are angels. Just as the weeds are collected and burned up with fire, so will it be at the end of the age. The Son of Man will send his angels, and they will collect out of his kingdom all causes of sin and all evildoers, and they will throw them into the furnace of fire, where there will be weeping and gnashing of teeth. Then the righteous will shine like the sun in the kingdom of their Father. Let anyone with ears listen!"

- Jesus is willing to keep teaching the disciples over and over again. He knows they are slow learners of discipleship, and so are we, because discipleship is heart-knowledge.
- We can learn from the words of Jesus, but miss their meaning if they have no effect in our lives. We can sing the song and never feel the melody. Jesus is always willing to explain to the willing heart what he says and who he is.

Wednesday 28th July   Matthew 13:44–46

Jesus said to the disciples, "The kingdom of heaven is like treasure hidden in a field, which someone found and hid; then in his joy he goes and sells all that he has and buys that field. Again, the kingdom of heaven is like a merchant in search of fine pearls; on finding one pearl of great value, he went and sold all that he had and bought it."

- Real and authentic discovery of God brings joy, the joy of being in love and of staying in love with the one who never changes.
- We may let go of other loves then—even of people who keep us from the love of God. We are committed only to the treasure in

the field, the fine pearl, the love of God and the love of people who bring us to God.

- Our concern is to bring alive the gospel of Jesus in the world. We pray that others may find this treasure through us.

Thursday 29th July   Jeremiah 18:1–6

The word that came to Jeremiah from the Lord: "Come, go down to the potter's house, and there I will let you hear my words." So I went down to the potter's house, and there he was working at his wheel. The vessel he was making of clay was spoiled in the potter's hand, and he reworked it into another vessel, as seemed good to him. Then the word of the Lord came to me: "Can I not do with you, O house of Israel, just as this potter has done?" says the Lord. "Just like the clay in the potter's hand, so are you in my hand, O house of Israel."

- Lord, this is my faith: I am clay in your loving hand. When I look back, I see times when I fell apart, could not keep my shape, and needed to be reworked by you, to be refired in the kiln.
- Even now I believe that your love is to be seen in the happenings of my life.

Friday 30th July   Matthew 13:54–58

Jesus came to his hometown and began to teach the people in their synagogue, so that they were astounded and said, "Where did this man get this wisdom and these deeds of power? Is not this the carpenter's son? Is not his mother called Mary? And are not his brothers James and Joseph and Simon and Judas? And are not all his sisters with us? Where then did this man get all this?" And they took offense at him. But Jesus said to them, "Prophets are not without honor except in their own country and in their own house." And he did not do many deeds of power there, because of their unbelief.

- Jesus' listeners were invited to hear his words as the words of God. To do so they had to get past the fact that he was a manual worker, and a familiar neighbor or a relative. They could not.
- Where do I stand here? Am I only listening for God's word in church? Or can it come to me in the innocent comment of the child or the barb of someone who criticizes me?

Saturday 31st July, St. Ignatius Loyola   Luke 9:23–25

Then Jesus said to the disciples, "If any want to become my followers, let them deny themselves and take up their cross daily and follow me. For those who want to save their life will lose it, and those who lose their life for my sake will save it. What does it profit them if they gain the whole world, but lose or forfeit themselves?"

- Let us sit with this prayer of Saint Ignatius: "Take Lord, and receive, my memory, my understanding, my entire will. All that I am, all that I have are you gift to me. I now return them to you. Give me only your love and your grace, with these I am rich enough, and desire no more."

Something to think and pray about each day this week:

The flame of compassion

The gospels speak of Jesus' compassion, a weighty word. It was much more than a warm feeling; it meant that you suffered with the other person, and did something about it. In feeding the multitudes, you did not fetch goodies from the sky like a magician. You started with what the apostles already had to hand, five loaves and a few small fish. Teach me, Lord, to use everything I am given. Save me from warm feelings that are a substitute for effective action. Lord, you never let me forget that love is shown in deeds, not words or feelings. I could fill notebooks with resolutions, and in the end be further from you. As William James put it, "A resolution that is a fine flame of feeling allowed to burn itself out without appropriate action, is not merely a lost opportunity, but a bar to future action."

The Presence of God
I pause for a moment
and reflect on God's life-giving presence
in every part of my body, in everything around me,
in the whole of my life.

Freedom
I ask for the grace to believe
in what I could be and do
if I only allowed God, my loving Creator,
to continue to create me, guide me and shape me.

Consciousness
In God's loving presence I unwind the past day,
starting from now and looking back, moment by moment.
I gather in all the goodness and light, in gratitude.
I attend to the shadows and what they say to me,
seeking healing, courage, forgiveness.

The Word
God speaks to each one of us individually. I need to listen to
what he is saying to me. (Please turn to your scripture on the
following pages. Inspiration points are there should you need
them. When you are ready, return here to continue.)

Conversation
How has God's word moved me? Has it left me cold?
Has it consoled me or moved me to act in a new way?
I imagine Jesus standing or sitting beside me,
I turn and share my feelings with him.

Conclusion
Glory be to the Father, and to the Son, and to the Holy Spirit,
As it was in the beginning, is now, and ever shall be,
World without end. Amen

254

Sunday 1st August,
Eighteenth Sunday in Ordinary Time　　　**Luke 12:13–21**

Someone in the crowd said to him, "Teacher, tell my brother to divide the family inheritance with me." But he said to him, "Friend, who set me to be a judge or arbitrator over you?" And he said to them, "Take care! Be on your guard against all kinds of greed; for one's life does not consist in the abundance of possessions." Then he told them a parable: "The land of a rich man produced abundantly. And he thought to himself, "What should I do, for I have no place to store my crops?" Then he said, "I will do this: I will pull down my barns and build larger ones, and there I will store all my grain and my goods. And I will say to my soul, Soul, you have ample goods laid up for many years; relax, eat, drink, be merry." But God said to him, "You fool! This very night your life is being demanded of you. And the things you have prepared, whose will they be?" So it is with those who store up treasures for themselves but are not rich towards God."

• "All kinds of greed . . ." How it creeps in. When I look at the time I spend worrying and planning, how much of it goes on increasing my money? When the cash rolls in, do I consider who will need it more than me?

Monday 2nd August　　　**Matthew 14:15–21**

When it was evening, the disciples came to him and said, "This is a deserted place, and the hour is now late; send the crowds away so that they may go into the villages and buy food for themselves." Jesus said to them, "They need not go away; you give them something to eat." They replied, "We have nothing here but five loaves and two fish." And he said, "Bring them here to me." Then he ordered the crowds to sit down on the grass. Taking the five loaves and the two fish, he looked up to heaven, and blessed and broke the loaves, and gave them to the disciples, and the disciples gave them to the crowds. And all ate and were filled; and they took up what was left over of the broken pieces, twelve baskets full. And those who ate were about five thousand men, besides women and children.

- Think of the food left over. The twelve baskets seem a lot, and we're not told what happened to them. The food had been the food of the poor—barley bread and sardine fish.
- In Jesus' mind, these "leftovers" feed us today. The apostles who fed the crowd still feed us today in the word of Jesus and each time we receive the bread of the eucharist.

Tuesday 3rd August   Matthew 14:22–33

Immediately Jesus made the disciples get into the boat and go on ahead to the other side, while he dismissed the crowds. And after he had dismissed the crowds, he went up the mountain by himself to pray. When evening came, he was there alone, but by this time the boat, battered by the waves, was far from the land, for the wind was against them. And early in the morning he came walking toward them on the sea. But when the disciples saw him walking on the sea, they were terrified, saying, "It is a ghost!" And they cried out in fear. But immediately Jesus spoke to them and said, "Take heart, it is I; do not be afraid." Peter answered him, "Lord, if it is you, command me to come to you on the water." He said, "Come." So Peter got out of the boat, started walking on the water, and came towards Jesus. But when he noticed the strong wind, he became frightened, and beginning to sink, he cried out, "Lord, save me!" Jesus immediately reached out his hand and caught him, saying to him, "You of little faith, why did you doubt?" When they got into the boat, the wind ceased. And those in the boat worshipped him, saying, "Truly you are the Son of God."

- Did Peter really walk on the water—leave the boat and trip across the waves in the headwind until he took his eyes off Jesus and sank? It sounds a bit magical or highly dramatic.
- The early Christians would not even have asked that question. To them it would mean that all of life is putting trust in God and that sinking in life begins in taking eyes off God.
- We, too, walk on water—all the time. We walk in trust and know that sometimes that trust in God is so real that we can give our lives to him forever.

Wednesday 4th August   **Matthew 15:21–28**

Jesus left that place and went away to the district of Tyre and Sidon. Just then a Canaanite woman from that region came out and started shouting, "Have mercy on me, Lord, Son of David; my daughter is tormented by a demon." But he did not answer her at all. And his disciples came and urged him, saying, "Send her away, for she keeps shouting after us." He answered, "I was sent only to the lost sheep of the house of Israel." But she came and knelt before him, saying, "Lord, help me." He answered, "It is not fair to take the children's food and throw it to the dogs." She said, "Yes, Lord, yet even the dogs eat the crumbs that fall from their masters' table." Then Jesus answered her, "Woman, great is your faith! Let it be done for you as you wish." And her daughter was healed instantly.

- May my prayer be like that woman's, Lord. I want to speak to you from my desire and from my frustration. I want to answer you back and make demands on you.
- This story gives me courage. You listen with good humor and heed my deepest desires.

Thursday 5th August Matthew 16:13–20

Now when Jesus came into the district of Caesarea Philippi, he asked his disciples, "Who do people say that the Son of Man is?" And they said, "Some say John the Baptist, but others Elijah, and still others Jeremiah or one of the prophets." He said to them, "But who do you say that I am?" Simon Peter answered, "You are the Messiah, the Son of the living God." And Jesus answered him, "Blessed are you, Simon son of Jonah! For flesh and blood has not revealed this to you, but my Father in heaven. And I tell you, you are Peter, and on this rock I will build my church, and the gates of Hades will not prevail against it. I will give you the keys of the kingdom of heaven, and whatever you bind on earth will be bound in heaven, and whatever you loose on earth will be loosed in heaven." Then he sternly ordered the disciples not to tell anyone that he was the Messiah.

- The traditional setting for this memorable encounter in Caesarea Philippi is a lovely riverbank under a huge rocky cliff. Peter's inspired confession leads Jesus to give him a new name and new role, to be leader of the people of God.
- Lord, you did not leave us orphans. We are the people of God, with a leader and the support of the Holy Spirit. I am not alone.

Friday 6th August,
Transfiguration of the Lord Luke 9:28b–36

Jesus took with him Peter and John and James, and went up on the mountain to pray. And while he was praying, the appearance of his face changed, and his clothes became dazzling white. Suddenly they saw two men, Moses and Elijah, talking to him. They appeared in glory and were speaking of his departure, which he was about to accomplish at Jerusalem. Now Peter and his companions were weighed down with sleep; but since they had stayed awake, they saw his glory and the two men who stood with him. Just as they were leaving him, Peter said to Jesus, "Master, it is good for us to be here; let us make three dwellings, one for you, one for Moses, and one for Elijah"—not knowing what he said. While he was saying this, a cloud came and overshadowed them; and they were terrified as they entered the cloud. Then from the cloud came a voice that said, "This is my Son, my Chosen; listen to him!" When the voice had spoken, Jesus was found alone. And they kept silent and in those days told no one any of the things they had seen.

- One of my favorite prayers is the "Glory Be to the Father." It dates from a time when I prayed over the gospel account of the transfiguration, and felt for a few moments the brightness of God come over me in a deep lightness of spirit and joy. I stayed like that, feeling a nearness to the brightness of God and praying the "Glory Be." That is why I say it many times every day.
- The words of praise to the Trinity have their source for me in a quiet prayer on a retreat about forty years ago! Strange how moments of prayer can last so long.

Saturday 7th August   Matthew 17:14–20

When they came to the crowd, a man came to Jesus, knelt before him, and said, "Lord, have mercy on my son, for he is an epileptic and he suffers terribly; he often falls into the fire and often into the water. And I brought him to your disciples, but they could not cure him." Jesus answered, "You faithless and perverse generation, how much longer must I be with you? How much longer must I put up with you? Bring him here to me." And Jesus rebuked the demon, and it came out of him, and the boy was cured instantly. Then the disciples came to Jesus privately and said, "Why could we not cast it out?" He said to them,

"Because of your little faith. For truly I tell you, if you have faith the size of a mustard seed, you will say to this mountain, 'Move from here to there,' and it will move; and nothing will be impossible for you."

- The man is nameless, a representative of the many parents who pray for their children, and each one of us who prays for someone we love. All human life is in the gospel of Jesus, the men and women who brought their own ailments or their cares about others to him.
- We know of their faith and of Jesus' positive response when people have faith. Faith may be small, like the smallest seed we know or like a drop of water. Joined to the power of Jesus, our faith can work small or great miracles.

august 8–14

Something to think and pray about each day this week:

The God beyond us

God is beyond our imagination. Every comparison, even with father or mother, limps. Saint Augustine said, "God is not what you imagine or think you understand. If you understand God, you have failed." The God we believe in is outside space and time, and surpasses all that we can conceive.

This also we know: that our faith is a mixture of light and darkness. We look to the holy people of history to give us some light on the quest for God. Saint John of the Cross, who reformed the Carmelites and was imprisoned for his pains, distrusted whatever removed the soul from the obscure faith where the understanding must be left behind in order to go to God by love. One of his greatest Carmelite followers, Thérèse of Lisieux, lived much of her religious life in darkness. Her biographer described her state in these words, "The whole area of religion seemed remote and unreal to her, not arousing the least response, either friendly or antagonistic, in her mind and heart. It was as though religion had become simply something remembered, grey, cold, and unimportant."

If that was the emotional condition of saints, what kept them going? It was the unemotional love that shows itself in fidelity. Both John and Thérèse had known enormous joy in the experience of God. But they had only a partial experience. So do we.

The Presence of God
The world is charged with the grandeur of God (Gerard Manley Hopkins).
I dwell for a moment on the presence of God
around me, in every part of my body,
and deep within my being.

Freedom
"In these days, God taught me
as a schoolteacher teaches a pupil" (St. Ignatius).
I remind myself that there are things God has to teach me yet,
and ask for the grace to hear them and let them change me.

Consciousness
Help me, Lord, to be more conscious of your presence.
Teach me to recognize your presence in others.
Fill my heart with gratitude for the times your love
has been shown to me through the care of others.

The Word
I read the word of God slowly, a few times over, and I listen to
what God is saying to me. (Please turn to your scripture on the
following pages. Inspirations points are there should you need
them. When you are ready, return here to continue.)

Conversation
What feelings are rising in me
as I pray and reflect on God's word?
I imagine Jesus himself sitting or standing beside me,
and open my heart to him.

Conclusion
Glory be to the Father, and to the Son, and to the Holy Spirit,
As it was in the beginning, is now, and ever shall be,
World without end. Amen

Sunday 8th August,
Nineteenth Sunday in Ordinary Time   Luke 12:32–34

"Do not be afraid, little flock, for it is your Father's good pleasure to give you the kingdom. Sell your possessions, and give alms. Make purses for yourselves that do not wear out, an unfailing treasure in heaven, where no thief comes near and no moth destroys. For where your treasure is, there your heart will be also."

- Some of this is ancient, natural wisdom. The Romans compared money to seawater: the more you drink, the thirstier you become.
- Your message, Lord, is not about insulating my heart against the shock of loss, but about treasuring what will last beyond this world, the love of you and of your kingdom. It is about extending love, not limiting it to what is perishable.
- Where is my treasure to be found?

Monday 9th August   Matthew 17:22–27

As they were gathering in Galilee, Jesus said to them, "The Son of Man is going to be betrayed into human hands, and they will kill him, and on the third day he will be raised." And they were greatly distressed. When they reached Capernaum, the collectors of the temple tax came to Peter and said, "Does your teacher not pay the temple tax?" He said, "Yes, he does." And when he came home, Jesus spoke of it first, asking, "What do you think, Simon? From whom do kings of the earth take toll or tribute? From their children or from others?" When Peter said, "From others." Jesus said to him, "Then the children are free. However, so that we do not give offence to them, go to the lake and cast a hook; take the first fish that comes up; and when you open its mouth, you will find a coin; take that and give it to them for you and me."

- This is a strange story about a coin in the mouth of a fish. We are not told that Peter actually found the coin. Michael Mullins writes, "It may well be another way of saying to those who were instructed to carry no gold, no silver, not even a few coppers in their purses, to trust in God who provides in unexpected ways."

Tuesday 10th August, St. Lawrence   John 12:24–26

"Very truly, I tell you, unless a grain of wheat falls into the earth and dies, it remains just a single grain; but if it dies, it bears much fruit. Those who love their life lose it, and those who hate their life in this world will keep it for eternal life. Whoever serves me must follow me, and where I am, there will my servant be also. Whoever serves me, the Father will honor."

- "Unless a grain of wheat falls into the earth and dies, it remains just a single grain." Jesus is speaking of his death, but he speaks for each of us, too. This seems to be a hard saying, but we know it is true, both from nature and from personal experience.
- Is there something I can "die" to today, some selfishness that is causing a rift with others? Can I follow Jesus in this?

Wednesday 11th August   Matthew 18:15–16

Jesus said to the disciples, "If another member of the church sins against you, go and point out the fault when the two of you are alone. If the member listens to you, you have regained that one. But if you are not listened to, take one or two others along with you, so that every word may be confirmed by the evidence of two or three witnesses."

- In caring and challenging the offending member, in gathering together in his name, the Lord is present. One of the first words of the gospel was "Emmanuel"—God is with us. The end of the gospel has Jesus' promise of being with us all days.

- In a church which may overemphasize the sacramental presence of the Lord, it is good to remind ourselves of the presence of Jesus among us all the time, in the hearts of his people.
- Can I be open to the Lord's presence in other people today?

Thursday 12th August   Ezekiel 12:1–4

The word of the Lord came to me: Mortal, you are living in the midst of a rebellious house, who have eyes to see but do not see, who have ears to hear but do not hear; for they are a rebellious house. Therefore, mortal, prepare for yourself an exile's baggage, and go into exile by day in their sight; you shall go like an exile from your place to another place in their sight. Perhaps they will understand, though they are a rebellious house. You shall bring out your baggage by day in their sight, as baggage for exile; and you shall go out yourself at evening in their sight, as those do who go into exile.

- This is one of the great themes of the prophets—confronting the people with their infidelity in the face of the Lord's constant faithfulness; to pull us back when we go off on our own.
- What are some of the things I refuse to see and hear? About myself, my way of life, my priorities? Am I too fixed in my ways?

Friday 13th August   Matthew 19:3–6

Some Pharisees came to him, and to test him they asked, "Is it lawful for a man to divorce his wife for any cause?" He answered, "Have you not read that the one who made them at the beginning 'made them male and female,' and said, 'For this reason a man shall leave his father and mother and be joined to his wife, and the two shall become one flesh'? So they are no longer two, but one flesh. Therefore what God has joined together, let no one separate."

- Again, in the face of a test case from lawyers, Jesus overturns current thinking: he went beyond the law of Moses back to God's creation. God made men and women, as people with equal dignity. Together, in the oneness ordained in God's creation, they form a new community.
- Lord, we know this ideal is so hard to achieve, that many struggle with it, as your disciples did. I know I can speak with you on this.

Saturday 14th August   Matthew 19:13–15

Then little children were being brought to Jesus in order that he might lay his hands on them and pray. The disciples spoke sternly to those who brought them; but Jesus said, "Let the little children come to me, and do not stop them; for it is to such as these that the kingdom of heaven belongs." And he laid his hands on them and went on his way.

- After discussing marriage, Jesus turns his attention to children. Laying on of hands is a sign of blessing and healing, and with this Jesus takes the youngest of the community into his care.
- The children are brought to Jesus by others—this can highlight that, like children, we go to God and to Jesus with the help and the guidance of others. In our prayer we remember those whom God has committed to our care.

august 15–21

Something to think and pray about each day this week:

Tending our wounds

Some holy pictures show Jesus with a wounded heart. The image can be so familiar that we do not notice that we too have wounded hearts. When you come to know any adult well, you nearly always discover a wound, a sense of having been badly and unjustly hurt at some stage. People live with their wounds and keep up a good front. Behind that front are all sorts of sorrows, and different ways of living with a wounded heart.

Often the most useful thing for yourself and everybody is to do nothing. It is also the most painful. We have a strong urge to act out, to deal with the anger that engulfs us by working it out in action. That can be destructive. The other destructive response is to turn the anger against oneself, and slump into depression. Those who have a streak of depression in the family may go this way. You may be facing an insoluble problem—as in the case of a person wrongly accused, or a mother suffering at her child's pain—but by turning it in on yourself, you are only adding to the trouble. It is in such a crisis that Jesus' heart can save our sanity and peace of soul. He showed the possibility of enduring the cruelest injustice, yet responding with love. This vision of a warm personal relationship with Jesus can sustain all Christians.

The Presence of God
As I sit here, God is present,
breathing life into me and into everything around me.
For a few moments, I sit silently,
and become aware of God's loving presence.

Freedom
If God were trying to tell me something, would I know?
If God were reassuring me or challenging me, would I notice?
I ask for the grace to be free of my own preoccupations
and open to what God may be saying to me.

Consciousness
How am I really feeling? Light-hearted? Heavy-hearted?
I may be very much at peace, happy to be here.
Equally, I may be frustrated, worried, or angry.
I acknowledge how I really am. It is the real me that the Lord loves.

The Word
I take my time to read the word of God, slowly, a few times,
allowing myself to dwell on anything that strikes me. (Please
turn to your scripture on the following pages. Inspiration points
are there should you need them. When you are ready, return
here to continue.)

Conversation
What is stirring in me as I pray?
Am I consoled, troubled, left cold?
I imagine Jesus himself standing or sitting at my side,
and share my feelings with him.

Conclusion
Glory be to the Father, and to the Son, and to the Holy Spirit,
As it was in the beginning, is now, and ever shall be,
World without end. Amen

Sunday 15th August,
Assumption of the Virgin Mary   Luke 1:46–55

And Mary said, "My soul magnifies the Lord, and my spirit rejoices in God my Savior, for he has looked with favor on the lowliness of his servant. Surely, from now on all generations will call me blessed; for the Mighty One has done great things for me, and holy is his name. His mercy is for those who fear him from generation to generation. He has shown strength with his arm; he has scattered the proud in the thoughts of their hearts. He has brought down the powerful from their thrones, and lifted up the lowly; he has filled the hungry with good things, and sent the rich away empty. He has helped his servant Israel, in remembrance of his mercy, according to the promise he made to our ancestors, to Abraham and to his descendants for ever."

- This is Mary's song of praise to God for all he has done and will do for her and for his people. Have you ever tried to write your own Magnificat—your prayer or song of thanks to God for all he has done for you?

- Perhaps you can start today. Begin prayerfully, with "Thanks" as your title; think back over the day, the week, the year; the past and the present; your personal gifts and all that others give you in life. The grateful heart is a heart open to love and to God.

Monday 16th August   Matthew 19:16–22

Then someone came to Jesus and said, "Teacher, what good deed must I do to have eternal life?" And he said to him, "Why do you ask me about what is good? There is only one who is good. If you wish to enter into life, keep the commandments." He said to him, "Which ones?" And Jesus said, "You shall not murder; You shall not commit adultery; You shall not steal; You shall not bear false witness; Honor your father and mother; also,

You shall love your neighbor as yourself." The young man said to him, "I have kept all these; what do I still lack?" Jesus said to him, "If you wish to be perfect, go, sell your possessions, and give the money to the poor, and you will have treasure in heaven; then come, follow me." When the young man heard this word, he went away grieving, for he had many possessions.

• To follow Jesus we need to shake off anything that binds us or any shackles that imprison us in a dependency on wealth, esteem or comfort.

• Any "wealth" which takes first place in life—even a person—can be a block to freedom in following the Lord. The wealth of the man who met Jesus in this incident made him sad, a sure sign that his possessions were imprisoning him.

• What are some of the things that block me from following Jesus?

Tuesday 17th August   **Matthew 19:23–26**

Jesus said to his disciples, "Truly I tell you, it will be hard for a rich person to enter the kingdom of heaven. Again I tell you, it is easier for a camel to go through the eye of a needle than for someone who is rich to enter the kingdom of God." When the disciples heard this, they were greatly astounded and said, "Then who can be saved?" But Jesus looked at them and said, "For mortals it is impossible, but for God all things are possible."

• There is high drama in the statement of Jesus about passing through the eye of a needle. Jesus does not mean it to be taken literally: he is highlighting a truth about wealth—it can ruin us.

• Wealth can leave us mistrustful of others or mean; it can also be the basis for service and generosity. To give away money or possessions regularly is a way to ensure wealth never ensnares us.

Wednesday 18th August   **Ezekiel 34:1–6**

The word of the Lord came to me: "Mortal, prophesy against the shepherds of Israel: prophesy, and say to them—to the shepherds: "Thus says the Lord God: Ah, you shepherds of Israel who have been feeding yourselves! Should not shepherds feed the sheep? You eat the fat, you clothe yourselves with the wool, you slaughter the fatlings; but you do not feed the sheep. You have not strengthened the weak, you have not healed the sick, you have not bound up the injured, you have not brought back the strayed, you have not sought the lost, but with force and harshness you have ruled them. So they were scattered, because there was no shepherd; and scattered, they became food for all the wild animals. My sheep were scattered, they wandered over all the mountains and on every high hill; my sheep were scattered over all the face of the earth, with no one to search or seek for them.""

- While Ezekiel's allegory is a call to conversion, directed at the failed leaders of Israel, we can also apply it to our own times and situation.
- Just as sheep need their shepherd, so do we humans need the trees, the water, the land, the animals, the sun, the snow.
- Or we can look at the way we provide leadership: clergy and their parishioners; managers and workers; parents and children; sons and daughters.
- Can I become a better shepherd in these things?

Thursday 19th August   **Matthew 22:1–2, 8–14**

Once more Jesus spoke to them in parables, saying: "The kingdom of heaven may be compared to a king who gave a wedding banquet for his son. Then he said to his slaves, 'The wedding is ready. Go therefore into the main streets, and invite everyone you find to the wedding banquet.' Those slaves went out into the streets and gathered all whom they found, both good and bad; so the wedding hall was filled with guests. But when the king came in to see the guests, he noticed a man there who was not wearing a wedding robe, and he said to him, 'Friend, how did you get in here without a wedding robe?' And he was speechless. Then the king said to the attendants, 'Bind him hand and foot, and throw him into the outer darkness, where there will be weeping and gnashing of teeth.' For many are called, but few are chosen."

- At the crossroads you are likely to find people of all sorts, from many places and backgrounds: good and bad, Jew and Gentile. All are invited to accept the call to change so that all might enter the kingdom.
- Churches are also called to be crossroad communities where all are welcome, all may meet and greet each other, and above all, in compassion and justice, take care of each other.
- How do I contribute to this now?
- What changes can I make here?

Friday 20th August   Matthew 22:34–40

When the Pharisees heard that Jesus had silenced the Sadducees, they gathered together, and one of them, a lawyer, asked him a question to test him. "Teacher, which commandment in the law is the greatest?" He said to him, "'You shall love the Lord your God with all your heart, and with all your soul, and with all your mind.' This is the greatest and first commandment. And a second is like it: 'You shall love your neighbor as yourself.' On these two commandments hang all the law and the prophets."

- At another time Jesus was asked, "Who is my neighbor?" His response was the story of the Good Samaritan (Lk 11). Jesus expands the meaning of neighbor to include everyone in need.
- It is an easy answer to say that the greatest commandment is to love God. The real insight of Jesus is to unite the two loves of life—God and others—into one big law of love.

Saturday 21st August · Matthew 23:8–12

Then Jesus said to the crowds and to his disciples, "You are not to be called rabbi, for you have one teacher, and you are all students. And call no one your father on earth, for you have one Father—the one in heaven. Nor are you to be called instructors, for you have one instructor, the Messiah. The greatest among you will be your servant. All who exalt themselves will be humbled, and all who humble themselves will be exalted."

- Jesus' message is that our teacher is God, and the true disciples learn only from God.
- We find very often in Jesus a dismissal of ostentatious religion. His followers are to be humble. Our church is to be a humble church, as we are to be in our dealings with each other. As we know, this is a constant and often difficult struggle.
- Lord, lead me by daily prayer into the mystery of being loved and called by God in Jesus Christ.

Something to think and pray about each day this week:

Journey through the desert

What does the desert signify in the story of the people of Israel, of John the Baptist, and then Jesus himself? It was not a destination, but a place for travelers going somewhere, journeying to a new life. Jesus had gone into the desert an unknown young carpenter from Nazareth, with thirty years of anonymity behind him. After the desert, he returned to Galilee with power of the Spirit in him and started to preach. Quickly he became a public figure, but he loved to withdraw to desert or mountain to recharge his energies by prayer. He moved forward like any of us, with no sure knowledge of what was to happen him. His life was shaped by the Spirit driving him forward, but shaped also by the accidents of his life, the enthusiasm of some of his listeners, and the resistance of others. After the quiet life of Nazareth, Jesus' public life was tumultuous. If we are to do justice to his humanity, we must accept that he did not know what would happen next, only that this was where God wanted him to be.

Most of us could point to a similar second calling, though we might not think of it in that way. A second journey like this is not an easy option. It means casting adrift from the security you have enjoyed, not knowing where the road will take you.

The Presence of God
As I sit here with my book, God is here.
Around me, in my sensations,
in my thoughts and deep within me.
I pause for a moment and become aware
of God's life-giving presence.

Freedom
I need to close out the noise, to rise above the noise;
The noise that interrupts, that separates,
The noise that isolates.
I need to listen to God again.

Consciousness
Knowing that God loves me unconditionally,
I can afford to be honest about how I am.
How has the last day been, and how do I feel now?
I share my feelings openly with the Lord.

The Word
God speaks to each one of us individually. I need to listen to
what he is saying to me. (Please turn to your scripture on the
following pages. Inspiration points are there should you need
them. When you are ready, return here to continue.)

Conversation
Do I notice myself reacting as I pray with the word of God?
Do I feel challenged, comforted, angry?
Imagining Jesus sitting or standing by me,
I speak out my feelings, as one trusted friend to another.

Conclusion
Glory be to the Father, and to the Son, and to the Holy Spirit,
As it was in the beginning, is now, and ever shall be,
World without end. Amen

Sunday 22nd August,
Twenty-first Sunday in Ordinary Time   Luke 13:22–30

Jesus went through one town and village after another, teaching as he made his way to Jerusalem. Someone asked him, "Lord, will only a few be saved?" He said to them, "Strive to enter through the narrow door; for many, I tell you, will try to enter and will not be able. When once the owner of the house has got up and shut the door, and you begin to stand outside and to knock at the door, saying, 'Lord, open to us', then in reply he will say to you, 'I do not know where you come from.' Then you will begin to say, 'We ate and drank with you, and you taught in our streets.' But he will say, 'I do not know where you come from; go away from me, all you evildoers!' There will be weeping and gnashing of teeth when you see Abraham and Isaac and Jacob and all the prophets in the kingdom of God, and you yourselves thrown out. Then people will come from east and west, from north and south, and will eat in the kingdom of God. Indeed, some are last who will be first, and some are first who will be last.'"

- When an Alpine guide was killed on the mountainside, they wrote on his grave: "He died climbing."
- Lord, I pray I may be pushing upwards to the end, never sitting back on presumed virtue, but keeping my eye and my efforts on that narrow gate.

Monday 23rd August   2 Thessalonians 1:1–4

Paul, Silvanus, and Timothy, To the church of the Thessalonians in God our Father and the Lord Jesus Christ: Grace to you and peace from God our Father and the Lord Jesus Christ. We must always give thanks to God for you, brothers and sisters, as is right, because your faith is growing abundantly, and the love of every one of you for one another is increasing. Therefore we ourselves boast of you among the churches of God for your steadfastness and faith during all your persecutions and the afflictions that you are enduring.

- Though there are some rebukes to follow, this letter starts with brotherly affection and acknowledges the community's active faith, love for each other, and hope in the face of persecution.
- When I have harsh words to deliver, do I take time to think about the positives, not just the negatives? Can I pray about this now?

Tuesday 24th August,
St. Bartholomew, Apostle   John 1:45–50

Philip found Nathanael and said to him, "We have found him about whom Moses in the law and also the prophets wrote, Jesus son of Joseph from Nazareth." Nathanael said to him, "Can anything good come out of Nazareth?" Philip said to him, "Come and see." When Jesus saw Nathanael coming towards him, he said of him, "Here is truly an Israelite in whom there is no deceit!" Nathanael asked him, "Where did you come to know me?" Jesus answered, "I saw you under the fig tree before Philip called you." Nathanael replied, "Rabbi, you are the Son of God! You are the King of Israel!" Jesus answered, "Do you believe because I told you that I saw you under the fig tree? You will see greater things than these."

- "Can anything good come out of Nazareth?" This is quite a cynical comment from Nathanael; or Bartholomew as he is called in the other gospels. No doubt he knew the place had a poor reputation.
- Yet Bartholomew still accepted the invitation to "come and see," and thus began a relationship with Jesus that changed his life. By his "yes," he found the gateway to a new life—the person, Jesus.

Wednesday 25th August   2 Thessalonians 3:6–10

Now we command you, beloved, in the name of our Lord Jesus Christ, to keep away from believers who are living in idleness and not according to the tradition that they received from us. For you yourselves know how you ought to imitate us; we were not idle when we were with you, and we did not eat anyone's bread without paying for it; but with toil and labor we worked night and day, so that we might not burden any of you. This was not because we do not have that right, but in order to give you an example to imitate. For even when we were with you, we gave you this command: Anyone unwilling to work should not eat.

- Some in the community, anticipating their harsh lives would be over as soon as Jesus came again, were having a "free ride" on the charity of others who continued to work hard.
- Lord, give me the energy to bring about change in this world in preparation for your coming: for refugees, social outcasts, the environment, public morality, etc. There is much still to do.

Thursday 26th August   Matthew 24:42–47

Jesus said to the people, "Keep awake therefore, for you do not know on what day your Lord is coming. But understand this: if the owner of the house had known in what part of the night the thief was coming, he would have stayed awake and would not have let his house be broken into. Therefore you also must be ready, for the Son of Man is coming at an unexpected hour. Who then is the faithful and wise slave, whom his master has put in charge of his household, to give the other slaves their allowance of food at the proper time? Blessed is that slave whom his master will find at work when he arrives. Truly I tell you, he will put that one in charge of all his possessions."

- "Keep awake." God can enter a life with vigor—as in those times, few though they may be, where we feel ourselves really strongly moved and called by God.
- Mostly the action of God is gentle, small, and insignificant callings in the ordinariness of life.
- Can you recall times when you felt close to God and God's calling? Recalling them in prayer can strengthen the love and call of God in our lives.

Friday 27th August   Matthew 25:1–13

Jesus said to his disciples, "Then the kingdom of heaven will be like this. Ten bridesmaids took their lamps and went to meet the bridegroom. Five of them were foolish, and five were wise. When the foolish took their lamps, they took no oil with them; but the wise took flasks of oil with their lamps. As the bridegroom was delayed, all of them became drowsy and slept. But at midnight there was a shout, 'Look! Here is the bridegroom! Come out to meet him.' Then all those bridesmaids got up and trimmed their lamps. The foolish said to the wise, 'Give us some of your oil, for our lamps are going out.' But the wise replied, 'No! there will not be enough for you and for us; you had better go to the dealers and buy some for yourselves.' And while they went to buy it, the bridegroom came, and those who were ready went with him into the wedding banquet; and the door was shut. Later the other bridesmaids came also, saying, 'Lord, lord, open to us.' But he replied, 'Truly I tell you, I do not know you.' Keep awake therefore, for you know neither the day nor the hour."

- The oil in the lamps is often understood as the good works that we do, which each of us may have to show when called to account. The answer from the wise virgins—"Buy some for yourselves"— implies reminds us that salvation does not come just from being attached to what some may consider "holy things," but is God's response to how we live.

- I am called to use my own wisdom and stand on my own record when I give an account of myself.
- Lord, I pray that you may know me when I present myself at your coming.

Saturday 28th August   1 Corinthians 1:26–31

Consider your own call, brothers and sisters: not many of you were wise by human standards, not many were powerful, not many were of noble birth. But God chose what is foolish in the world to shame the wise; God chose what is weak in the world to shame the strong; God chose what is low and despised in the world, things that are not, to reduce to nothing things that are, so that no one might boast in the presence of God. He is the source of your life in Christ Jesus, who became for us wisdom from God, and righteousness and sanctification and redemption, in order that, as it is written, "Let the one who boasts, boast in the Lord."

- Paul certainly knows how to cut away the dross and get to the point! There is nothing flattering to the ego here—it is all about God and not about me, except that we have been chosen.
- If I have truly answered the Lord's call then I may well "boast in the Lord" because Jesus is the source of my life.

august 29–september 4

Something to think and pray about each day this week:

Letting go

A friend consoled me after a fire destroyed my records and possessions. "We manage to accumulate so much in our lives. It is only when someone close dies and you have to deal with their affairs, that all the things that meant so much to them are seen in a different light. I used to love our silver. It was all family stuff. When we were relieved of it all some years ago by someone who felt they had to have it, I was greatly saddened. However, since then we have replaced some and inherited some more. But I can no longer invest any emotion into things."

We seem to desire to hold onto so many things that are precious to us—the things that remind us of people we loved, of past achievements, and of beauty. But in the end these things are within our minds and our hearts. Everything on this earth is dynamic. When one amazing sunset disappears for ever, another glorious sunrise appears elsewhere.

The Presence of God
I pause for a moment, aware that God is here.
I think of how everything around me,
the air I breathe, my whole body,
is tingling with the presence of God.

Freedom
I will ask God's help,
to be free from my own preoccupations,
to be open to God in this time of prayer,
to come to love and serve him more.

Consciousness
In the presence of my loving Creator,
I look honestly at my feelings over the last day,
the highs, the lows, and the level ground.
Can I see where the Lord has been present?

The Word
I read the word of God slowly, a few times over, and I listen to
what God is saying to me. (Please turn to your scripture on the
following pages. Inspiration points are there should you need
them. When you are ready, return here to continue.)

Conversation
Remembering that I am still in God's presence,
I imagine Jesus himself standing or sitting beside me,
and say whatever is on my mind, whatever is in my heart,
speaking as one friend to another.

Conclusion
Glory be to the Father, and to the Son, and to the Holy Spirit,
As it was in the beginning, is now, and ever shall be,
World without end. Amen

Sunday 29th August,
Twenty-second Sunday in Ordinary Time   Luke 14:1, 7–11

On one occasion when Jesus was going to the house of a leader of the Pharisees to eat a meal on the sabbath, they were watching him closely. When he noticed how the guests chose the places of honor, he told them a parable. "When you are invited by someone to a wedding banquet, do not sit down at the place of honor, in case someone more distinguished than you has been invited by your host; and the host who invited both of you may come and say to you, 'Give this person your place,' and then in disgrace you would start to take the lowest place. But when you are invited, go and sit down at the lowest place, so that when your host comes, he may say to you, 'Friend, move up higher'; then you will be honored in the presence of all who sit at the table with you. For all who exalt themselves will be humbled, and those who humble themselves will be exalted."

- Jesus, how often my giving is corrupted by self-interest and the hope of favors in return. You gave to me without hope of return.
- I can do you no favors, but you taught me that love means giving without expectations, that there is more happiness in giving than in receiving.

Monday 30th August   Luke 4:16–22a

When he came to Nazareth, where he had been brought up, he went to the synagogue on the sabbath day, as was his custom. He stood up to read, and the scroll of the prophet Isaiah was given to him. He unrolled the scroll and found the place where it was written: "The Spirit of the Lord is upon me, because he has anointed me to bring good news to the poor. He has sent me to proclaim release to the captives and recovery of sight to the blind, to let the oppressed go free, to proclaim the year of the Lord's favor." And he rolled up the scroll, gave it back to the attendant, and sat down. The eyes of all in the synagogue were fixed on him. Then he began to say to them, "Today this scripture has been fulfilled in your hearing." All spoke well of him and were amazed at the gracious words that came from his mouth.

- The beginning of Jesus' public life and mission starts in the local gathering place—the synagogue in his small village. It comes as no surprise that the local people wondered where Jesus got his wisdom.
- Perhaps he found this wisdom among these people and in his prayerful relationship with his Father. They, without knowing it, were the teachers of Jesus in faith. Without knowing it, we also are teachers of faith in what we say and do.

Tuesday 31st August   Luke 4:31–37

He went down to Capernaum, a city in Galilee, and was teaching them on the sabbath. They were astounded at his teaching, because he spoke with authority. In the synagogue there was a man who had the spirit of an unclean demon, and he cried out with a loud voice, "Let us alone! What have you to do with us, Jesus of Nazareth? Have you come to destroy us? I know who you are, the Holy One of God." But Jesus rebuked him, saying, "Be silent, and come out of him!" When the demon had thrown him down before them, he came out of him without having done him any harm. They were all amazed and kept saying to one another, "What kind of utterance is this? For with authority and power he commands the unclean spirits, and out they come!" And a report about him began to reach every place in the region.

- Jesus seems to live within a world of hostility; political and family divisions, as well as the conflict of good and evil, were a constant of his life.

- Somehow Jesus transcends but is involved in the conflicts. He seems to face conflict head-on.
- He does so, not only with the power of his own personality, but with the power of his Father so that he can command evil, and it flees.
- Some of our evils can be dealt with only through prayer in the power of the risen Lord.

Wednesday 1st September — Luke 4:38–39

After leaving the synagogue Jesus entered Simon's house. Now Simon's mother-in-law was suffering from a high fever, and they asked him about her. Then he stood over her and rebuked the fever, and it left her. Immediately she got up and began to serve them.

- At a synagogue Jesus was sure of meeting everyone. He sought people out, so he went to where they were. This is the Incarnation continuing daily.
- God in Jesus came from eternity and heaven to find the lost and to save all. He is constantly trying to find us. He wants to be part of our lives, as a true friend does.
- Prayer is giving time to God, so I'm home when he calls.

Thursday 2nd September — Luke 5:4–11

When Jesus had finished speaking, he said to Simon, "Put out into the deep water and let down your nets for a catch." Simon answered, "Master, we have worked all night long but have caught nothing. Yet if you say so, I will let down the nets." When they had done this, they caught so many fish that their nets were beginning to break. So they signaled their partners in the other boat to come and help them. And they came and filled both boats, so that they began to sink. But when Simon Peter saw it, he fell down at Jesus' knees, saying, "Go away from me, Lord, for I am a sinful man!" For he and all who were with him were amazed at the catch of fish that they had taken; and so also were James and John, sons of Zebedee, who were partners with Simon. Then Jesus said to Simon, "Do not be afraid; from now on you will be catching people." When they had brought their boats to shore, they left everything and followed him.

- Peter invited Jesus into one of his most precious and important possessions, his boat. Peter also allowed Jesus tell him where to fish, handing over control of the boat, his own livelihood and his life, to Jesus.
- In prayer we invite Jesus into the most personal and important places of our lives. We also allow him take possession of us, giving all that we can to him. From Peter's boat, he spoke to the crowds; from our lives he speaks to people today.

Friday 3rd September   Luke 5:33–38
Then the Pharisees and the scribes said to Jesus, "John's disciples, like the disciples of the Pharisees, frequently fast and pray, but your disciples eat and drink." Jesus said to them, "You cannot make wedding guests fast while the bridegroom is with them, can you? The days will come when the bridegroom will be taken away from them, and then they will fast in those days." He also told them a parable: "No one tears a piece from a new garment and sews it on an old garment; otherwise the new will be torn, and the piece from the new will not match the old. And no one puts new wine into old wineskins; otherwise the new wine will burst the skins and will be spilled, and the skins will be destroyed. But new wine must be put into fresh wineskins.'"

- Jesus has come to bring something radically new to the people he met. He would offer a new understanding of their religion. He would refer back to times past, but move onto the future, even though it meant parting company with John the Baptist and his disciples.

- Many of his words and actions were intended to bring something new into the lives of his people.
- Am I open to the love of Jesus and the challenge of the gospel every day?

Saturday 4th September   Luke 6:1–5

One sabbath while Jesus was going through the grainfields, his disciples plucked some heads of grain, rubbed them in their hands, and ate them. But some of the Pharisees said, "Why are you doing what is not lawful on the sabbath?" Jesus answered, "Have you not read what David did when he and his companions were hungry? He entered the house of God and took and ate the bread of the Presence, which it is not lawful for any but the priests to eat, and gave some to his companions?" Then he said to them, "The Son of Man is lord of the sabbath."

- The link between faith and human needs is strong; religion and humanity are intrinsically linked. Hunger for ordinary food is taken seriously by Jesus so that religious laws may be set aside.
- I can bring to mind the reality of starvation for many millions in our world. What is our role here? Can we ensure that the bread of ordinary life is more equally shared among the loved ones of God?

september 5–11

Something to think and pray about each day this week:

The Spirit of prayer

"Abba," meaning Daddy, is one of the Hebrew words we may have all heard, not just in the name of the Swedish pop group, but in Saint Paul's letter to the Romans. "The Spirit you have received is the spirit of children, and it makes us cry out, 'Abba! Father!'" (Rom 8:15).

At times we can feel lost and think that nobody cares if we are alive or dead. Prayer becomes difficult, and we are thrown back on our own weakness. Saint Paul takes up the theme, "The Spirit comes to help us in our weakness. For when we cannot choose words in order to pray properly, the Spirit himself expresses our plea in a way that could never be put into words, and God who knows everything in our hearts knows perfectly well what he means" (Rom 8:26).

In old age, and in sickness, prayer does not become easier, and Saint Paul's words matter more and more. We have a place in God's mind. God knows everything in our hearts. There is a constant bond of love and communication between the Holy Spirit in us and God in heaven. When we pray we try to tune in to that communication.

The Presence of God

For a few moments, I think of God's veiled presence in things:
in the elements, giving them existence;
in plants, giving them life; in animals, giving them sensation;
and finally, in me, giving me all this and more,
making me a temple, a dwelling-place of the Spirit.

Freedom

God is not foreign to my freedom.
Instead the Spirit breathes life into my most intimate desires,
gently nudging me towards all that is good.
I ask for the grace to let myself be enfolded by the Spirit.

Consciousness

Knowing that God loves me unconditionally,
I look honestly over the last day, its events, and my feelings.
Do I have something to be grateful for? Then I give thanks.
Is there something I am sorry for? Then I ask forgiveness.

The Word

I take my time to read the word of God, slowly, a few times,
allowing myself to dwell on anything that strikes me. (Please
turn to your scripture on the following pages. Inspiration points
are there should you need them. When you are ready, return
here to continue.)

Conversation

How has God's word moved me? Has it left me cold?
Has it consoled me or moved me to act in a new way?
I imagine Jesus standing or sitting beside me,
I turn and share my feelings with him.

Conclusion

Glory be to the Father, and to the Son, and to the Holy Spirit,
As it was in the beginning, is now, and ever shall be,
World without end. Amen

Sunday 5th September,
Twenty-third Sunday in Ordinary Time   Luke 14:25, 27

Now large crowds were traveling with him; and he turned and said to them, "Whoever does not carry the cross and follow me cannot be my disciple."

- Lord, as you spoke, you were on your way to Jerusalem and the passion. The cross was not a little ornament to wear round the neck, but a terrifying symbol of evil, torture and death.

- There may be feel-good times in my piety, but I must be ready for the feel-fear times, too, when I join you in your darkest hour.

Monday 6th September   Luke 6:6–11

On another sabbath he entered the synagogue and taught, and there was a man there whose right hand was withered. The scribes and the Pharisees watched him to see whether he would cure on the sabbath, so that they might find an accusation against him. Even though he knew what they were thinking, he said to the man who had the withered hand, "Come and stand here." He got up and stood there. Then Jesus said to them, "I ask you, is it lawful to do good or to do harm on the sabbath, to save life or to destroy it?" After looking around at all of them, he said to him, "Stretch out your hand." He did so, and his hand was restored. But they were filled with fury and discussed with one another what they might do to Jesus.

- There is something almost comforting about knowing what the "right thing to do" is, even if we struggle to always do it. It is deep within most of us; we act as our own policeman and feel guilty even if no one else knows what we've done wrong.

- Jesus turns it all upside down—he breaks the religious laws and challenges the lawmakers and the custodians of "right" behavior.

- Where do I stand on this? Do I value the law before people? Do I give life to bring others or oppress them to freedom as Jesus did?

Tuesday 7th September   Luke 6:12–16

Now during those days he went out to the mountain to pray; and he spent the night in prayer to God. And when day came, he called his disciples and chose twelve of them, whom he also named apostles: Simon, whom he named Peter, and his brother Andrew, and James, and John, and Philip, and Bartholomew, and Matthew, and Thomas, and James son of Alphaeus, and Simon, who was called the Zealot, and Judas son of James, and Judas Iscariot, who became a traitor.

- Big events in Jesus' life were preceded by prayer. Choosing the apostles was a big event; it would impact on the life of his community forever.
- Time in prayer is joining in the prayer of Christ, and can help us discern what is best, most human, and most loving in our lives.

Wednesday 8th September,
Birthday of the Blessed Virgin Mary   Matthew 1:18–23

Now the birth of Jesus the Messiah took place in this way. When his mother Mary had been engaged to Joseph, but before they lived together, she was found to be with child from the Holy Spirit. Her husband Joseph, being a righteous man and unwilling to expose her to public disgrace, planned to dismiss her quietly. But just when he had resolved to do this, an angel of the Lord appeared to him in a dream and said, "Joseph, son of David, do not be afraid to take Mary as your wife, for the child conceived in her is from the Holy Spirit. She will bear a son, and you are to name him Jesus, for he will save his people from their sins." All this took place to fulfill what had been spoken by the Lord through the prophet: "Look, the virgin shall conceive and bear a son, and they shall name him Emmanuel," which means, "God is with us."

- The name of Jesus, "Emmanuel," "God is with us," is like a mantra which will be a name for Jesus. We can look at everything he does and everything that happens to him with these words echoing like a chorus or featured like a backdrop.
- Through him we are all Emmanuel; God is with us still in a special way because he was in Jesus in a special way.

Thursday 9th September   Luke 6:27a, 31–36

Jesus said to his disciples, "But I say to you that listen, Do to others as you would have them do to you. If you love those who love you, what credit is that to you? For even sinners love those who love them. If you do good to those who do good to you, what credit is that to you? For even sinners do the same. If you lend to those from whom you hope to receive, what credit is that to you? Even sinners lend to sinners, to receive as much again. But love your enemies, do good, and lend, expecting nothing in return. Your reward will be great, and you will be children of the Most High; for he is kind to the ungrateful and the wicked. Be merciful, just as your Father is merciful."

- Jesus expects more from us than the "do unto others" attitude, which of itself is a high moral standard. He asks for generosity and charity, and beyond that, he also asks for mercy and justice.
- The central quality of the Christian stance to others is the mercy which covers over faults and fallings; not to deny them, but always to offer another chance.

Friday 10th September   Luke 6:39–42

He also told them a parable: "Can a blind person guide a blind person? Will not both fall into a pit? A disciple is not above the teacher, but everyone who is fully qualified will be like the teacher. Why do you see the speck in your neighbor's eye, but do not notice the log in your own eye? Or how can you say to your neighbor, 'Friend, let me take out the speck in your eye,' when you yourself do not see the log in your own eye? You hypocrite, first take the log out of your own eye, and then you will see clearly to take the speck out of your neighbor's eye."

- Did it ever happen that you realized you were condemning another person for their faults and then remembered that your own faults were just as many or more?
- "Friend, let me take out the speck in your eye . . ." It's just human to be like that. The ability to recognize our personal shortcomings can come to us in prayer.

Saturday 11th September   Luke 6:47–49

Jesus said to the disciples, "I will show you what someone is like who comes to me, hears my words, and acts on them. That one is like a man building a house, who dug deeply and laid the foundation on rock; when a flood arose, the river burst against that house but could not shake it, because it had been well built. But the one who hears and does not act is like a man who built a house on the ground without a foundation. When the river burst against it, immediately it fell, and great was the ruin of that house."

- Prayer puts nourishment into the roots of our Christian life. What we say and do for God and in the name of Christ comes from what is inside us.
- We nourish the gifts of God and the faith we have in prayer and in doing good. Prayer is one of the foundations of a life of faith; it is a rock which helps us remain constant in times of struggle and temptation.

Something to think and pray about each day this week:

The prodigal father

The scriptures do not offer much advice on family problems, but we can pick up clues. In the father of the prodigal son we have Jesus' model of what it is to be a parent. He is not overprotective. He allows his son the freedom to follow his own dream rather than his father's, to take risks and to make mistakes. He is still there for the son who has made a fool of himself and brought shame on the family. He absorbs the jealousy and anger of the older son but does not yield to him. He shows what it is to be a man: there when he is needed; faithful to wife and children; able to sustain his lifelong commitment; nurturing, forgiving, patient, and aware that children can learn from their mistakes.

He does not blame himself. When the boy is bursting with re-hearsed self-reproaches ("I have sinned against heaven. I am not worthy to be called your son." Luke 15:21), the father has no time for them. Instead he blesses and heals. Children shy away from parents who blame themselves for their children's failures. We hate to be made to feel a disappointment to those we love. And we hate them to feel guilty over happenings that were not their fault. But we warm to the parent who, without any illusions about what has happened, is still ready to fall on our necks and kill the fatted calf.

The Presence of God
Jesus waits silent and unseen to come into my heart.
I will respond to His call.
He comes with His infinite power and love.
May I be filled with joy in His presence.

Freedom
Everything has the potential to draw forth from me a fuller love
and life.
Yet my desires are often fixed, caught, on illusions of fulfillment.
I ask that God, through my freedom, may orchestrate
my desires in a vibrant loving melody rich in harmony.

Consciousness
How do I find myself today?
Where am I with God? With others?
Do I have something to be grateful for? Then I give thanks.
Is there something I am sorry for? Then I ask forgiveness.

The Word
God speaks to each one of us individually. I need to listen to
what he is saying to me. (Please turn to your scripture on the
following pages. Inspiration points are there should you need
them. When you are ready, return here to continue.)

Conversation
What feelings are rising in me
as I pray and reflect on God's word?
I imagine Jesus himself sitting or standing beside me,
and open my heart to him.

Conclusion
Glory be to the Father, and to the Son, and to the Holy Spirit,
As it was in the beginning, is now, and ever shall be,
World without end. Amen

Sunday 12th September,
Twenty-fourth Sunday in Ordinary Time   Luke 15:20–24

(The prodigal son) set off and went to his father. But while he was still far off, his father saw him and was filled with compassion; he ran and put his arms around him and kissed him. Then the son said to him, "Father, I have sinned against heaven and before you; I am no longer worthy to be called your son." But the father said to his slaves, "Quickly, bring out a robe—the best one—and put it on him; put a ring on his finger and sandals on his feet. And get the fatted calf and kill it, and let us eat and celebrate; for this son of mine was dead and is alive again; he was lost and is found!" And they began to celebrate.

- This is the point at which my prayer begins: the father (Jesus' most developed image of God) is not sitting at home brooding about the "mistake" of financing his younger son's follies, but standing at his doorway, scanning the road by which the boy may come back; running to embrace him, silencing his apologies, calling a party to celebrate his own joy.

- Lord, you are watching out for me. I do not need to make speeches to you, but simply to enjoy your embrace.

Monday 13th September   1 Corinthians 11:23–26

For I received from the Lord what I also handed on to you, that the Lord Jesus on the night when he was betrayed took a loaf of bread, and when he had given thanks, he broke it and said, "This is my body that is for you. Do this in remembrance of me." In the same way he took the cup also, after supper, saying, "This cup is the new covenant in my blood. Do this, as often as you drink it, in remembrance of me." For as often as you eat this bread and drink the cup, you proclaim the Lord's death until he comes.

- When the mother of James and John asks Jesus to give her sons a special place, Jesus replies, "Are you able to drink the cup that I am about to drink?" (Mt 20:22).
- Jesus' invitation to drink the cup is a radical challenge. The cup is full of life, full of joys and sorrows. As we grasp the cup, he is there with us.

Tuesday 14th September,
Triumph of the Holy Cross   John 3:12–17

Jesus said, "And just as Moses lifted up the serpent in the wilderness, so must the Son of Man be lifted up, that whoever believes in him may have eternal life. For God so loved the world that he gave his only Son, so that everyone who believes in him may not perish but may have eternal life. Indeed, God did not send the Son into the world to condemn the world, but in order that the world might be saved through him."

- The cross, a sign of shame, is also a sign of hope. For many people it is for a sign that Jesus has shared the worst of life.
- The figure on the cross in the early church was usually the risen Jesus. This is something of the origin of this feast: it is the sign that love triumphs over hatred, that the compassion of God is so strong that Jesus forgives all who harmed him. "Indeed this was the son of God."

Wednesday 15th September   Luke 7:31–35

Jesus said to the people, "To what then will I compare the people of this generation, and what are they like? They are like children sitting in the market-place and calling to one another, 'We played the flute for you, and you did not dance; we wailed, and you did not weep.' For John the Baptist has come eating no bread and drinking no wine, and you say, 'He has a demon;' the Son of Man has come eating and drinking, and you say, 'Look,

a glutton and a drunkard, a friend of tax-collectors and sinners!'
Nevertheless, wisdom is vindicated by all her children."

- Jesus is trying to obtain a hearing from the people he is talking to.
- We can always find reasons for not listening to others. Jesus asks
  that we look into our own hearts and find the way to conversion
  from there, without comparisons or condemnation with regard to
  others. Can I do that today?

Thursday 16th September   **1 Corinthians 15:1–8**

Now I should remind you, brothers and sisters, of the good
news that I proclaimed to you, which you in turn received,
in which also you stand, through which also you are being saved,
if you hold firmly to the message that I proclaimed to you—
unless you have come to believe in vain. For I handed on to you
as of first importance what I in turn had received: that Christ
died for our sins in accordance with the scriptures, and that he
was buried, and that he was raised on the third day in accordance
with the scriptures, and that he appeared to Cephas, then to the
twelve. Then he appeared to more than five hundred brothers
and sisters at one time, most of whom are still alive, though some
have died. Then he appeared to James, then to all the apostles.
Last of all, as to someone untimely born, he appeared also to
me.

- This is a wonderful and early testimony of Christian faith. This is
  what Paul himself has received, what he experienced himself, and
  what he now passes on.
- Let me sit quietly and take it in, step by step. How might I meet
  Jesus in my life today?

Friday 17th September Luke 8:1–3

Soon afterwards he went on through cities and villages, proclaiming and bringing the good news of the kingdom of God. The twelve were with him, as well as some women who had been cured of evil spirits and infirmities: Mary, called Magdalene, from whom seven demons had gone out, and Joanna, the wife of Herod's steward Chuza, and Susanna, and many others, who provided for them out of their resources.

- The presence of women among Jesus' disciples was unusual. Even more, one was formerly possessed by demons; another had been attached to Herod's court. Their presence in Jesus' company made others uncomfortable and critical.
- Jesus friendship with women was among the most significant examples of how he turned convention on its head.

Saturday 18th September Luke 8:4–8

When a great crowd gathered and people from town after town came to him, Jesus said in a parable: "A sower went out to sow his seed; and as he sowed, some fell on the path and was trampled on, and the birds of the air ate it up. Some fell on the rock; and as it grew up, it withered for lack of moisture. Some fell among thorns, and the thorns grew with it and choked it. Some fell into good soil, and when it grew, it produced a hundredfold." As he said this, he called out, "Let anyone with ears to hear listen!"

- We want our community to be good soil for the seed, the word of God. To do that, we must nourish well the soil which is itself the gift of God.
- Nourishment for our faith comes with prayer, service, and love. It all makes sense only if the way we live our lives make sense of the gospel.

september 19–25

Something to think and pray about each day this week:

Making the effort

Zacchaeus was a small man, used to being despised and spat upon, feeling he deserved it because of his greed and extortions as a tax-collector. His motives were mixed in seeking Jesus (Lk 19:1-10). He wanted just to see him, not engage with him. But that faint beginning of desire was enough. It met a greater desire in Jesus to meet him, call him by name, "Zacchaeus make haste and come down; for I must stay at your house today."

In my prayer, Lord, I am often like Zacchaeus, making huge efforts to catch a glimpse of you, but perhaps still wanting to keep my distance, to keep "safe." But I find that you are waiting for me, calling me by name, inviting yourself into my heart. Once I let go and am with you, I find happiness in putting things right, ordering my life, finding the springs of generosity and justice that have been stifled by old habits.

The Presence of God

I reflect for a moment on God's presence around me and in me.
Creator of the universe, the sun and the moon, the earth,
every molecule, every atom, everything that is:
God is in every beat of my heart. God is with me, now.

Freedom

There are very few people
who realize what God would make of them
if they abandoned themselves into his hands,
and let themselves be formed by his grace. (St. Ignatius)
I ask for the grace to trust myself totally to God's love.

Consciousness

I remind myself that I am in the presence of the Lord.
I will take refuge in His loving heart.
He is my strength in times of weakness.
He is my comforter in times of sorrow.

The Word

I read the word of God slowly, a few times over, and I listen to
what God is saying to me. (Please turn to your scripture on the
following pages. Inspiration points are there should you need
them. When you are ready, return here to continue.)

Conversation

What is stirring in me as I pray?
Am I consoled, troubled, left cold?
I imagine Jesus himself standing or sitting at my side,
and share my feelings with him.

Conclusion

Glory be to the Father, and to the Son, and to the Holy Spirit,
As it was in the beginning, is now, and ever shall be,
World without end. Amen

Sunday 19th September,
Twenty-fifth Sunday in Ordinary Time   Luke 16:10–13

Then Jesus said to the disciples, "Whoever is faithful in a very little is faithful also in much; and whoever is dishonest in a very little is dishonest also in much. If then you have not been faithful with the dishonest wealth, who will entrust to you the true riches? And if you have not been faithful with what belongs to another, who will give you what is your own? No slave can serve two masters; for a slave will either hate the one and love the other, or be devoted to the one and despise the other. You cannot serve God and wealth."

- There are practical lessons here: first, that whatever the value of our worldly goods, we must be faithful in our stewardship; and second, that the Christian should take the long-term view of this world, with an eye always on the "true riches" of the kingdom.
- The only things we take with us from our life on earth are those which we have given away.

Monday 20th September   Luke 8:16–18

Jesus said to his disciples, "No one after lighting a lamp hides it under a jar, or puts it under a bed, but puts it on a lampstand, so that those who enter may see the light. For nothing is hidden that will not be disclosed, nor is anything secret that will not become known and come to light. Then pay attention to how you listen; for to those who have, more will be given; and from those who do not have, even what they seem to have will be taken away."

- God's love, God's word is a lamp for our steps, a lamp that shines from the inside of our personalities. Nothing can put it out.
- Sometimes we struggle to believe in this love. It is always there, shining in darkness, doubt, meanness, and sin.
- Do we keep the light a secret? Do we hide our goodness from others?

Tuesday 21st September,
St. Matthew, Apostle and Evangelist   Matthew 9:9–13

As Jesus was walking along, he saw a man called Matthew sitting at the tax booth; and he said to him, "Follow me." And he got up and followed him. And as he sat at dinner in the house, many tax collectors and sinners came and were sitting with him and his disciples. When the Pharisees saw this, they said to his disciples, "Why does your teacher eat with tax collectors and sinners?" But when he heard this, he said, "Those who are well have no need of a physician, but those who are sick. Go and learn what this means, 'I desire mercy, not sacrifice.' For I have come to call not the righteous but sinners."

- In Hebrew, his name means "gift from God," but the gospel labels him quite directly as a "tax collector"; thus Matthew was viewed by many as a public sinner. To him Jesus said, "Follow me."
- Jesus does not exclude a single one of us from his friendship, but offers each of us the same invitation, to a new life with him.

Wednesday 22nd September   Luke 9:1–6

Jesus called the twelve together and gave them power and authority over all demons and to cure diseases, and he sent them out to proclaim the kingdom of God and to heal. He said to them, "Take nothing for your journey, no staff, nor bag, nor bread, nor money—not even an extra tunic. Whatever house you enter, stay there, and leave from there. Wherever they do not welcome you, as you are leaving that town shake the dust off your feet as a testimony against them." They departed and went through the villages, bringing the good news and curing diseases everywhere.

- God is not to be forced on people. God's love and care are an invitation, not a direction or command. The disciples of Jesus are to move on if they are not welcomed.
- Hostility can cling like dust to the feet, and hinder further growth. Prayer invites us to let go of hostility, both from us to another, and from another to ourselves. The invitation is to a future of hope and freedom.

Thursday 23rd September   Luke 9:7–9

Now Herod the ruler heard about all that had taken place, and he was perplexed, because it was said by some that John had been raised from the dead, by some that Elijah had appeared, and by others that one of the ancient prophets had arisen. Herod said, "John I beheaded; but who is this about whom I hear such things?" And he tried to see him.

- Somehow Herod wanted to see Jesus. He would try a few times in the course of the public ministry of Jesus. Was it to argue? To listen? To get rid of him?
- Do I really want to "see" Jesus; to know what he is like, to know the love he offers me, to be changed by him? Seeing Jesus means being willing to live forever with what we "see."

Friday 24th September   Luke 9:18–22

Once when Jesus was praying alone, with only the disciples near him, he asked them, "Who do the crowds say that I am?" They answered, "John the Baptist; but others, Elijah; and still others, that one of the ancient prophets has arisen." He said to them, "But who do you say that I am?" Peter answered, "The Messiah of God." He sternly ordered and commanded them not to tell anyone, saying, "The Son of Man must undergo great suffering, and be rejected by the elders, chief priests, and scribes, and be killed, and on the third day be raised."

- People often prayed with Jesus, prayed near him at his prayer. Something of his prayer and relationship with his father must have rubbed off on them.
- It helps us to pray together, even in silence. A child learns to pray by watching a parent, a grandparent, or another adult. Praying together gives us courage to face difficulties together.

Saturday 25th September   Luke 9:43–45

And all were astounded at the greatness of God. While everyone was amazed at all that he was doing, he said to his disciples, "Let these words sink into your ears: The Son of Man is going to be betrayed into human hands." But they did not understand this saying; its meaning was concealed from them, so that they could not perceive it. And they were afraid to ask him about this saying.

- Some of Jesus' words make us feel afraid, uneasy, and challenged. Anything to do with his death had this effect on those close to him and on his disciples.
- There is a time for going to the words and the events of Jesus' life which we enjoy and also to those which disturb us. Lord, you are always loving and compassionate.

september 26–october 2

Something to think and pray about each day this week:

Making preparations
There is a somber air about this week's readings. Jesus has set his face to go up to Jerusalem, knowing that trouble awaits him there. In a series of meetings, he teaches his disciples to control their anger, to choose effective action over sweet words, to keep their inner peace despite the insecurities which dog them.

What is my Jerusalem, Lord? What is the place and time and circumstance in which I will have to face my own weakness, the hostility of others, and the destiny to which you call me? You are always lifting me out of the humdrum, the dull routine of survival, and making me aware of my vocation as your friend.

The Presence of God
I remind myself that, as I sit here now,
God is gazing on me with love and holding me in being.
I pause for a moment and think of this.

Freedom
Lord, grant me the grace to be free from the excesses of this life.
Let me not get caught up with the desire for wealth.
Keep my heart and mind free to love and serve you.

Consciousness
How am I really feeling? Light-hearted? Heavy-hearted?
I may be very much at peace, happy to be here.
Equally, I may be frustrated, worried, or angry.
I acknowledge how I really am. It is the real me that the Lord
loves.

The Word
I take my time to read the word of God, slowly, a few times,
allowing myself to dwell on anything that strikes me. (Please
turn to your scripture on the following pages. Inspiration points
are there should you need them. When you are ready, return
here to continue.)

Conversation
Do I notice myself reacting as I pray with the word of God?
Do I feel challenged, comforted, angry?
Imagining Jesus sitting or standing by me,
I speak out my feelings, as one trusted friend to another.

Conclusion
Glory be to the Father, and to the Son, and to the Holy Spirit,
As it was in the beginning, is now, and ever shall be,
World without end. Amen

310

Sunday 26th September,
Twenty-sixth Sunday in Ordinary Time   Amos 6:1, 4–7

Alas for those who are at ease in Zion, and for those who feel secure on Mount Samaria, the notables of the first of the nations, to whom the house of Israel resorts! Alas for those who lie on beds of ivory, and lounge on their couches, and eat lambs from the flock, and calves from the stall; who sing idle songs to the sound of the harp, and like David improvise on instruments of music; who drink wine from bowls, and anoint themselves with the finest oils, but are not grieved over the ruin of Joseph! Therefore they shall now be the first to go into exile, and the revelry of the loungers shall pass away.

• This powerful prophecy of Amos, and the parable of Dives and Lazarus in today's gospel, are about thoughtless luxury, the enjoyment of riches without any sense of responsibility towards those who have little.

• Lord, keep me mindful of those that I can help. Keep me alert to the needs around me, and save me from the indifference of "those who feel secure."

Monday 27th September   Luke 9:46–50

An argument arose among them as to which one of them was the greatest. But Jesus, aware of their inner thoughts, took a little child and put it by his side, and said to them, "Whoever welcomes this child in my name welcomes me, and whoever welcomes me welcomes the one who sent me; for the least among all of you is the greatest." John answered, "Master, we saw someone casting out demons in your name, and we tried to stop him, because he does not follow with us." But Jesus said to him, "Do not stop him; for whoever is not against you is for you."

- In the Christian faith tradition, the angels look after us, guide us, and guard us from unseen dangers. Whatever this may mean, it is a belief that God, through all sorts of beings, looks after us.
- In a culture where children were ignored and treated badly, Jesus highlights their importance as loved children of God.

Tuesday 28th September   **Luke 9:51–56**

When the days drew near for him to be taken up, Jesus set his face to go to Jerusalem. And he sent messengers ahead of him. On their way they entered a village of the Samaritans to make ready for him; but they did not receive him, because his face was set toward Jerusalem. When his disciples James and John saw it, they said, Lord, do you want us to command fire to come down from heaven and consume them?" But he turned and rebuked them. Then they went on to another village.

- The antagonism between Jews and Samaritans was strong. It highlights the worst of religious intolerance and racism.
- Jesus seems to want to break through the barriers and walls separating these people. Sometimes it worked, as with the woman of Samaria. Other times, he moves on, knowing that for one time at least, nothing could be done.

Wednesday 29th September,
Sts. Michael, Gabriel, and Raphael   **John 1:47–51**

When Jesus saw Nathanael coming toward him, he said of him, "Here is truly an Israelite in whom there is no deceit!" Nathanael asked him, "Where did you get to know me?" Jesus answered, "I saw you under the fig tree before Philip called you." Nathanael replied, "Rabbi, you are the Son of God! You are the King of Israel!" Jesus answered, "Do you believe because I told you that I saw you under the fig tree? You will see greater things than these." And he said to him, "Very truly, I tell you,

you will see heaven opened and the angels of God ascending and descending upon the Son of Man."

- Nathanael's approach was prompted by Philip's challenge to "come and see" this Jesus, son of Joseph from Nazareth. Like Philip before him, Nathanael—or Bartholomew as he is called in the other gospels—becomes personally involved.
- Are we like these apostles, and like the angels, God's messengers of salvation? How do we invite others to meet Jesus, to come into relationship with the son of Joseph?

Thursday 30th September   Luke 10:1–7

After this the Lord appointed seventy others and sent them on ahead of him in pairs to every town and place where he himself intended to go. He said to them, "The harvest is plentiful, but the laborers are few; therefore ask the Lord of the harvest to send out laborers into his harvest. Go on your way. See, I am sending you out like lambs into the midst of wolves. Carry no purse, no bag, no sandals; and greet no one on the road. Whatever house you enter, first say, 'Peace to this house!' And if anyone is there who shares in peace, your peace will rest on that person; but if not, it will return to you. Remain in the same house, eating and drinking whatever they provide, for the laborer deserves to be paid."

- Jesus did not send out the disciples alone but in pairs, for mutual support. We lean on one another, and on the community of faith, and worship which we call the church.
- On our own, it may be seem almost impossible to keep our end up. Sacred Space is one way of keeping in touch with other believers.

Friday 1st October   Luke 10:13–16

"Woe to you, Chorazin! Woe to you, Bethsaida! For if the deeds of power done in you had been done in Tyre and

Sidon, they would have repented long ago, sitting in sackcloth and ashes. But at the judgment it will be more tolerable for Tyre and Sidon than for you. And you, Capernaum, will you be exalted to heaven? No, you will be brought down to Hades." "Whoever listens to you listens to me, and whoever rejects you rejects me, and whoever rejects me rejects the one who sent me."

- Jesus entrusts his mission to the disciples; listening to them is like listening to him. He promises that he will always be faithful to his disciples, that they are united like vine and branches.
- We are those disciples now, and through the community of his followers, Jesus spreads his gospel message today. Prayer is a time of offering ourselves as listeners to him.

Saturday 2nd October   Luke 10:21–24

At that same hour Jesus rejoiced in the Holy Spirit and said, "I thank you, Father, Lord of heaven and earth, because you have hidden these things from the wise and the intelligent and have revealed them to infants; yes, Father, for such was your gracious will. All things have been handed over to me by my Father; and no one knows who the Son is except the Father, or who the Father is except the Son and anyone to whom the Son chooses to reveal him." Then turning to the disciples, Jesus said to them privately, "Blessed are the eyes that see what you see! For I tell you that many prophets and kings desired to see what you see, but did not see it, and to hear what you hear, but did not hear it."

- Jesus seems here to be rejoicing in his disciples, happy that they are with him. He is happy too with what God his Father has given to his followers.
- He rejoices in us as friends rejoice together, as parents rejoice in the talents and gifts of their children. Maybe we can rejoice in each other? Lord, help me to do that today.

october 3–9

Something to think and pray about each day this week:

The mystery of evil

The prophet Habakuk (1:13) voiced the bafflement of believers at the mystery of evil, "God, why do you look on where there is tyranny?" When I read the papers, hear the news, and learn of people who get away with being corrupt, cruel, and malicious, I am still pulled up short by this mystery. Why do the wicked prosper?

Lord, you told Habakuk to have patience, "The upright man will live by his faithfulness." Jesus said the same; the cockle will grow with the wheat, but in the end God will harvest both. More than that, Jesus showed how to face suffering and death, treachery and evil, with a love that conquers both. Give me some share in that patience and that love.

The Presence of God

In the silence of my innermost being,
in the fragments of my yearned-for wholeness,
can I hear the whispers of God's presence?
Can I remember when I felt God's nearness?
When we walked together and I let myself be embraced by
God's love.

Freedom

I ask for the grace
to let go of my own concerns
and be open to what God is asking of me,
to let myself be guided and formed by my loving Creator.

Consciousness

I exist in a web of relationships—links to nature, people, God.
I trace out these links, giving thanks for the life that flows
through them.
Some links are twisted or broken: I may feel regret, anger,
disappointment.
I pray for the gift of acceptance and forgiveness.

The Word

The word of God comes down to us through the scriptures.
May the Holy Spirit enlighten my mind and my heart to
respond to the gospel teachings. (Please turn to your scripture
on the following pages. Inspiration points are there should you
need them. When you are ready, return here to continue.)

Conversation

Remembering that I am still in God's presence,
I imagine Jesus himself standing or sitting beside me,
and say whatever is on my mind, whatever is in my heart,
speaking as one friend to another.

Conclusion

Glory be to the Father, and to the Son, and to the Holy Spirit,
As it was in the beginning, is now, and ever shall be,
World without end. Amen

316

Sunday 3rd October,
Twenty-seventh Sunday in Ordinary Time   Luke 17:5–6

The apostles said to the Lord, "Increase our faith!" The Lord replied, "If you had faith the size of a mustard seed, you could say to this mulberry tree, 'Be uprooted and planted in the sea,' and it would obey you."

- "Increase our faith," begged the apostles. For most of us, said Francis Thompson, God is a belief; for the saints, a touch.
- Lord, let me feel your touch in prayer.

Monday 4th October,
St. Francis of Assisi   Matthew 11:25–27

Jesus said, "I thank you, Father, Lord of heaven and earth, because you have hidden these things from the wise and the intelligent and have revealed them to infants; yes, Father, for such was your gracious will. All things have been handed over to me by my Father; and no one knows the Son except the Father, and no one knows the Father except the Son and anyone to whom the Son chooses to reveal him."

- Here we see Jesus in prayer. Five times he says, "Father," as he give profound thanks for the way God unites us as his children. In his own way, this intimate relationship was one Francis sought to share, to the point of embracing Jesus' wounds in his own body.
- Can I sit and talk with my Father, Abba, Dad?

Tuesday 5th October   Luke 10:38–42

Now as they went on their way, Jesus entered a certain village, where a woman named Martha welcomed him into her home. She had a sister named Mary, who sat at the Lord's feet and listened to what he was saying. But Martha was distracted by her many tasks; so she came to him and asked, "Lord, do you not care that my sister has left me to do all the work by myself? Tell her then to help me." But the Lord answered her, "Martha, Martha, you are worried and distracted by many things; there is need of only one thing. Mary has chosen the better part, which will not be taken away from her."

- Jesus highlights the potential of the present moment. He is not praising contemplation over work; but that is not the point of the story. It is reminding us to grab cherish the better part of the "moments" in life. At this point, the better moment for Martha was to listen to the word of God.
- Sometimes the better moment is service in the name of the Lord.

Wednesday 6th October   Luke 11:1–4

Jesus was praying in a certain place, and after he had finished, one of his disciples said to him, "Lord, teach us to pray, as John taught his disciples." He said to them, "When you pray, say: Father, hallowed be your name. Your kingdom come. Give us each day our daily bread. And forgive us our sins, for we ourselves forgive everyone indebted to us. And do not bring us to the time of trial."

- Jesus calls God by the intimate name of "Abba" or "Dad." He knows that the loving God is as close to us as the air we breathe.
- Because of love, we want what Abba wants, and these are the first two prayers of the Our Father. The rest is to tell what we want ourselves. Many spend time in prayer just saying over and over again the words of the "Our Father."

Thursday 7th October   Luke 11:5–10

And Jesus said to them, "Suppose one of you has a friend, and you go to him at midnight and say to him, 'Friend, lend me three loaves of bread; for a friend of mine has arrived, and I have nothing to set before him.' And he answers from within, 'Do not bother me; the door has already been locked, and my children are with me in bed; I cannot get up and give you anything.' I tell you, even though he will not get up and give him anything because he is his friend, at least because of his persistence he will get up and give him whatever he needs. So I say to you, Ask, and it will be given you; search, and you will find; knock, and the door will be opened for you. For everyone who asks receives, and everyone who searches finds, and for everyone who knocks, the door will be opened."

- Prayer is its own reward to the extent that we always receive when we pray. We are closer to God's love, and the door is always opened to new hope and new confidence in our lives.

- We may not get all we want, or specific things we ask for. We get what God wants to give, at a time that is good for our lives. What we are always given in prayer is the gift of God's Holy Spirit.

Friday 8th October   Luke 11:15–23

Some of the crowd said of Jesus, "He casts out demons by Beelzebul, the ruler of the demons." Others, to test him, kept demanding from him a sign from heaven. But he knew what they were thinking and said to them, "Every kingdom divided against itself becomes a desert, and house falls on house. If Satan also is divided against himself, how will his kingdom stand?—for you say that I cast out the demons by Beelzebul. Now if I cast out the demons by Beelzebul, by whom do your exorcists cast them out? Therefore they will be your judges. But if it is by the finger of God that I cast out the demons, then the kingdom of God has come to you. When a strong man, fully armed, guards his castle, his property is safe. But when one stronger than he attacks him and overpowers him, he takes away his armor in which he trusted and divides his plunder. Whoever is not with me is against me, and whoever does not gather with me scatters."

- The casting out of demons was a particularly cultural activity of Jesus. Demons were the names given to what possesses us in a violent way in our lives. Maybe today it would be the obsessions that make for control of others, addictions, greed, violence, and abuse of others in any way.
- We might name our demons in prayer and ask for help with what leads us away from God and sometimes leads us to harm others.

Saturday 9th October   **Luke 11:27–28**

While Jesus was speaking, a woman in the crowd raised her voice and said to him, "Blessed is the womb that bore you and the breasts that nursed you!" But he said, "Blessed rather are those who hear the word of God and obey it!"

- To receive the word of God is a greater gift in the eyes of Jesus than to receive the body of Jesus in the womb. Mary is richly blessed—more for her receiving the word of God in her life and living by it, than being the physical mother of God.
- Prayer is the time we give in our lives, even daily, to receiving the word of God.

october 10–16

Something to think and pray about each day this week:

Who am I?

It is extraordinary to hear that question from Jesus, "Who do you say that I am?" (Mk 8:27–30). Of all human beings, he is the one who knew who he was and who knew his role, yet it mattered to him to hear it from his friends. We live in one another's eyes. We are curious to hear, "What are they saying about me?" This can be threatening, "Am I the target of gossip or critical talk?" But how we see one another can be constructive to an extraordinary degree. It always matters to us how our mother or father see us. And not just parents; a married woman once told a group of her friends: "When my husband looks at me, I am so much greater and richer than when I look at myself. I sense so much more potential in me." Her husband added, "When I experience my wife's loving gaze, I feel a sense of inner growth which seems to be lacking if I just look at myself in the mirror."

So we ask the Lord, "Give me the grace to look at others with the eye of love, with a constructive eye. Never let me forget that my eye and my mind can enrich and support others."

The Presence of God
God is with me, but more,
God is within me, giving me existence.
Let me dwell for a moment on God's life-giving presence
in my body, my mind, my heart
and in the whole of my life.

Freedom
I ask for the grace to believe
in what I could be and do
if I only allowed God, my loving Creator,
to continue to create me, guide me, and shape me.

Consciousness
Knowing that God loves me unconditionally,
I can afford to be honest about how I am.
How has the last day been, and how do I feel now?
I share my feelings openly with the Lord.

The Word
I read the word of God slowly, a few times over, and I listen to
what God is saying to me. (Please turn to your scripture on the
following pages. Inspiration points are there should you need
them. When you are ready, return here to continue.)

Conversation
How has God's word moved me? Has it left me cold?
Has it consoled me or moved me to act in a new way?
I imagine Jesus standing or sitting beside me,
I turn and share my feelings with him.

Conclusion
Glory be to the Father, and to the Son, and to the Holy Spirit,
As it was in the beginning, is now, and ever shall be,
World without end. Amen

322

Sunday 10th October,
Twenty-eighth Sunday in Ordinary Time   Luke 17:11–19

On the way to Jerusalem Jesus was going through the region between Samaria and Galilee. As he entered a village, ten lepers approached him. Keeping their distance, they called out, saying, "Jesus, Master, have mercy on us!" When he saw them, he said to them, "Go and show yourselves to the priests." And as they went, they were made clean. Then one of them, when he saw that he was healed, turned back, praising God with a loud voice. He prostrated himself at Jesus' feet and thanked him. And he was a Samaritan. Then Jesus asked, "Were not ten made clean? But the other nine, where are they? Was none of them found to return and give praise to God except this foreigner?" Then he said to him, "Get up and go on your way; your faith has made you well."

- I can take kindness for granted, and do not bother to say thanks. It was the stranger, the Samaritan, who took the trouble to go back to Jesus. The other nine went off happily, feeling, "Sure that's only what the rabbis/doctors/healers are there for."
- Thank you, Lord, that I am alive and able to speak to you; that I have access to your word in Sacred Space. May I always count my blessings.

Monday 11th October   Luke 11:29–32

When the crowds were increasing, Jesus began to say, "This generation is an evil generation; it asks for a sign, but no sign will be given to it except the sign of Jonah. For just as Jonah became a sign to the people of Nineveh, so the Son of Man will be to this generation. The Queen of the South will rise at the judgment with the people of this generation and condemn them, because she came from the ends of the earth to listen to the wisdom of Solomon, and see, something greater than Solomon is here! The people of Nineveh will rise up at the judgment with this generation and condemn it, because they repented at the proclamation of Jonah, and see, something greater than Jonah is here!"

- The sign Jesus refers to is not the mysterious sign of Jonah in the whale's belly, but the sign of repentance which Jonah preached to the people, and which the Queen of the South with all her finery accepted.
- They listened to the word of God; this is the new sign of Jesus. All scripture can lead us to repentance—to a change of mind and heart to be more like the heart and mind of Jesus.

Tuesday 12th October   Luke 11:37–41

While Jesus was speaking, a Pharisee invited him to dine with him; so he went in and took his place at the table. The Pharisee was amazed to see that he did not first wash before dinner. Then the Lord said to him, "Now you Pharisees clean the outside of the cup and of the dish, but inside you are full of greed and wickedness. You fools! Did not the one who made the outside make the inside also? So give for alms those things that are within; and see, everything will be clean for you."

- We are introduced in these chapters of Luke to some sayings of Jesus about being clean on the inside as well as the outside.
- God sees the heart, and judges us on what we try to be, and understands that much of the meanness and even the sin of everyone has to do with the human weakness all of us inherit at birth and gather during our lives.

Wednesday 13th October   Luke 11:42–46

"But woe to you Pharisees! For you tithe mint and rue and herbs of all kinds, and neglect justice and the love of God; it is these you ought to have practiced, without neglecting the others. Woe to you Pharisees! For you love to have the seat of honor in the synagogues and to be greeted with respect in the market-places. Woe to you! For you are like unmarked graves, and people walk over them without realizing it." One of the lawyers answered him, "Teacher, when you say these things, you insult us too." And he said, "Woe also to you lawyers! For you load people with burdens hard to bear, and you yourselves do not lift a finger to ease them."

- Jesus encourages a consistency between what we say and what we do, between who we are and who we advertise ourselves to be. He condemns those who exploit the poverty and the weakness of others; they are "like unmarked graves."
- Am I "dead" already, not living as I should, following the pack, not following my conscience? Prayer can bring this dead side of ourselves to life.

Thursday 14th October   **Luke 11:47–51**

Jesus said to the lawyers, "Woe to you! For you build the tombs of the prophets whom your ancestors killed. So you are witnesses and approve of the deeds of your ancestors; for they killed them, and you build their tombs. Therefore also the Wisdom of God said, 'I will send them prophets and apostles, some of whom they will kill and persecute,' so that this generation may be charged with the blood of all the prophets shed since the foundation of the world, from the blood of Abel to the blood of Zechariah, who perished between the altar and the sanctuary. Yes, I tell you, it will be charged against this generation."

- Many professional religious people of Jesus' time remembered only the law, but forgot what the law was for. Jesus is tough on them for killing the words of the prophets, for their pomposity and religious pride.

- He knew this would spark off their hostility. He was prepared to engage the opposition of anyone as he wanted to proclaim always the love of God his Father for all.

Friday 15th October, St. Teresa of Avila Romans 8:26–27

The Spirit helps us in our weakness; for we do not know how to pray as we ought, but that very Spirit intercedes with sighs too deep for words. And God, who searches the heart, knows what is the mind of the Spirit, because the Spirit intercedes for the saints according to the will of God.

- According to Paul's view the Spirit is crucial in our relationship with God; it is in the Spirit that we pray with the confidence of a trusting child, "Abba, Father."
- Our response to God, our prayer, may be inadequate because of our human failings, but not in our Father's eyes, for "the Spirit helps us in our weakness."

Saturday 16th October Luke 12:8–12

"And I tell you, everyone who acknowledges me before others, the Son of Man also will acknowledge before the angels of God; but whoever denies me before others will be denied before the angels of God. And everyone who speaks a word against the Son of Man will be forgiven; but whoever blasphemes against the Holy Spirit will not be forgiven. When they bring you before the synagogues, the rulers, and the authorities, do not worry about how you are to defend yourselves or what you are to say; for the Holy Spirit will teach you at that very hour what you ought to say."

- Jesus speaks to his disciples, knowing there is conflict and ahead.
- When I read these words, am I encouraged and challenged, or am I frightened and beaten? Why do I react like that?
- What can I take out of these words today?

october 17–23

Something to think and pray about each day this week:

A child's needs

You remember the Gospel scene (Mk 10:13) where Jesus encountered noisy children. A crowd of them interrupted his preaching, and the apostles were moving them away. They were boisterous, energetic, enjoying life, running instinctively towards someone who also enjoyed it. The apostles spoke sternly to those who brought them. ("These kids are not serious people. We are here to listen to the Sermon on the Mount, and we can't hear him properly with all this noise and commotion.") Jesus intervened, invited the children closer, and laid his hands on them. He gave them two precious things that cost no money: time and affection. These days, parents often experience a famine of time, so that children suffer from too little attention. Concern about children's safety means that children suffer from not being touched—as too-careful adults and teachers avoid responsibility. Yet children's needs remain the same.

The Presence of God
To be present is to arrive as one is and open up to the other.
At this instant, as I arrive here, God is present waiting for me.
God always arrives before me, desiring to connect with me
even more than my most intimate friend.
I take a moment and greet my loving God.

Freedom
"In these days, God taught me
as a schoolteacher teaches a pupil" (St. Ignatius).
I remind myself that there are things God has to teach me yet,
and ask for the grace to hear them and let them change me.

Consciousness
In the presence of my loving Creator,
I look honestly at my feelings over the last day,
the highs, the lows and the level ground.
Can I see where the Lord has been present?

The Word
I take my time to read the word of God, slowly, a few times,
allowing myself to dwell on anything that strikes me. (Please
turn to your scripture on the following pages. Inspiration points
are there should you need them. When you are ready, return
here to continue.)

Conversation
What feelings are rising in me
as I pray and reflect on God's word?
I imagine Jesus himself sitting or standing beside me,
and open my heart to him.

Conclusion
Glory be to the Father, and to the Son, and to the Holy Spirit,
As it was in the beginning, is now, and ever shall be,
World without end. Amen

328

Sunday 17th October,
Twenty-ninth Sunday in Ordinary Time   Luke 18:1–8

Then Jesus told them a parable about their need to pray always and not to lose heart. He said, "In a certain city there was a judge who neither feared God nor had respect for people. In that city there was a widow who kept coming to him and saying, 'Grant me justice against my opponent.' For a while he refused; but later he said to himself, 'Though I have no fear of God and no respect for anyone, yet because this widow keeps bothering me, I will grant her justice, so that she may not wear me out by continually coming.' And the Lord said, "Listen to what the unjust judge says. And will not God grant justice to his chosen ones who cry to him day and night? Will he delay long in helping them? I tell you, he will quickly grant justice to them. And yet, when the Son of Man comes, will he find faith on earth?"

- Lord, you puzzle me. I hear you telling me to persist, I hear you say, "God will quickly grant justice." But then I think of good people suffering, of children dying, of Jews in Auschwitz, still singing the psalms as they walked into the gas chambers. Surely there are times when you delay in helping us?
- At times like this I turn to the memory of your passion, and your agonized prayer in the garden. You have faced a dark and apparently empty heaven, yet stayed faithful. Keep me with you.

Monday 18th October,
St. Luke, Evangelist   2 Timothy 4:16–17b

At my first defence no one came to my support, but all deserted me. May it not be counted against them! But the Lord stood by me and gave me strength, so that through me the message might be fully proclaimed and all the Gentiles might hear it.

- Like Paul or Job, we can feel isolated, alone, even abandoned—by family, friends, loved ones, even by God. Does God really know or care about me? Surely God does not need the likes of me.
- Lord, you know and need each one of us. It is through each of us that your word is proclaimed. Just as Luke and Timothy stood with Paul, so we are called to stand with you, Lord; you give us the strength we need.

Tuesday 19th October   Luke 12:35–38

Jesus said to his disciples, "Be dressed for action and have your lamps lit; be like those who are waiting for their master to return from the wedding banquet, so that they may open the door for him as soon as he comes and knocks. Blessed are those slaves whom the master finds alert when he comes; truly I tell you, he will fasten his belt and have them sit down to eat, and he will come and serve them. If he comes during the middle of the night, or near dawn, and finds them so, blessed are those slaves."

- Being ready was a big theme for the writers of the gospel. For us it means being open to the ways that Jesus comes among us.
- Where we are alive to God's creation, in nature, love, and prayer, we are ready to meet the "God of surprises." If we ask ourselves what we are truly grateful for in our lives, there is a good chance that we will find God there.

Wednesday 20th October   Luke 12:39–44

Jesus said, "But know this: if the owner of the house had known at what hour the thief was coming, he would not have let his house be broken into. You also must be ready, for the Son of Man is coming at an unexpected hour." Peter said, "Lord, are you telling this parable for us or for everyone?" And the Lord said, "Who then is the faithful and prudent manager whom his master will put in charge of his slaves, to give them their allowance of food at the proper time? Blessed is that slave whom his master will find at work when he arrives. Truly I tell you, he will put that one in charge of all his possessions."

- We have been trusted with the gospel of Jesus. We have been entrusted with his eucharistic presence. A eucharistic prayer of the Roman church speaks of "the paschal mystery entrusted to us." Without the people, there would be no word, no bread, no memory of God.
- Would any of us entrust the future of our family and the meaning of our lives to the sort of people many of us are? Yet God does. In prayer we ask the grace to be worthy receivers of the gifts of God.

Thursday 21st October   Luke 12:49–53

" I came to bring fire to the earth, and how I wish it were already kindled! I have a baptism with which to be baptized, and what stress I am under until it is completed! Do you think that I have come to bring peace to the earth? No, I tell you, but rather division! From now on five in one household will be divided, three against two and two against three; they will be divided: father against son and son against father, mother against daughter and daughter against mother, mother-in-law against her daughter-in-law and daughter-in-law against mother-in-law."

- Jesus seems to know that his life will cause huge divisions, even in one of the most sacred communities of all—the family. He calls his mission "a fire."
- Fire destroys and leaves its marks forever. It can also strengthen with its huge energy. Through baptism, we enter with Jesus into the fire of love, commitment, and conviction.

Friday 22nd October **Luke 12:54–59**

J esus also said to the crowds, "When you see a cloud rising in the west, you immediately say, 'It is going to rain'; and so it happens. And when you see the south wind blowing, you say, 'There will be scorching heat'; and it happens. You hypocrites! You know how to interpret the appearance of earth and sky, but why do you not know how to interpret the present time? And why do you not judge for yourselves what is right? Thus, when you go with your accuser before a magistrate, on the way make an effort to settle the case, or you may be dragged before the judge, and the judge hand you over to the officer, and the officer throw you in prison. I tell you, you will never get out until you have paid the very last penny."

- The realism of Jesus comes across in these sayings, which advise us to take notice of what is going on and interpret what may happen in the future—with a recommendation, if in a legal dispute, to settle out of court if possible!

- It is not always easy to pray some of Jesus' sayings—here we ask his help in the difficulties we face, and the humility and energy to take the human steps we need to deal with the dilemmas we face.

Saturday 23rd October **Luke 13:6–9**

J esus told this parable: "A man had a fig tree planted in his vineyard; and he came looking for fruit on it and found none. So he said to the gardener, 'See here! For three years I have come looking for fruit on this fig tree, and still I find none. Cut it down! Why should it be wasting the soil?' He replied, 'Sir, let it alone for one more year, until I dig round it and put manure on it. If it bears fruit next year, well and good; but if not, you can cut it down.'"

- The end of the story about the fig tree is about the patience of God, our need for time to repent and grow in our faith and prayer, and it is about the "God of the many chances."
- All of us carry faults and failings through life, and even though we try our best, find that they stay with us. God sees our efforts to change and be renewed. Lord, help us to believe in ourselves.

Something to think and pray about each day this week:

Future costs

As Jesus began his ministry, he looked hard at the group of possible disciples who were attracted to him and who wanted to belong with him (Mt 10:37). He cautioned them, "Hold on. Don't start something you cannot finish. The cost could be high." The dearest part of that cost is to our ego, our centering of our energies on our own desires. Eleven of the twelve apostles counted the cost and eventually paid it, though they stumbled on the way—think of Peter denying Jesus and hiding during the Crucifixion. Poor Judas stumbled and never found his way back.

Lord, I want to be serious in following you, but I do not trust myself. I pray with Philip Neri: "Lord, beware of this Philip or he will betray you! Lay your hand upon my head, for without you there is not a sin I may not commit this day."

Presence of God

What is present to me is what has a hold on my becoming.
I reflect on the presence of God always there in love,
amidst the many things that have a hold on me.
I pause and pray that I may let God
affect my becoming in this precise moment.

Freedom

If God were trying to tell me something, would I know?
If God were reassuring me or challenging me, would I notice?
I ask for the grace to be free of my own preoccupations
and open to what God may be saying to me.

Consciousness

Knowing that God loves me unconditionally,
I look honestly over the last day, its events, and my feelings.
Do I have something to be grateful for? Then I give thanks.
Is there something I am sorry for? Then I ask forgiveness.

The Word

God speaks to each one of us individually. I need to listen to
what he is saying to me. (Please turn to your scripture on the
following pages. Inspiration points are there should you need
them. When you are ready, return here to continue.)

Conversation

What is stirring in me as I pray?
Am I consoled, troubled, left cold?
I imagine Jesus himself standing or sitting at my side,
and share my feelings with him.

Conclusion

Glory be to the Father, and to the Son, and to the Holy Spirit,
As it was in the beginning, is now, and ever shall be,
World without end. Amen

336

Sunday 24th October,
Thirtieth Sunday in Ordinary Time   **Luke 18:9–14**

He also told this parable to some who trusted in themselves that they were righteous and regarded others with contempt: 'Two men went up to the temple to pray, one a Pharisee and the other a tax-collector. The Pharisee, standing by himself, was praying thus, "God, I thank you that I am not like other people: thieves, rogues, adulterers, or even like this tax-collector. I fast twice a week; I give a tenth of all my income." But the tax-collector, standing far off, would not even look up to heaven, but was beating his breast and saying, "God, be merciful to me, a sinner!" I tell you, this man went down to his home justified rather than the other; for all who exalt themselves will be humbled, but all who humble themselves will be exalted.'

- The contrast between Pharisee and publican has entered so deeply into our culture that it is sometimes reversed; those who go to church may be more anxious to be at the back of the church than to be in the front pews.
- How does the story hit me? I would hate to be the object of people's contempt. But Lord, if they knew me as you do, they might be right to feel contempt. And I have no right to look down on those whose sins are paraded in the media as public sinners. Be merciful to me.

Monday 25th October   **Luke 13:10–17**

Now Jesus was teaching in one of the synagogues on the sabbath. And just then there appeared a woman with a spirit that had crippled her for eighteen years. She was bent over and was quite unable to stand up straight. When Jesus saw her, he called her over and said, "Woman, you are set free from your ailment." When he laid his hands on her, immediately she stood up straight and began praising God. But the leader of the synagogue, indignant because Jesus had cured on the sabbath, kept saying to the crowd, "There are six days on which work ought to be done; come on those days and be cured, and not on the sabbath day." But the Lord answered him and said, "You hypocrites! Does not each of you on the sabbath untie his ox or his donkey from the manger, and lead it away to give it water? And ought not this woman, a daughter of Abraham whom Satan bound for eighteen long years, be set free from this bondage on the sabbath day?" When he said this, all his opponents were put to shame; and the entire crowd was rejoicing at all the wonderful things that he was doing.

- Jesus has no choice when faced with the bondage of the law over human compassion: he must set us free.
- That is the call of the church and of Christians: to be people receiving the healing and the justice of Jesus and being willing to spread the kingdom of God within the world.

Tuesday 26th October — Luke 13:18–21

He said therefore, "What is the kingdom of God like? And to what should I compare it? It is like a mustard seed that someone took and sowed in the garden; it grew and became a tree, and the birds of the air made nests in its branches." And again he said, "To what should I compare the kingdom of God? It is like yeast that a woman took and mixed in with three measures of flour until all of it was leavened."

- "What is the kingdom of God like?" It does not seem like a place or a glittering "heaven" but seems founded on what is ordinary, simple, nourishing, protective, small—with the power to grow stronger.
- What do I think the kingdom is like?
- Can I see signs of the kingdom around me?

Wednesday 27th October   Luke 13:22–30

Jesus went through one town and village after another, teaching as he made his way to Jerusalem. Someone asked him, "Lord, will only a few be saved?" He said to them, "Strive to enter through the narrow door; for many, I tell you, will try to enter and will not be able. When once the owner of the house has got up and shut the door, and you begin to stand outside and to knock at the door, saying, 'Lord, open to us,' then in reply he will say to you, 'I do not know where you come from.' Then you will begin to say, 'We ate and drank with you, and you taught in our streets.' But he will say, 'I do not know where you come from; go away from me, all you evildoers!' There will be weeping and gnashing of teeth when you see Abraham and Isaac and Jacob and all the prophets in the kingdom of God, and you yourselves thrown out. Then people will come from east and west, from north and south, and will eat in the kingdom of God. Indeed, some are last who will be first, and some are first who will be last."

- Jesus does not give a direct answer to the question, "Will only a few be saved?" There is a challenging image here: a narrow door, like a turnstile in a stadium. As Paul says, God wants all to be saved, but we cannot take salvation for granted. I need to keep my eye on that turnstile, keep pushing towards it.

- Jesus does not point towards the law but points inside; the narrow door is the door of the heart. It can be opened by everyone, of any race or color.

Thursday 28th October,
Sts. Simon and Jude, Apostles   Luke 6:12–16

Now during those days he went out to the mountain to pray; and he spent the night in prayer to God. And when day

came, he called his disciples and chose twelve of them, whom
he also named apostles: Simon, whom he named Peter, and his
brother Andrew, and James, and John, and Philip, and Bartholomew, and Matthew, and Thomas, and James son of Alphaeus,
and Simon, who was called the Zealot, and Judas son of James,
and Judas Iscariot, who became a traitor.

- Jesus prayed before he called the twelve. We also bring our confu-
  sions and decisions to prayer; we don't get easy answers, but we
  look to God when we make important decisions.
- Lord, encourage me to place the important decisions of my day in
  the context of love of God and love of my neighbour.

Friday 29th October   Luke 14:1–6

On one occasion when Jesus was going to the house of a
leader of the Pharisees to eat a meal on the sabbath, they
were watching him closely. Just then, in front of him, there was a
man who had dropsy. And Jesus asked the lawyers and Pharisees,
"Is it lawful to cure people on the sabbath, or not?" But they were
silent. So Jesus took him and healed him, and sent him away.
Then he said to them, "If one of you has a child or an ox that
has fallen into a well, will you not immediately pull it out on a
sabbath day?" And they could not reply to this.

- This religious meal on the Sabbath is invaded by a sick man who
  seems to be hoping for healing. No words are spoken between him
  and Jesus, but he moves to put compassion before the law.
- Can I bring people to mind and see them with the compassionate
  eye of Jesus? Compassion reaches deeply into our hearts, both the
  giver and the receiver. To suffer with the other person makes all of
  us stronger.

340

Saturday 30th October Luke 14:1, 7–11

On one occasion when Jesus was going to the house of a leader of the Pharisees to eat a meal on the sabbath, they were watching him closely. When he noticed how the guests chose the places of honor, he told them a parable. "When you are invited by someone to a wedding banquet, do not sit down at the place of honor, in case someone more distinguished than you has been invited by your host; and the host who invited both of you may come and say to you, 'Give this person your place,' and then in disgrace you would start to take the lowest place. But when you are invited, go and sit down at the lowest place, so that when your host comes, he may say to you, 'Friend, move up higher'; then you will be honored in the presence of all who sit at the table with you. For all who exalt themselves will be humbled, and those who humble themselves will be exalted."

- Stories about Jesus eating at table are common in Luke, who often uses them to pose the question, "Who do you invite to share your meal; who is invited to belong to the faith community?" Jesus' answer is clear: "All are invited, without exception."
- Do I make exceptions? How do I discriminate or create division? Is it by my actions, by inaction, by my words?
- Can I talk with the Lord about this?

october 2010

october 31–november 6

Something to think and pray about each day this week:

Giving and receiving

"There is more happiness in giving than in receiving." This comment of Jesus is quoted by St. Paul (Acts 20:35) though it is not in the gospels. We know its truth from experience—there is such joy in giving to the one we love. "Giving" does not mean just transferring property; that can be done (think of corporate donations), with little emotion. Part of the joy of giving is that it costs us. Remember King David's protest, "I will not offer sacrifices that cost me nothing" (II Sm 24:24). Whether what we are giving is money, or a gift, or care, or time, there must be something of ourselves in it. I love the old Dean's wisdom in Babette's Feast: "The only things we take with us from our life on earth are those which we have given away."

The Presence of God
God is with me, but more, God is within me.
Let me dwell for a moment on God's life-giving presence
in my body, in my mind, in my heart,
as I sit here, right now.

Freedom
I need to close out the noise, to rise above the noise;
The noise that interrupts, that separates,
The noise that isolates.
I need to listen to God again.

Consciousness
I remind myself that I am in the presence of the Lord.
I will take refuge in His loving heart.
He is my strength in times of weakness.
He is my comforter in times of sorrow.

The Word
I read the word of God slowly, a few times over, and I listen to
what God is saying to me. (Please turn to your scripture on the
following pages. Inspiration points are there should you need
them. When you are ready, return here to continue.)

Conversation
Do I notice myself reacting as I pray with the word of God?
Do I feel challenged, comforted, angry?
Imagining Jesus sitting or standing by me,
I speak out my feelings, as one trusted friend to another.

Conclusion
Glory be to the Father, and to the Son, and to the Holy Spirit,
As it was in the beginning, is now, and ever shall be,
World without end. Amen

Sunday 31st October,
Thirty-first Sunday in Ordinary Time   Luke 19:1–10

He entered Jericho and was passing through it. A man was there named Zacchaeus; he was a chief tax-collector and was rich. He was trying to see who Jesus was, but on account of the crowd he could not, because he was short in stature. So he ran ahead and climbed a sycamore tree to see him, because he was going to pass that way. When Jesus came to the place, he looked up and said to him, "Zacchaeus, hurry and come down; for I must stay at your house today." So he hurried down and was happy to welcome him. All who saw it began to grumble and said, "He has gone to be the guest of one who is a sinner." Zacchaeus stood there and said to the Lord, "Look, half of my possessions, Lord, I will give to the poor; and if I have defrauded anyone of anything, I will pay back four times as much." Then Jesus said to him, "Today salvation has come to this house, because he too is a son of Abraham. For the Son of Man came to seek out and to save the lost."

- In my prayer, Lord, I am often like Zacchaeus, making great efforts to catch a glimpse of you, only to find that you are already there, waiting for me, calling me by name, inviting yourself in.
- Once I am with you, I find happiness in putting things right, ordering my life, finding the springs of generosity and justice that I have stifled by my habits.

Monday 1st November, Feast of All Saints   Matthew 5:2–12

He began to speak, and taught them, saying: "Blessed are the poor in spirit, for theirs is the kingdom of heaven. Blessed are those who mourn, for they will be comforted. Blessed are the meek, for they will inherit the earth. Blessed are those who hunger and thirst for righteousness, for they will be filled. Blessed are the merciful, for they will receive mercy. Blessed are the pure in heart, for they will see God. Blessed are the peacemakers, for they will be called children of God. Blessed are those who are persecuted for righteousness' sake, for theirs is the kingdom of heaven. Blessed are you when people revile you and persecute you and utter all kinds of evil against you falsely on my account. Rejoice and be glad, for your reward is great in heaven, for in the same way they persecuted the prophets who were before you."

- A child was asked for a definition of a saint. She said, "A stained glass window!" Asked why, she explained, "The different colours let in the light, and every saint is a different colour of God."
- Every one of our unknown saints coloured God in a new way in his or her corner of the globe. Today we are grateful for the lives of so many people of every age, church, and century who have done their best to live in the spirit of the gospel of Jesus Christ.

Tuesday 2nd November,
Feast of All Souls   Matthew 25:31–40

"When the Son of Man comes in his glory, and all the angels with him, then he will sit on the throne of his glory. All the nations will be gathered before him, and he will separate people one from another as a shepherd separates the sheep from the goats, and he will put the sheep at his right hand and the goats at the left. Then the king will say to those at his right hand, 'Come, you that are blessed by my Father, inherit the kingdom prepared for you from the foundation of the world; for I was hungry and you gave me food, I was thirsty and you gave me something to drink, I was a stranger and you welcomed me, I was naked and you gave me clothing, I was sick and you took care of me, I was in prison and you visited me.' Then the righteous will answer him, 'Lord, when was it that we saw you hungry and gave you food, or thirsty and gave you something to drink? And when was it that we saw you a stranger and welcomed you, or naked and gave you clothing? And when was it that we saw you sick or in prison and visited you?' And the king will answer them, 'Truly I tell you, just as you did it to one of the least of these who are members of my family, you did it to me.'"

- The custom of the church today has been to pray for the dead.
- Let me sit and recall people who have died, and pray for them.

Wednesday 3rd November   Luke 14:25–27

Now large crowds were traveling with him; and he turned and said to them, "Whoever comes to me and does not hate father and mother, wife and children, brothers and sisters, yes, and even life itself, cannot be my disciple. Whoever does not carry the cross and follow me cannot be my disciple."

- The way of speaking in Jesus' time was often in stark contrasts, so the contrast of discipleship and possessions is his way of valuing discipleship over all else, not of rubbishing possessions.
- The cost of discipleship is high for Jesus.

Thursday 4th November,
St. Charles Borromeo   John 10:11–16

Jesus said to the Pharisees, "I am the good shepherd. The good shepherd lays down his life for the sheep. The hired hand, who is not the shepherd and does not own the sheep, sees the wolf coming and leaves the sheep and runs away—and the wolf snatches them and scatters them. The hired hand runs away because a hired hand does not care for the sheep. I am the good shepherd. I know my own and my own know me, just as the Father knows me and I know the Father. And I lay down my life for the sheep. I have other sheep that do not belong to this fold.

I must bring them also, and they will listen to my voice. So there will be one flock, one shepherd."

- "I know my own, and my own know me." Jesus calls himself the Good Shepherd to show the great intimacy that must exist between leaders and those entrusted to them.
- Do I allow Jesus to call me by name? Do I embrace this intimacy, or do I step back from it?

Friday 5th November   **Luke 16:1–8**

Then Jesus said to the disciples, "There was a rich man who had a manager, and charges were brought to him that this man was squandering his property. So he summoned him and said to him, 'What is this that I hear about you? Give me an accounting of your management, because you cannot be my manager any longer.' Then the manager said to himself, 'What will I do, now that my master is taking the position away from me? I am not strong enough to dig, and I am ashamed to beg. I have decided what to do so that, when I am dismissed as manager, people may welcome me into their homes.' So, summoning his master's debtors one by one, he asked the first, 'How much do you owe my master?' He answered, 'A hundred jugs of olive oil.' He said to him, 'Take your bill, sit down quickly, and make it fifty.' Then he asked another, 'And how much do you owe?' He replied, 'A hundred containers of wheat.' He said to him, 'Take your bill and make it eighty.' And his master commended the dishonest manager because he had acted shrewdly; for the children of this age are more shrewd in dealing with their own generation than are the children of light."

- This is one of those strange stories we find in the gospels. Jesus praises shrewdness which is lawful and expects us to use our heads and our hearts in our decisions for him. Martin Luther King said

348

that we need "hard heads and soft hearts, not soft heads and hard hearts."

- Does this story trouble me? Can I talk with the Lord about it?

Saturday 6th November   Luke 16:9–15

Jesus said to the disciples, "And I tell you, make friends for yourselves by means of dishonest wealth so that when it is gone, they may welcome you into the eternal homes. Whoever is faithful in a very little is faithful also in much; and whoever is dishonest in a very little is dishonest also in much. If then you have not been faithful with the dishonest wealth, who will entrust to you the true riches? And if you have not been faithful with what belongs to another, who will give you what is your own? No slave can serve two masters; for a slave will either hate the one and love the other, or be devoted to the one and despise the other. You cannot serve God and wealth." The Pharisees, who were lovers of money, heard all this, and they ridiculed him. So he said to them, "You are those who justify yourselves in the sight of others; but God knows your hearts; for what is prized by human beings is an abomination in the sight of God."

- These words of Jesus encourage us to integrity and consistency in our lives. We try to live what we believe, "walk the talk," in a oft-used phrase.
- Lovers of money and people suffering from greed resist these words. Time in prayer, speaking with the Lord, purifies our intentions and makes us aware of inconsistency. It gives the grace and help to live consistently.

november 7–13

Something to think and pray about each day this week:

Hearing God

I imagine myself visiting the Jewish Temple as Jesus enters (Jn 2:13). I am accustomed to the money-changers and hucksters who provide a service to the worshippers by selling cattle, sheep and doves for the ritual sacrifices. The fury of Jesus startles and upsets me. I think to myself, "Surely these people are making honest money? They are just offering a service." But commerce tends to grow and grow when it finds a market, so the temple, the place of prayer, degenerated into a sort of marketplace. This is the house of God. When money creeps in, it tends to take over. Jesus needed to challenge the drift and reassert the holiness of the temple.

Does it happen in my life, Lord? Is there any of the Christian sacraments untouched by commercialism? We grow accustomed to the souvenir shops in Lourdes, the event managers of weddings, and the organizers of first communion parties and outfits. We take for granted there will be Christening parties, first communion gifts, wedding feasts, etc. These occasions are meant to be the touch of God at key moments in our lives; but can God get a hearing amid the clatter of coins?

The Presence of God
As I sit here, the beating of my heart,
the ebb and flow of my breathing, the movements of my mind
are all signs of God's ongoing creation of me.
I pause for a moment and become aware
of this presence of God within me.

Freedom
Lord, grant me the grace to be free from the excesses of this life.
Let me not get caught up with the desire for wealth.
Keep my heart and mind free to love and serve you.

Consciousness
In God's loving presence I unwind the past day,
starting from now and looking back, moment by moment.
I gather in all the goodness and light, in gratitude.
I attend to the shadows and what they say to me,
seeking healing, courage, forgiveness.

The Word
I take my time to read the word of God, slowly, a few times,
allowing myself to dwell on anything that strikes me. (Please
turn to your scripture on the following pages. Inspiration points
are there should you need them. When you are ready, return
here to continue.)

Conversation
Remembering that I am still in God's presence,
I imagine Jesus himself standing or sitting beside me,
and say whatever is on my mind, whatever is in my heart,
speaking as one friend to another.

Conclusion
Glory be to the Father, and to the Son, and to the Holy Spirit,
As it was in the beginning, is now, and ever shall be,
World without end. Amen

Sunday 7th November,
Thirty-second Sunday in Ordinary Time   Luke 20:27–38

Some Sadducees, those who say there is no resurrection, came to him and asked him a question, "Teacher, Moses wrote for us that if a man's brother dies, leaving a wife but no children, the man shall marry the widow and raise up children for his brother. Now there were seven brothers; the first married, and died childless; then the second and the third married her, and so in the same way all seven died childless. Finally the woman also died. In the resurrection, therefore, whose wife will the woman be? For the seven had married her." Jesus said to them, "Those who belong to this age marry and are given in marriage; but those who are considered worthy of a place in that age and in the resurrection from the dead neither marry nor are given in marriage. Indeed they cannot die any more, because they are like angels and are children of God, being children of the resurrection. And the fact that the dead are raised Moses himself showed, in the story about the bush, where he speaks of the Lord as the God of Abraham, the God of Isaac, and the God of Jacob. Now he is God not of the dead, but of the living; for to him all of them are alive."

- The Sadducees try to trick Jesus who then lifts them above the human tangles in which they are trapped, to a cosmic vision.
- "He is God not of the dead but of the living, for to him all are alive." We are part of that cosmos that embraces Abraham, Isaac, and Jacob as well as our ancestors to the beginning of creation. In the resurrection we will share the eternal now of God.

Monday 8th November   Luke 17:1–6

Jesus said to his disciples, "Occasions for stumbling are bound to come, but woe to anyone by whom they come! It would be better for you if a millstone were hung around your neck and you were thrown into the sea than for you to cause one of these little ones to stumble. Be on your guard! If another disciple sins, you must rebuke the offender, and if there is repentance, you must forgive. And if the same person sins against you seven times a day, and turns back to you seven times and says, 'I repent,' you must forgive." The apostles said to the Lord, "Increase our faith!" The Lord replied, "If you had faith the size of a mustard seed, you could say to this mulberry tree, 'Be uprooted and planted in the sea,' and it would obey you."

- Religion is meant to be expansive and widen the heart of love within us. If we sin in any way, God forgives.
- The faith that is strong enough to move us in love through life is born in forgiveness. Sometimes prayer is a space to relax into the mystery of the forgiving God.

Tuesday 9th November,
Dedication of the Lateran Basilica   John 2:13–22

The Passover of the Jews was near, and Jesus went up to Jerusalem. In the temple he found people selling cattle, sheep, and doves, and the money changers seated at their tables. Making a whip of cords, he drove all of them out of the temple, both the sheep and the cattle. He also poured out the coins of the money changers and overturned their tables. He told those who were selling the doves, "Take these things out of here! Stop making my Father's house a marketplace!" His disciples remembered that it was written, "Zeal for your house will consume me." The Jews then said to him, "What sign can you show us for doing this?" Jesus answered them, "Destroy this temple, and in three days I will raise it up." The Jews then said, "This temple has been under construction for forty-six years, and will you raise it up in three days?" But he was speaking of the temple of his body. After he was raised from the dead, his disciples remembered that he had said this; and they believed the scripture and the word that Jesus had spoken.

- For Jesus to compare his body and himself to the temple and to declare that he was greater than the temple was taken as an insult and would bring him to death.
- Later they would remember and realise that he foretold his resurrection.
- Is there a message for me in this? Am I blind, reluctant to "see," pushing Jesus aside because I don't want to change the way I am?

Wednesday 10th November   **Luke 17:11–19**

On the way to Jerusalem Jesus was going through the region between Samaria and Galilee. As he entered a village, ten lepers approached him. Keeping their distance, they called out, saying, "Jesus, Master, have mercy on us!" When he saw them, he said to them, "Go and show yourselves to the priests." And as they went, they were made clean. Then one of them, when he saw that he was healed, turned back, praising God with a loud voice. He prostrated himself at Jesus' feet and thanked him. And he was a Samaritan. Then Jesus asked, "Were not ten made clean? But the other nine, where are they? Was none of them found to return and give praise to God except this foreigner?" Then he said to him, "Get up and go on your way; your faith has made you well."

- Praising God is not limited to any one people or religion, to those who sing psalms. Jesus highlights here that a foreigner was the one to return in praise.
- We all share our faith in the God who creates us and the world day by day. All prayer echoes Mary: "my soul glorifies the Lord and my spirit rejoices in God my Savior" (Lk 1:46).

Thursday 11th November   Luke 17:20–25

Once Jesus was asked by the Pharisees when the kingdom of God was coming, and he answered, "The kingdom of God is not coming with things that can be observed; nor will they say, 'Look, here it is!' or 'There it is!' For, in fact, the kingdom of God is among you." Then he said to the disciples, "The days are coming when you will long to see one of the days of the Son of Man, and you will not see it. They will say to you, 'Look there!' or 'Look here!' Do not go, do not set off in pursuit. For as the lightning flashes and lights up the sky from one side to the other, so will the Son of Man be in his day. But first he must endure much suffering and be rejected by this generation."

- Rejection was a big part of the life of Jesus. From his first days he had many occasions of violent rejection, of people trying to injure and kill him.
- At the centre of his death and resurrection was final rejection by his own people. Where do I stand in all of this?

Friday 12th November   Luke 17:26–36

Just as it was in the days of Noah, so too it will be in the days of the Son of Man. They were eating and drinking, and marrying and being given in marriage, until the day Noah entered the ark, and the flood came and destroyed all of them. Likewise, just as it was in the days of Lot: they were eating and drinking, buying and selling, planting and building, but on the day that Lot left Sodom, it rained fire and sulfur from heaven and destroyed all of them—it will be like that on the day that the Son of Man is revealed. On that day, anyone on the housetop who has belongings in the house must not come down to take them away; and likewise anyone in the field must not turn back. Remember Lot's wife. Those who try to make their life secure will lose it, but those who lose their life will keep it. I tell you, on that night there will be two in one bed; one will be taken and the other left. There will be two women grinding meal together; one will be taken and the other left.

- Praying the last days can be difficult. In the centre of all the texts about the end time is the call to trust God.
- We are invited to center our lives not just on ourselves but on God to whom we belong, by birth and by death. Can I respond?

Saturday 13th November   Luke 18:1–8

Then Jesus told them a parable about their need to pray always and not to lose heart. He said, "In a certain city there was a judge who neither feared God nor had respect for people. In that city there was a widow who kept coming to him and saying, 'Grant me justice against my opponent.' For a while he refused; but later he said to himself, 'Though I have no fear of God and no respect for anyone, yet because this widow keeps bothering me, I will grant her justice, so that she may not wear me out by continually coming.'" And the Lord said, "Listen to what the unjust judge says. And will not God grant justice to his chosen ones who cry to him day and night? Will he delay long in helping them? I tell you, he will quickly grant justice to them. And yet, when the Son of Man comes, will he find faith on earth?"

- The judge was meant to look after the widow and the orphan— this was part of his role in society. It might be said that the woman had a right to pester and bother him.
- It is never too often to ask God for something. Prayer can be answered through persistence. The more we pray, the more we can learn something about ourselves, and grow closer to God.

november 14–20

Something to think and pray about each day this week:

Hearing the voice

"They will listen to my voice," said Jesus (Jn 10:16). How do I imagine that voice? A hectoring father? A nagging mother? A moralizing preacher? A roaring sergeant-major?

No, it is the voice of a lover, who knows me in my uniqueness and calls me by name. Of all that you say here, Lord, your last words hearten me most: "I must bring the other sheep also, so there will be one flock, one shepherd." As humankind grows older, we long for unity, for an end to the needless divisions that cripple us. Be a good shepherd to all who come to Sacred Space. We find here a unity in hearing your words and communing with you.

The Presence of God

As I sit here, the beating of my heart,
the ebb and flow of my breathing, the movements of my mind
are all signs of God's ongoing creation of me.
I pause for a moment, and become aware
of this presence of God within me.

Freedom

I will ask God's help,
to be free from my own preoccupations,
to be open to God in this time of prayer,
to come to love and serve him more.

Consciousness

Help me, Lord, to be more conscious of your presence.
Teach me to recognize your presence in others.
Fill my heart with gratitude for the times your love
has been shown to me through the care of others.

The Word

I take my time to read the word of God, slowly, a few times, allowing myself to dwell on anything that strikes me. (Please turn
to your scripture on the following pages. Inspiration points are
there should you need them. When you are ready, return here
to continue.)

Conversation

Remembering that I am still in God's presence,
I imagine Jesus himself standing or sitting beside me,
and say whatever is on my mind, whatever is in my heart,
speaking as one friend to another.

Conclusion

Glory be to the Father, and to the Son, and to the Holy Spirit,
As it was in the beginning, is now, and ever shall be,
World without end. Amen

Sunday 14th November,
Thirty-third Sunday in Ordinary Time   Luke 21:5–19

When some were speaking about the temple, how it was adorned with beautiful stones and gifts dedicated to God, he said, "As for these things that you see, the days will come when not one stone will be left upon another; all will be thrown down." They asked him, "Teacher, when will this be, and what will be the sign that this is about to take place?" And he said, "Beware that you are not led astray; for many will come in my name and say, 'I am he!' and, 'The time is near!' Do not go after them. "When you hear of wars and insurrections, do not be terrified; for these things must take place first, but the end will not follow immediately." Then he said to them, "Nation will rise against nation, and kingdom against kingdom; there will be great earthquakes, and in various places famines and plagues; and there will be dreadful portents and great signs from heaven. But before all this occurs, they will arrest you and persecute you; they will hand you over to synagogues and prisons, and you will be brought before kings and governors because of my name. This will give you an opportunity to testify. So make up your minds not to prepare your defence in advance; for I will give you words and a wisdom that none of your opponents will be able to withstand or contradict. You will be betrayed even by parents and brothers, by relatives and friends; and they will put some of you to death. You will be hated by all because of my name. But not a hair of your head will perish. By your endurance you will gain your souls."

- The temple was not just the centre of the Jews' civilization: it was the place where God lived among them. Jesus told them that it was all going to fall apart!

- Is there any way in which my secure center—either personal or national—threatens to collapse? The key words from Jesus in all of this are, "Do not be terrified."
- Can I allow Jesus, the Consoler, to speak to me, wherever I am?

Monday 15th November   Luke 18:35–43

As he approached Jericho, a blind man was sitting by the roadside begging. When he heard a crowd going by, he asked what was happening. They told him, "Jesus of Nazareth is passing by." Then he shouted, "Jesus, Son of David, have mercy on me!" Those who were in front sternly ordered him to be quiet; but he shouted even more loudly, "Son of David, have mercy on me!" Jesus stood still and ordered the man to be brought to him; and when he came near, he asked him, "What do you want me to do for you?" He said, "Lord, let me see again." Jesus said to him, "Receive your sight; your faith has saved you." Immediately he regained his sight and followed him, glorifying God; and all the people, when they saw it, praised God.

- Wouldn't it be great to get really excited like the blind man because Jesus is near? He kept shouting a welcome and a request to Jesus. In his blindness he recognised Jesus, whom others with sight had missed.
- This incident happened on the edge of the town. Maybe we need to go to the edge of our being to find God. What does that mean for me today?

Tuesday 16th November   Luke 19:1–10

Jesus entered Jericho and was passing through it. A man was there named Zacchaeus; he was a chief tax-collector and was rich. He was trying to see who Jesus was, but on account of the crowd he could not, because he was short in stature. So he ran ahead and climbed a sycamore tree to see him, because he was going to pass that way. When Jesus came to the place, he looked up and said to him, "Zacchaeus, hurry and come down; for I must stay at your house today." So he hurried down and was happy to welcome him. All who saw it began to grumble and said, "He has gone to be the guest of one who is a sinner." Zacchaeus stood there and said to the Lord, "Look, half of my possessions, Lord, I will give to the poor; and if I have defrauded anyone of anything, I will pay back four times as much." Then Jesus said to him, "Today salvation has come to this house, because he too is a son of Abraham. For the Son of Man came to seek out and to save the lost."

- Jesus' hangers-on could be surprising. First comes a blind man of Jericho; next is one of the richest and most hated men of the town, a man who has cheated many people, the cause of many a family's poverty. The home of the one most hated was the place Jesus chose to stay.
- The despised man was converted; he turned around; he changed his ways and gave back what was wrongfully his. Jesus' words always challenge us to change our ways.

Wednesday 17th November, St. Elizabeth of Hungary   Psalm 33(34):1–4

I will bless the Lord at all times; his praise shall continually be in my mouth. My soul makes its boast in the Lord; let the humble hear and be glad. O magnify the Lord with me, and let us exalt his name together. I sought the Lord, and he answered me, and delivered me from all my fears.

- There are times when something so significant has been done for us that we want to do more that say a simple, "Thank you." We want to show in a special way that we really mean it.
- Do I see God's love in this way?
- How do I give thanks to the God who gives me hope each day?

Thursday 18th November Luke 19:41–44

A s he came near and saw the city, he wept over it, saying, "If you, even you, had only recognized on this day the things that make for peace! But now they are hidden from your eyes. Indeed, the days will come upon you, when your enemies will set up ramparts around you and surround you, and hem you in on every side. They will crush you to the ground, you and your children within you, and they will not leave within you one stone upon another; because you did not recognize the time of your visitation from God."

- The future of Jerusalem brings tears to the eyes of Jesus. His love for this city was strong; he knew that something awful would happen to it.
- Jerusalem is the name for many a city now. As Jesus was sorrowful that they did not recognise the visit of God when he came, so now the heart of Jesus longs for our love and recognition of who he is, and who we all are because of him.

Friday 19th November Luke 19:45–48

T hen Jesus entered the temple and began to drive out those who were selling things there; and he said, "It is written, 'My house shall be a house of prayer'; but you have made it a den of robbers." Every day he was teaching in the temple. The chief priests, the scribes, and the leaders of the people kept looking for a way to kill him; but they did not find anything they could do, for all the people were spellbound by what they heard.

- "Every day he was teaching in the temple." Despite the opposition he faced, Jesus did not step back. He needed to challenge the drift away from God and reassert its holiness of the temple.
- I face this same challenge on this day, to keep my face turned towards you, Lord.

Saturday 20th November
Luke 20:27–38

Some Sadducees, those who say there is no resurrection, came to him and asked him a question, "Teacher, Moses wrote for us that if a man's brother dies, leaving a wife but no children, the man shall marry the widow and raise up children for his brother. Now there were seven brothers; the first married, and died childless; then the second and the third married her, and so in the same way all seven died childless. Finally the woman also died. In the resurrection, therefore, whose wife will the woman be? For the seven had married her." Jesus said to them, "Those who belong to this age marry and are given in marriage; but those who are considered worthy of a place in that age and in the resurrection from the dead neither marry nor are given in marriage. Indeed they cannot die any more, because they are like angels and are children of God, being children of the resurrection. And the fact that the dead are raised Moses himself showed, in the story about the bush, where he speaks of the Lord as the God of Abraham, the God of Isaac, and the God of Jacob. Now he is God not of the dead, but of the living; for to him all of them are alive."

- Jesus was facing the watered-down faith of the Sadducees, who disputed the existence of spirits and the resurrection of the dead. Their question sounds complicated to us. Jesus answers them in language they would understand, and leads them from their limited view to a vision of the God of the living.

- Teach me, Lord, to speak of you in language that is simple and understandable yet tries to do you justice.

Something to think and pray about each day this week:

Joy in moderation

Jesus used a curious phrase to his disciples, "Be on guard so that your hearts are not weighed down with dissipation and drunkenness" (Lk 21:34). The warning fits. Drink is a narcotic; it dulls our hearts and blunts our reactions. Dissipation may be sold as fun and having a laugh, but the morning-after hangover helps us to realize with Nietzsche that "the mother of dissipation is not joy but joylessness." Joy and moderation go hand in hand. When our hearts are happy, in our own skins are good place to be, and we do not need to be blown out of our minds by alcohol or other drugs. Aquinas observed that a joyful heart is a sure sign of temperance.

The Presence of God
I pause for a moment
and reflect on God's life-giving presence
in every part of my body, in everything around me,
in the whole of my life.

Freedom
God is not foreign to my freedom.
Instead the Spirit breathes life into my most intimate desires,
gently nudging me towards all that is good.
I ask for the grace to let myself be enfolded by the Spirit.

Consciousness
I exist in a web of relationships—links to nature, people, God.
I trace out these links, giving thanks for the life that flows
through them.
Some links are twisted or broken: I may feel regret, anger,
disappointment.
I pray for the gift of acceptance and forgiveness.

The Word
God speaks to each one of us individually. I need to listen to
what he is saying to me. (Please turn to your scripture on the
following pages. Inspiration points are there should you need
them. When you are ready, return here to continue.)

Conversation
How has God's word moved me? Has it left me cold?
Has it consoled me or moved me to act in a new way?
I imagine Jesus standing or sitting beside me,
I turn and share my feelings with him.

Conclusion
Glory be to the Father, and to the Son, and to the Holy Spirit,
As it was in the beginning, is now, and ever shall be,
World without end. Amen

Sunday 21st November,
Feast of Christ the King   Luke 23:35–43

And the people stood by, watching; but the leaders scoffed at him, saying, "He saved others; let him save himself if he is the Messiah of God, his chosen one!" The soldiers also mocked him, coming up and offering him sour wine, and saying, "If you are the King of the Jews, save yourself!" There was also an inscription over him, "This is the King of the Jews." One of the criminals who were hanged there kept deriding him and saying, "Are you not the Messiah? Save yourself and us!" But the other rebuked him, saying, "Do you not fear God, since you are under the same sentence of condemnation? And we indeed have been condemned justly, for we are getting what we deserve for our deeds, but this man has done nothing wrong." Then he said, "Jesus, remember me when you come into your kingdom." He replied, "Truly I tell you, today you will be with me in Paradise."

- We know him as the good thief, Dismas, and bless him for that extraordinary prayer: "Jesus, remember me when you come into your kingdom." In the throes of your final agony, Lord, you welcomed him into paradise: "You will be with me."

- I lean on that promise, Lord. To call you a king is to use a human metaphor. It is enough for me that you are my Lord, and that my strongest hope is to be with you when death claims me.

Monday 22nd November   Luke 21:1–4

Jesus looked up and saw rich people putting their gifts into the treasury; he also saw a poor widow put in two small copper coins. He said, "Truly I tell you, this poor widow has put in more than all of them; for all of them have contributed out of their abundance, but she out of her poverty has put in all she had to live on."

- Jesus asks for a generous heart. He does not praise what this woman gave, but her wholehearted giving. She gave till it hurt.
- Do I give until it hurts, or only when I have more than enough? Lord, encourage me to give of myself, as much as I can.

Tuesday 23rd November   Luke 21:5–9

When some were speaking about the temple, how it was adorned with beautiful stones and gifts dedicated to God, Jesus said, "As for these things that you see, the days will come when not one stone will be left upon another; all will be thrown down." They asked him, "Teacher, when will this be, and what will be the sign that this is about to take place?" And he said, "Beware that you are not led astray; for many will come in my name and say, 'I am he!' and, 'The time is near!' Do not go after them. When you hear of wars and insurrections, do not be terrified; for these things must take place first, but the end will not follow immediately."

- As we pray, the gospels of the end times call us to trust in the presence and love of God when the end of life comes, or the end of the world—however that might be.
- Let me take time to reflect on the mystery of trust and give thanks for those I have trusted and can trust.

Wednesday 24th November   Luke 21:12–19

Jesus said to his disciples, "But before all this occurs, they will arrest you and persecute you; they will hand you over to synagogues and prisons, and you will be brought before kings and governors because of my name. This will give you an opportunity to testify. So make up your minds not to prepare your defense in advance; for I will give you words and a wisdom that none of your opponents will be able to withstand or contradict. You will be betrayed even by parents and brothers, by relatives and friends; and they will put some of you to death. You will be hated by all because of my name. But not a hair of your head will perish. By your endurance you will gain your souls."

- The God who cares for the growth of every hair on our head will keep us in safety, love and protection. This is the promise of God at the beginning of life, the promise at baptism for Christians.
- Can I be more open to God's promise so that this protection becomes more deeply a part of my life?

Thursday 25th November   Luke 21:20–28

Jesus said to the disciples, "When you see Jerusalem surrounded by armies, then know that its desolation has come near. Then those in Judea must flee to the mountains, and those inside the city must leave it, and those out in the country must not enter it; for these are days of vengeance, as a fulfillment of all that is written. Woe to those who are pregnant and to those who are nursing infants in those days! For there will be great distress on the earth and wrath against this people; they will fall by the edge of the sword and be taken away as captives among all nations; and Jerusalem will be trampled on by the Gentiles, until the times of the Gentiles are fulfilled. There will be signs in the sun, the moon, and the stars, and on the earth distress among nations confused by the roaring of the sea and the waves. People will faint from fear and foreboding of what is coming upon the world, for the powers of the heavens will be shaken. Then they will see 'the Son of Man coming in a cloud' with power and great glory. Now when these things begin to take place, stand up and raise your heads, because your redemption is drawing near."

- The worst of life can be a sign for the best. Turmoil and destruction in creation can herald the coming of the Lord. In the worst of times, the Lord is found to be near. This can be in the life of a people and in the life of each one of us.

- Let me take the time to recall when I felt the Lord was present, in the midst of turmoil, either in my life or in the life of someone I know. Can I pray to the Lord about this?

Friday 26th November   Luke 21:29–31

Then Jesus told them a parable: "Look at the fig tree and all the trees; as soon as they sprout leaves you can see for yourselves and know that summer is already near. So also, when you see these things taking place, you know that the kingdom of God is near."

- The words of God, the faithfulness and the promises of God, and the love of God will never leave us. Just as fig trees ripen every year and bear fruit, God is true and certain.
- Praying with the words of scripture gives us a security and a love in life that nothing can move.

Saturday 27th November   Luke 21:34–36

Jesus said to his disciples, "Be on guard so that your hearts are not weighed down with dissipation and drunkenness and the worries of this life, and that day catch you unexpectedly, like a trap. For it will come upon all who live on the face of the whole earth. Be alert at all times, praying that you may have the strength to escape all these things that will take place, and to stand before the Son of Man."

- The cares of life can lead us to God or away from God. We can look to alcohol and other escapes to help us cope with what is difficult in life.
- As we end this year, we know that God's strength is with us at all times. In prayer we are in touch with the strong love of God, which supports us and gives us courage.